First World War
and Army of Occupation
War Diary
France, Belgium and Germany

59 DIVISION
Divisional Troops
Royal Army Medical Corps
2/3 North Midland Field Ambulance
2 February 1916 - 1 August 1919

WO95/3018/3

The Naval & Military Press Ltd
www.nmarchive.com
Published in association with The National Archives

Published by

The Naval & Military Press Ltd

Unit 10 Ridgewood Industrial Park,
Uckfield, East Sussex,
TN22 5QE England
Tel: +44 (0) 1825 749494

www.naval-military-press.com

www.nmarchive.com

This diary has been reprinted in facsimile from the original. Any imperfections are inevitably reproduced and the quality may fall short of modern type and cartographic standards.

© Crown Copyright
Images reproduced by permission of The National Archives, London, England, 2015.

Contents

Document type	Place/Title	Date From	Date To
Heading	WO95/3018-3		
Heading	59th Division 2-3rd (N.M) Field Ambnce Feb 1917-1919 Jly		
Heading	War Diary Of O.C. 2/3rd North Midland Field Ambulance, From February 1st, 1916, To Feb 29th, 1916.		
War Diary	St Albans	02/02/1916	17/02/1916
Heading	War Diary Of O.C. 2/3rd North Mid. Fd. Ambulance. From 25/2/14 To 28/2/14 Volume II		
War Diary	Gillingham Dorset	25/02/1917	25/02/1917
War Diary	Southampton	25/02/1917	25/02/1917
War Diary	Lehavre	26/02/1917	27/02/1917
War Diary	Logneau (Amiens)	28/02/1917	28/02/1917
Heading	War Diary Of The 2/3rd North Midland Field Ambulance Month Ending March 31st 1917.		
War Diary	Glissy	01/03/1917	01/03/1917
War Diary	Warfusee-Abancourt	02/03/1917	06/03/1917
War Diary	Villers-Bretonneux	08/03/1917	08/03/1917
War Diary	Proyart	11/03/1917	11/03/1917
War Diary	Villers-Bretonneux	12/03/1917	31/03/1917
Heading	War Diary Of O.C. 2/3rd Nth Mid Fd Ambce From April 1st 1917 To April 30th 1917 Volume IV		
War Diary	Villers-Carbonnel	01/04/1917	30/04/1917
Heading	War Diary Of 2/3rd North Mid. Fd. Ambulance From 1/5/17 To 31/5/17 Volume V		
War Diary	Villers-Carbonnel	03/05/1917	25/05/1917
War Diary	Neuville Bonjourval	31/05/1917	31/05/1917
Diagram etc	2/3 N.M. Field Ambulance		
Operation(al) Order(s)	Operation Order No. 1. by Lieut Colonel C.A. Stidston Commanding 2/3rd North Midland Field Ambulance	24/05/1917	24/05/1917
Heading	2/3rd North Midland F.A.		
Heading	War Diary Of 2/3rd North Midland Field Ambulance From June 1st 1917 To June 31st 1917 Volume 6		
War Diary	Neuville Bonjourval Metz-En-Couture	01/06/1917	30/06/1917
Map	Appendix 4		
Heading	War Diary Of 2/3rd N.M Fd Amb July 1917 Vol 6		
War Diary	Neuville Bourjonval	02/07/1917	10/07/1917
War Diary	Barastre Map 57c	15/07/1917	31/07/1917
Operation(al) Order(s)	Operation Orders No. 2 by Lieut Colonel C.A. Stidston Commanding 2/3rd North Midland Field Ambulance 59th Division		
Operation(al) Order(s)	Operations Order No. 1 By Lieut Col C.A. Stidston. Commanding 2/3rd North Mid Field Amblce	24/07/1917	24/07/1917
Map	Map		
Miscellaneous	O/c 2/3rd North Midland Field Ambulance	27/07/1917	27/07/1917
Miscellaneous	Standing Orders. for Transport Attached 2/3rd North Midland Field Ambulance		
Heading	War Diary Of 2/3rd North Midland Field Ambulance For August 1917 Vol 7		
War Diary	Barastre	02/08/1917	22/08/1917

War Diary	Millencourt	23/08/1917	23/08/1917
War Diary	Senlis	26/08/1917	31/08/1917
Operation(al) Order(s)	Operation Order No. 4 by Lieut Colonel C.A. Stidston Commanding 2/3rd North Midland Field Ambulance R.A.M.C. TF	27/08/1917	27/08/1917
Heading	War Diary Of 2/3rd North Midland Field Ambulance September 1917 Vol 9		
War Diary	Luna Park Sheet 27 L.9.B. 2.1.	18/09/1917	18/09/1917
War Diary	Poperinghe Sheet 27 F.6.c.9.4	19/09/1917	22/09/1917
War Diary	Poperinghe	23/09/1917	23/09/1917
War Diary	Moated Farm Vlamertinghe 28 Sheet 4.2.d.b.1.	24/09/1917	24/09/1917
War Diary	Vlamertinghe Sheet 28.H.d.6.1	23/09/1917	30/09/1917
Heading	War Diary Of The 2/3rd North Midland Field Ambulance R.A.M.C. T.F. For The Month Of October 1917. Vol 10		
War Diary	Vlamertinghe	01/10/1917	01/10/1917
War Diary	Steenbecque Map Hazebrouck 5.A.4,7,7,1.5.	02/10/1917	02/10/1917
War Diary	St. Martin Hazebrouck 5.A.5.E.7.8	02/10/1917	04/10/1917
War Diary	Covecque Hazebrouck (Hazebrouck 5.a.5.c.2.2.5)	05/10/1917	08/10/1917
War Diary	Tangry (Lens 11.E.1.26.)	10/10/1917	10/10/1917
War Diary	Marest (Lens.11.E.1.9.6.)	11/10/1917	11/10/1917
War Diary	Barlin (Lens.11.E.J.3.5)	12/10/1917	12/10/1917
War Diary	Souchez (36.c.S.8.a.2.3.)	13/10/1917	27/10/1917
Operation(al) Order(s)	Operation Order No. 8. by Lieut Col C.A. Stidston Commanding 2/3rd N.M. Field Amb	10/10/1917	10/10/1917
Operation(al) Order(s)	Operation Order No. 9 by Lieut Colonel C.A. Stidston Commanding 2/3rd North Mid F Amb	11/10/1917	11/10/1917
Operation(al) Order(s)	Operation Orders No. 10 by Lieut Col C.A. Stidston Commanding 2/3rd North Midland Field Amb	12/10/1917	12/10/1917
Operation(al) Order(s)	Operation Order No. 11 by Lieut Col C.A. Stidston Commanding 2/3rd North Mid Field Amb	13/10/1917	13/10/1917
Map	Map		
Heading	War Diary Of O.C. 2/3rd North Midland Field Ambulance From 1/11/17 To 30/11/17 Vol 11		
War Diary	Souchez	04/11/1917	18/11/1917
War Diary	Bernaville (Lens.11. 1\100.000 3.I.0.2.)	19/11/1917	21/11/1917
War Diary	Courcelles-Le-Comte Lens.11.5.J.	21/11/1917	23/11/1917
War Diary	Heudicourt 57.C.W.21.A.1.9.	24/11/1917	27/11/1917
War Diary	Ribecourt 57.L.25.C.7.6	27/11/1917	28/11/1917
War Diary	Flesquieres 57.C.K.24.b.3.7	29/11/1917	30/11/1917
Diagram etc	Diagram		
Miscellaneous	2/3rd North Midland Field Ambulance		
Operation(al) Order(s)	Operation Order No. 12 by Lieut Col C.A. Stidston Commanding 2/3rd North Mid Field Amb	17/11/1917	17/11/1917
Heading	2/3rd North Midland F.A.		
War Diary	Flesquieres 57.c.k.24.b.3.7.	01/12/1917	04/12/1917
War Diary	Ruyaulcourt 57.c.p.10.b.22	05/12/1917	20/12/1917
War Diary	Barastre 57.c.0.16.d 7.3	22/12/1917	23/12/1917
War Diary	Barastre 57.c.0.16.d 7.3.	22/12/1917	23/12/1917
War Diary	Berlencourt	25/12/1917	31/12/1917
Heading	2/3rd North Midland F.A.		
War Diary	Berlencourt (Lens 11 3.F.10.30.	04/01/1918	31/01/1918
Miscellaneous	Appendix No. 17 Commendation Cards as Under Have Been Received From The G.O.C. 59th Division. And Were Presented on Parade on January 6th. 1918		

Heading	War Diary Of 2/3rd North Midland Field Ambulance From February 1st 1918 To February 28th 1918 (Volume II)		
War Diary	Berlencourt (Map Lens.11.3.10.30.)	01/02/1918	07/02/1918
War Diary	Berles-Aux-Bois	08/02/1918	12/02/1918
War Diary	Hamelincourt	13/02/1918	28/02/1918
Miscellaneous	2/3rd North Midland Field Ambulance		
Operation(al) Order(s)	Operation Order No. 13 by Lieut Colonel C.A. Stidston D.S.O. Officer Commanding 2/3rd North Midland Field Ambulance	07/02/1918	07/02/1918
Operation(al) Order(s)	Operation Order No. 14 by Lieut Col C.A. Stidston D.S.O. Comdg	11/02/1918	11/02/1918
Diagram etc	Diagram		
Miscellaneous	2/3rd North Midland Field Ambulance		
Operation(al) Order(s)	Operation Order No. 15 by Captain Alexander Mearns A/Officer Commanding 2/3rd N.M. Field Ambulance	01/03/1918	01/03/1918
Heading	2/3rd North Mid. F.A.		
Heading	War Diary Of 2/3rd (N.M.) Field Ambulance 59th Division March 1918 (Volume 3)		
War Diary	Hamelincourt	01/03/1918	01/03/1918
War Diary	Behagnies 57.C.H.I. (Central)	02/03/1918	21/03/1918
War Diary	Courcelles-Le-Comte 57.C.A.21.A.28.	21/03/1918	21/03/1918
War Diary	Ablainzeville	22/03/1918	22/03/1918
War Diary	57.D.F.16.D.8.2	22/03/1918	23/03/1918
War Diary	Aveluy 57.d.w.16.b.5.2.	24/03/1918	24/03/1918
War Diary	Behencourt (Amiens.17.1.f 35.70)	25/03/1918	25/03/1918
War Diary	Pion Trelet Mah. Lens. 11. (5.c.75.10)	26/03/1918	26/03/1918
War Diary	Montrelet (Lens. 11. 5.c. 75. 10)	27/03/1918	28/03/1918
War Diary	Cambligneul	29/03/1918	31/03/1918
Miscellaneous	2/3rd North Midland Field Ambulance		
Heading	2/3rd North Midland F.A.		
Heading	War Diary Of The 2/3rd North Midland Field Ambulance For The Month April 1918 (Volume 4.)		
War Diary	Clifford Camp	01/04/1918	04/04/1918
Map	Map Sheet 28. Ed 3		
War Diary	Vlamertinghe 28.H.a.9.9	05/04/1918	07/04/1918
War Diary	The Mill Vlamertinghe	08/04/1918	12/04/1918
War Diary	Godewaersvelde	13/04/1918	14/04/1918
War Diary	Locre Sheet 28 M.29 B.6.9	14/04/1918	15/04/1918
War Diary	Sheet 28.m.17.c.36	16/04/1918	17/04/1918
War Diary	Kokereele Farm Sheet 27.r17.b.7.3	18/04/1918	20/04/1918
War Diary	Dozinghem	20/04/1918	21/04/1918
War Diary	Houtkerque	21/04/1918	27/04/1918
War Diary	Clifford Camp 27 Sheet F.19.7.5.8	27/04/1918	29/04/1918
War Diary	Houtkerque	30/04/1918	30/04/1918
Operation(al) Order(s)	Operation Order No. 17 by Lieut-Col C.A. Stidston D.S.O. Commanding 2/3rd North Midland Field Ambulance	01/04/1918	01/04/1918
Operation(al) Order(s)	Operation Order No 18 by Lieut-Col C.A. Stidston D.S.O. Commanding 2/3rd North Midland Field Ambulance 59th Div	03/04/1918	03/04/1918
Miscellaneous	Clinical Chart		
Miscellaneous	A.D.M.S. 59th Division. Appendix XVIII		
Heading	2/3rd North Midland F.A.		
War Diary	Houtkerque	01/05/1918	05/05/1918
War Diary	St. Omer	06/05/1918	08/05/1918

War Diary	Ecques	09/05/1918	10/05/1918
War Diary	Bours	10/05/1918	13/05/1918
Heading	War Diary Of Officer Commanding 2/3rd North Midland Field Ambulance From 1-5-18 To 31-5-18 Vol 5		
War Diary	Bours	14/05/1918	29/05/1918
War Diary	Rely	30/05/1918	31/05/1918
Operation(al) Order(s)	Operation Order No. 19 by Lt Col C.A. Stidston D.S.O. Commanding	05/05/1918	05/05/1918
Operation(al) Order(s)	Operation Order No. 20 by O.C. 2/3rd North Midland Field Ambulance	09/05/1918	09/05/1918
Miscellaneous	2/3rd North Midland Field Ambulance	27/03/1918	27/03/1918
Miscellaneous	The Undermentioned General Routine Orders Are Published For Your Information		
Heading	2/3rd North Mid. F.A. June 1918		
Heading	War Diary Of The 2/3rd North Midland Field Amblce For The Month Of June 1918 Vol 6		
War Diary	Rely	01/06/1918	15/06/1918
War Diary	Boyaval	16/06/1918	29/06/1918
Miscellaneous	Operation Order No. By Major T.S. Elliot Commanding 2/3rd N.M.F. Amb	16/06/1918	16/06/1918
Heading	War Diary Of O.C. 2/3rd North Midland Field Ambulance From July 1st 1918 To July 31st 1918 (Volume 7)		
War Diary	Boyaval	01/07/1918	21/07/1918
War Diary	Barly	23/07/1918	29/07/1918
Operation(al) Order(s)	R.A.M.C. Orders No. 50. By A.D.M.S 59th Division	23/07/1918	23/07/1918
Heading	War Diary Of The 2/3rd North Midland Field Ambulance August 31st 1918 (Volume 8.)		
War Diary	Wailly	01/08/1918	24/08/1918
War Diary	Melanoy Farm	25/08/1918	31/08/1918
Miscellaneous	Inspection by D.M.S., Third Army. Appendix No. I		
Miscellaneous	Special Order Of The Day By Field-Marshal Sir Douglas Haig K.T. G.C.B. G.C.V.O. K.C.I.E. Commander In Chief British Armies In France	04/08/1918	04/08/1918
Operation(al) Order(s)	59th Division Special Order No. 152.	23/08/1918	23/08/1918
Operation(al) Order(s)	R.A.M.C. Orders No 53 By A.D.M.S. 59th Division	26/08/1918	26/08/1918
Heading	War Diary Of 2/3rd North Midland Field Amblce For Month Of September 1918 Vol 9		
War Diary	Ligne	01/09/1918	30/09/1918
Heading	War Diary Of 2/3rd North Midland Field Ambulance From October 1st 1918 To October 31st 1918 Vol 10		
War Diary	Ligne	01/10/1918	04/10/1918
War Diary	Le Nouveau Monde (Estaires)	05/10/1918	11/10/1918
War Diary	Fleurbaix H.22.C.0.7 Sheet 36	12/10/1918	18/10/1918
War Diary	K.19.b Central (Sheet 36)	19/10/1918	19/10/1918
War Diary	Flers L.32.C.6.4. [Sheet 36	19/10/1918	20/10/1918
War Diary	Hems Hems q.25.b.7.7	21/10/1918	21/10/1918
War Diary	Templeuve H. 32B b Hemt	21/10/1918	25/10/1918
War Diary	Chateau de Wasmes Sheet 37	26/10/1918	26/10/1918
War Diary	Toufflers	27/10/1918	31/10/1918
Miscellaneous	Orders By Major T.S. Elliot, M.C. Commanding		
Miscellaneous	Operation Orders By Major T.S. Elliot, M.C. Comdg.		
Miscellaneous	59th Division. App 3		
Miscellaneous	Operation Order By Lieut. Col. O. Steel., M.C. Comdg. 2/3rd North MID. Field Amblce.	24/10/1918	24/10/1918

Heading	2/3rd North Mid Fd Nov 1918		
War Diary	Toufflers 9.23.a. [Sheet 37	01/11/1918	09/11/1918
War Diary	Bailleul H.8.b. [Sheet 37	09/11/1918	14/11/1918
War Diary	La Marais M.16.a.Central [Sheet 37	15/11/1918	16/11/1918
War Diary	Seclin [V.30.Central Sheet 36.	16/11/1918	30/11/1918
Heading	War Diary Of The 2/3rd North Midland Field Ambulance R.A.M.C. T.F. For The Month Of December 1918		
War Diary	Seclin V.30.Sheet 36	01/12/1918	05/12/1918
War Diary	Noeux Les Mines K.18.B.5. Sheet 44 b	05/12/1918	31/12/1918
Operation(al) Order(s)	R.A.M.C. Orders No. 58. By A.D.M.S 59th Division	03/12/1918	03/12/1918
Miscellaneous	A.D.M.S., 59th Division No. S.39		
Heading	War Diary Of The 2/3rd North Midland Field Ambulance R.A.M.C. (T.F.) For The Month Of January 1919 (Vol I)		
War Diary	Noeux-Les-Mines k.18.b.6.2 442	01/01/1919	31/01/1919
Heading	War Diary Of The 2/3rd North Midland Field Ambulance For The Month Of February 1919 (Vol. 2)		
War Diary	Noeux Les Mines K.18.b.6.2 (44 b)	01/02/1919	15/02/1919
War Diary	Minx K.6.a. Central (44 B)	16/02/1919	19/02/1919
War Diary	Minx K.18.b. 6.2 (44 B)	20/02/1919	28/02/1919
Heading	War Diary Of 2/3rd North Midland Field Ambulance From March 1st 1919 To March 31st 1919		
War Diary	Minx Camp	01/03/1919	08/03/1919
War Diary	En.Route	09/03/1919	10/03/1919
War Diary	Balinghem	11/03/1919	31/03/1919
Heading	2/3rd Nth. Mid. F.A.		
Heading	War Diary Of The 2/3rd North Midland Field Ambulance From April 1st 1919 To April 30th 1919		
War Diary	Balinghem	01/04/1919	30/04/1919
Heading	War Diary Of 2/3rd North Midland Field Ambulance From 1st May 1919 To 31st May 1919		
War Diary	Balinghem	01/05/1919	19/05/1919
War Diary	Dunkerque	20/05/1919	31/05/1919
Miscellaneous	Appendix I		
Heading	War Diary Of 2/3rd North Midland Field Ambulance From June 1st 1919 To June 30th 1919		
War Diary	Dunkerque	01/06/1919	30/06/1919
Heading	2/3rd N. Mid. F.A.		
War Diary	Mardyck Dunkirk	01/07/1919	31/07/1919
War Diary	Mardyck Dunkirk	01/08/1919	01/08/1919

was Back

59TH DIVISION

2-3RD (N.M) FIELD AMBNCE.

FEB 1917-DEC 1918

1919 JLY

(also 1916 FEB)

59th NM Division

CONFIDENTIAL.

War Diary

of

O.C. 2/3rd North Midland Field Ambulance,

From February 1st, 1916, to Feb 29th, 1916.

(Volume 2.)

Army Form C. 2118.

WAR DIARY
or
INTELLIGENCE SUMMARY.
(Erase heading not required.)

Place	Date	Hour	Summary of Events and Information	Remarks and references to Appendices
St Albans	2/2/16	—	Lieut General Codrington inspected the Division whilst on Route march. The Ambulance paraded as strong as possible, seeing it as finding personnel for three Hospitals at St Albans. All Transport was present.	W.
"	14/2/16	—	Major-General A.E. Sandbach C.B. D.S.O. took over Command of the Division	W.
"	17/2/16	—	Colonel Lee. R.M.S. A.D.M.S. 3rd Army inspected Bricket House and Reception Hospital, Victoria Street.	W.

Amy W Cockhill
LIEUT. COL. R.A.M.C.
O.C. 2/3 NORTH MIDLAND FIELD AMBULANCE

Confidential

War Diary
of 2/3rd North. Mid. Fd. Amb.
From 25/2/17   To 28/2/17

Volume II

COMMITTEE FOR THE
MEDICAL HISTORY OF THE WAR
Date 11 MAY 1917

Army Form C. 2118.

WAR DIARY
or
INTELLIGENCE SUMMARY.
(Erase heading not required.)

Instructions regarding War Diaries and Intelligence Summaries are contained in F. S. Regs., Part II. and the Staff Manual respectively. Title pages will be prepared in manuscript.

Hour, Date, Place		Summary of Events and Information	Remarks and references to Appendices
6.40 A.M. 25/2/17	GILLINGHAM DORSET	Left Gillingham Station for SOUTHAMPTON arrived SOUTHAMPTON Docks 9.20 A.M. C.N.D.	MOVES
8 P.M. 25/2/17	SOUTHAMPTON	2 OFFICERS + 62 O.R. embarked on S.S. MANCHESTER IMPORTER TRANSPORT complete on same Ship. 4 Officers + remainder of unit embarked on S.S. KING EDWARD. C.N.D	"
2.30 P.M. 26/2/17	LE HAVRE	Arrival of S.S. KING EDWARD at LE HAVRE C.N.D	"
9.40 A.M. "	"	Disembarkation complete. Proceeded to No.1 Rest Camp C.N.D	"
26/2/17 C.N.D	"	Disembarkation of remainder of unit proceeded to No.1 Rest Camp from S.S. MANCHESTER IMPORTER C.N.D	"
27/2/17 C.N.D	"	Entire unit entrained LE HAVRE, left station 10.30 A.M. C.N.D	"
28/2/17 1.35 A.M.	LOGNEAU (AMIENS)	Arrival + detrainment at LOGNEAU (AMIENS) marched 2½ miles to GLISSY + billeted there C.N.D	"O.M.C(P.S)" Field Ambulance 2/3 (N.Mid) 59 Division

February 1917 Endo Ceuter O Gartaster Lt. 2/3 (N. Mid) 59 Division

CONFIDENTIAL

WAR DIARY OF THE

2/3RD NORTH MIDLAND FIELD

AMBULANCE

MONTH ENDING MARCH 31ST.1917.

COMMITTEE FOR THE
MEDICAL HISTORY OF THE WAR
Date 11 MAY. 1917

WAR DIARY or INTELLIGENCE SUMMARY.

Army Form C. 2118.

(Erase heading not required.)

Instructions regarding War Diaries and Intelligence Summaries are contained in F.S. Regs., Part II. and Staff Manual respectively. Title pages will be prepared in manuscript.

Hour, Date, Place	Summary of Events and Information	Remarks and references to Appendices
MAR.1.17. Glisy.	The Unit marched to "BLANGY-TRONVILLE" 1½ mls. and there billetted for the night. C.M.D.	MOVE
MAR-2-17 WARFUSEE-ABANCOURT	The Unit marched (8 miles) to WARFUSEE ABANCOURT and there billetted in two Adrian huts C.M.D. Horses in open C.M.D. Arrival of 5 motor amt. Cars C.M.D.	" " " " " . Motor Amb. Cars
MAR-4-17 " "	The C.O., O.C.'s 3 Section & 4 R.M.O.'s of 178 Infy Bde proceeded to meeting of army Medical Society at Amiens (or "Spontay") C.M.D.	Medical Meeting.
"-5-17 " "	Bearer subdivision of 'A' Section proceded to CERISY to help in pioneer work on Corps Rest Station there being constructed C.M.D.	DUTY
" 6 " 17 " "	"B" section complete with section transport marched to Corps Rest Station VILLERS = BRETONNEUX as advance party to learn routine of work C.M.D.	MOVE

WAR DIARY
or
INTELLIGENCE SUMMARY.
(Erase heading not required.)

Army Form C. 2118.

Instructions regarding War Diaries and Intelligence Summaries are contained in F.S. Regs., Part II. and the Staff Manual respectively. Title pages will be prepared in manuscript.

Hour, Date, Place	Summary of Events and Information	Remarks and references to Appendices
VILLERS-BRETONNEUX MAR. 8. 1917	Remainder of Unit proceeded from WARFUSEE-ABANCOURT to 3RD CORPS REST STATION at VILLERS-BRETONNEUX and took over same from 1st NORTHUMBRIAN FIELD AMBULANCE. This last Unit proceeded to our vacated billets. CAD Total of patients taken over, including those in	MOVE
PROYART. MAR. 11. 17	readmis section to 692. CAD Meeting of COs of 3. 7 Ambce. 59 Division CWD	NO. IN. HOSPITALS CONFERENCE.
VILLERS-BRETONNEUX MAR. 12. 17	CAPT. HEGGS, 1 NCO, 10 O.R. proceed to Div. School at Montigny for Medical States CWO	STRENGTH
" MAR. 13. 17.	Inspection of Hospitals by D.D.M.S. III CORPS. CWO	INSPECTION.
" MAR. 14. 17.	Opened Canteen for head personnel CWO	CANTEEN.
" " 20. 17	LIEUT. HENDERSON EVERILL of this unit reported from HQ A.D.M.S. 59 DN. for duty. CWO	STRENGTH
" " " "	Pte. Thompson, O.H.B. reported for duty (water) to D.C. 59 DIV. Supply Column.	" "

(73959) W4141-463. 400,000. 9/14. H.&J.Ltd. Forms/C. 2118/10.

WAR DIARY or INTELLIGENCE SUMMARY.

Army Form C. 2118.

(Erase heading not required.)

Hour, Date, Place	Summary of Events and Information	Remarks and references to Appendices
MAR. 24. 1917 VILLERS BRETTONNEUX	2 N.C.O's & 25 men on duty at 3rd Corps Rest Station (in course of erection) reported from base to duty at Cerisy.	MOVES.
	Have 4 day party to A.D.M.S 59 Div. Auth: D.D.M.S. III Corps C.A.O	TIME
MAR. 28. 1917.	11 P.M. Friesnes 12 Midnight CAO	STRENGTH
	Lieut. Henderson Everitt returned from duty with 7th 2/1 N.M. F. Ambce CAO. Return of 10 men detailed for duty to A.D.M.S. 59 Div CAO.	DUTY
	Ceased to admit patients at 3rd Corps Rest Station CAO Started to evacuate material to 3rd Corps Rest Station at Cerisy, & patients to CAS. on duty. CAO	
	2 water carts, personnel horses, & one man went to Clayton disinfector, report from this unit for duty at 3rd C.R.S. CERISY. (Authority D.D.M.S. 3rd Corps) CAO	DUTY
" 29. 1917 "	Arrival of Advance Party 141 7 Ambce. CAO	MOVES
" 30. 1917 "		
" 31. 1917 "	CAPT J.E.S. SMITH & 3 M. Ambces & advance party of 120.R forward to & arrive at M.D.S. at VILLERS CARBONNEL taking over from 2/1 N.M.F. AMBCE. CAO CAPT JOHNSTON & LT H. EVERILL & one complete section proceed en route to VILLERS CARBONNEL & slept tonight at Bois St Martin OCO Winton Lieut Col RAMSETT 4. Ambce A/ag 2/3 N. Mid. (59 Div.)	MOVES

Confidential

War Diary

of

O.C. 2/3rd Nth. Mid. Fd. Ambce.

From April 1st 1917.   To April 30th 1917.

(Volume IV)

[stamp: COMMITTEE FOR THE MEDICAL HISTORY OF THE WAR — Date 6 JUN. 1917]

Army Form C. 2118.

WAR DIARY
or
INTELLIGENCE SUMMARY.
(Erase heading not required.)

Instructions regarding War Diaries and Intelligence Summaries are contained in F. S. Regs., Part II. and the Staff Manual respectively. Title pages will be prepared in manuscript.

Hour, Date, Place	Summary of Events and Information	Remarks and references to Appendices
VILLERS-CARBONNEL AP.1.1917	1. N.C.O. + 2 men sent to A.D.P. at MISERY C.U.S. H.Q. Established VILLERS-CARBONNEL. Arrival of 2.Officers + One section from BOIS-ST.MARTIN. 1 Officer Reconnoitered of unit Dus via party near VILLERS-BRETONNEUX for BOIS-ST.MARTIN C.U.O.	Duty.
" AP.1.1917	CAPT W. JOHNSTON reports to O.C. 9/5 N. STAFFS for duty @ H.Q.	MOVES
" AP.2.1917	1 N.C.O. + 2 D.R. to A.D.P. MISERY C.U.O. Arrival at VILLERS CARBONNEL of Remainder of unit less tim party C.U.O. LT HENDERSON EVERIEL Transferred sick from this unit to III Corps Rest Station at CERISY C.U.O. Withdrew 1N.C.O. + 2 O.R. from A.D.P. @ REST. MISERY C.U.O.	DUTY STRENGTH MOVE. STRENGTH
" AP.3.17	36 Bearers report for duty to O.C. 9/ N.M. + Andre C.U.O	Duty.
" AP.4.17	Captain Lee reports for duty to O.C. 9/N.M. + Andre C.U.O	" "
" "	14 Additional Bearers report for duty to O.C. 9/N.M.+Andre C.U.O	" "
" "	Erection of a hut in village 50 yards long 5 ft high of 50,000 bricks stored by tanks, roofed with corrugate to hold 130 Personnel having eleven "rooms" C.U.O	Billets

WAR DIARY
or
INTELLIGENCE SUMMARY.

(Erase heading not required.)

Army Form C. 2118.

Hour, Date, Place	Summary of Events and Information	Remarks and references to Appendices
Ap. 6.17 Villers Carbonnel	14 Bearers return from duty with 2/1 N.M.F. Ambce C.C.S.	Duty
" 7.17 "	Completion of 50 yards horselines made of wooden framework filled in with bricks. C.C.P.	Horselines
" 10.17 "	Completion of 2nd Adrian Hut. Horseslong of two huts from neighbouring German dug-outs with lathes, forms + chairs C.C.P.	Rest station
" " "	Opened as 59 Div. Rest station C.C.P.	Duty
12 midnight " " "	Return of Pte 2565 Penny from working day for Disinfector for No.1. F. Ambce III Corps R.S. CERISY C.C.O.	Strength
11.17 " "		" "
16.17 " "	Return of Lieut Errill from Hospital (III C.R.S. CERISY) C.C.O.	" "
17.17 " "	Captain Smith evacuated to C.C.S. Heilly with "Rose" Measles. O.C.	" "
" " " "	Visit of General Sir H. Rawlinson Bt Comy. IV Army.	Inspection (informal)
18 " " "	Inspection by General Romer. G.O.C. 59 Division	" "
23 " " "	Surgeon General O'Keefe. D.M.S. IV Army	" "

Army Form C. 2118.

WAR DIARY
or
INTELLIGENCE SUMMARY.
(Erase heading not required.)

Hour, Date, Place	Summary of Events and Information	Remarks and references to Appendices
AP. 24. 17. VILLERS CARBONNEL	Return of Captain Heggs from duty with III Corps Training School MONTIGNY. C.A.O.	DUTY
" 25. 17. "	Arrival of Reinforcements :- Lieut S.F.H. OWENS to O.R. No 38 C.C.S. C.A.O.	REINFORCEMENTS.
" 26. 17. "	Return of CAPT. J.E.S. SMITH from C.C.S. HEILLY discharged following "nose" measles.	STRENGTH C.A.O.
" 28. 17. "	Arrival of Lieut Ferguson & No 19 Mobile Laboratory to investigate cases of diarrhoea. Provision of a ward & medium-making apartment. C.A.O.	No 19. MOBILE LABORATORY
" 30 " " "	Arrival of Captain Gemmell from No 38 C.C.S. HEILLY in connection with the treatment of cases of diarrhoea & their investigation C.A.O.	59 Divisional Branches

C. A. Didston (?) N.M. A Freshwater
Lieut Col. O.C. 2/3 (59 Division)

Confidential

War Diary

of

2/3rd Nth. Mid. Fd. Ambce

From: 1/5/17   To: 31/5/17

(Volume V.)

Army Form C. 2118.

WAR DIARY
or
INTELLIGENCE SUMMARY.
(Erase heading not required.)

Instructions regarding War Diaries and Intelligence Summaries are contained in F. S. Regs., Part II. and the Staff Manual respectively. Title pages will be prepared in manuscript.

Hour, Date, Place	Summary of Events and Information	Remarks and references to Appendices
MAY. 3. 1917. VILLERS-CARBONNEL. Mob. (Rowie Control) N.30.d.6.7	Completion of Village Baths. Three lines V.C. rifles. Presentation by General C.T. Romer. C.B., C.M.G. P.D.C. G.O.C. to No 2491 Pte. S. Arnold 2/3 NORTH MIDLAND FIELD AMBULANCE, on parade, of a copy of IV Army R.O. No 64. Vide Appendix '2'.	19th Infantry. HONOURS & AWARDS Appendix "2". STRENGTH DUTY
MAY. 11 " "	CAPTAIN R.H. HEGGS proceeds as M.O. to III Corps Training School FOUCAUCOURT. CAP.	" "
MAY. 12 " "	CAPTAIN J.E.S. SMITH relieves LIEUT AITKEN as M.O. 2/6 S. STAFFS B.M. at quarry E. of Templeux. 62.C.L.3.d.7.3. CAP.	" "
" " " "	Visit of D.D.M.S. CAVALRY CORPS and A.D.M.S. V CAVALRY DIV. CAP	" "
" 18 " "	Return of CAPTAIN J.E.S. SMITH from 2/6 S. STAFFS CAP.	" "
" 22 " "	Loan of party of 6 men B.O.C. No 55 C.C.S July to help erect an Adrian Hut. CAP.	

(73969) W4141—463. 400,000. 9/14. H.&J.Ltd. Forms/C. 2118/10.

WAR DIARY or INTELLIGENCE SUMMARY

Army Form C. 2118.

Hour, Date, Place	Summary of Events and Information	Remarks and references to Appendices
VILLERS-CARBONNEL MAY 25, 1917	Mon went to NEUVILLE - BONJOURVAL + METZ 57C P 22 (1/40,000) + 57 C Q 20. (1/40,000) Again	MOTS! MOVE
NEUVILLE-BONJOURVAL 57C P 22 (1/40,000) MAY 31.	Move completed as per Operation order No.1. and A.D.S. (Mets. 57C Q.20 1/40,000), Relay Post, Loading Post + Reg. mounted Aid Post opened. Completed map appears in diary of JUNE 1917. (JP)	→ Appendix No 3

(Signature)

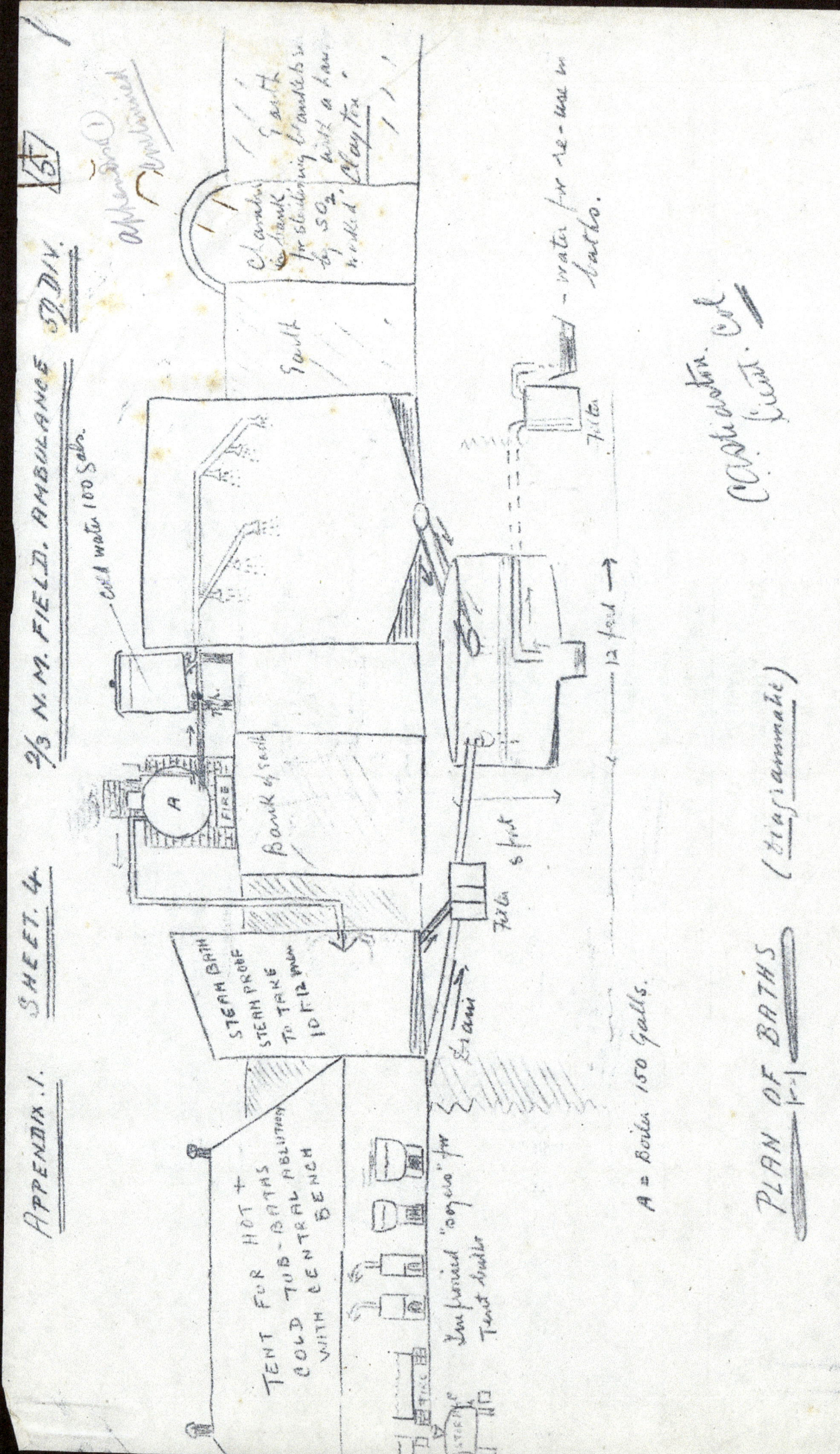

COPY NO. 6

OPERATION ORDER NO 1.

by Lieut Colonel C.A.Stidston.. Commanding

2/3rd North Midland Field Ambulance...

=:=

VILLERS=CARBONNEL.

May 24th.1917..

MAP REFERENCES..
No 1. FRANCE. 57c.. 1/40000
No 2. FRANCE. 62c.. 1/40000.

1. MOVEMENT.

(a) A & C.Sections complete, and with one days Rations will proceed by March, Route; to the Rest Camp (Map 1. V 16.B.2.5.) South of EQUANCOURT. via PERONNE - NURLU .. on Friday May 25th 1917.

(b) On Saturday May 26th.1917, A.Section will proceed by Route March to NEUVILLE BOURJONVAL (Map 1. P.22.0.7.) and establish there, the Headquarters.

(c) On Saturday May 26th.1917 C.Section complete, will proceed to METZ-EN-COUTURE (Map 1. Q 20.D.5.2.) and will serve the following Regimental Aid Posts, Loading Post and Relay Posts, all on Ref Map 1..

Regimental Aid Posts.   Q.15. C.central.
                            Q.16. C.central.
Loading Post.   Q.28. C.central.   Stretchers
Relay Posts.   Q.23.C.8.8. (10 Bearers and 3 Wheeled
                            Q.21.B.2.6.

2. DETAIL OF MAIN DRESSING STATION.   3 Medical Officers.
                                                 1 Bearer sub-division.
                                                 4 Motor Ambulances.

3. RELIEF.   Relief will be completed by the 27th instant at 6-0 p.m.

4. DETAIL ORDERS.   Detailed Orders will be issued after I have inspected the M.D.S., R.A.P. and Relay Post.

5. MOVEMENT.
B.Section will remain at VILLERS-CARBONNEL, Divisional Rest Station and complete evacuation of patients, under details to be notified later, and on or after May 28th will proceed by Route March to the Rest Camp, above mentioned, and the following day to Headquarters at NEUVILLE-BOURJONVAL.
Capt Lee of B.Section will rejoin the Unit, under orders to be issued later.

6. RATIONS.   Refilling Point will be notified when received..

C.A.Stidston
Lieut.Col.R.A.M.C.(TF)
O/C 2/3rd North Midland Field Ambulance..

DISTRIBUTION.
Copy No 1. A.D.M.S. 59th Division.
     2. O/C A.Section.
     3. O/C B.Section.
     4. O/C C.Section.
     5. O/C T.Section.
     6. File.   7 &8. War Diary..

140/2230

2/3rd North Midland F.A.

June 1917

51/

COMMITTEE FOR THE
MEDICAL HISTORY OF THE WAR
Date - 7 AUG. 1917

CONFIDENTIAL

WAR DIARY

OF

2/3rd NORTH MIDLAND FIELD AMBULANCE.

From.....June 1st, 1917
To.......June 31st, 1917.

(Volume 6.)

Army Form C. 2118.

WAR DIARY
or
INTELLIGENCE SUMMARY.
(Erase heading not required.)

Instructions regarding War Diaries and Intelligence Summaries are contained in F. S. Regs., Part II. and the Staff Manual respectively. Title pages will be prepared in manuscript.

Hour, Date, Place	Summary of Events and Information	Remarks and references to Appendices
June 1. 1917 NEUVILLE-BONJOURVAL (57.c P.22) (H.Q.) METZ-EN-COUTURE (57.c Q.20) A.D.S.	System of collecting & evacuating wounded to complete. See working order. m/s reference in Appendix (4), and tracing one from 1/1 E. LANCS. F. AMBCE completed. C.P.O.	Collectors details. Appendice (4)
June 3. 1917	11.15 p.m. False gas alarm. C.P.O.	Gas alarm
June -4- 1917	LIEUT. S. H. KINGSTON R.A.M.C. taken on strength.	Strength
" 5 " 1917	CAPT. B. M. ZOOTNER transports to No. 3 Cap. General Hospital. Treport an M.O. C.P.O.	" "
" 6 "	LT OWEN relieves M.O. o/c SHERWOOD FORESTERS C.P.O	July
" 9 "	CAPT. W. JOHNSTON relieves M.O. 4/5 SOUTH STAFFS C.P.O	Ing

(73959) W4141—463. 400,000. 9/14. H.&J.Ltd. Forms/C. 2118/10.

WAR DIARY
or
INTELLIGENCE SUMMARY.
(Erase heading not required.)

Army Form C. 2118.

Hour, Date, Place	Summary of Events and Information	Remarks and references to Appendices
NEUVILLE - BON JOURVAL METZ EN = COUTURE JUNE 14. 1917	Every available man in the unit has been apart from medical work, employed in taking out German dug-outs & inverting them at, & forward of the A.D.S. Inside of the A.D.S. (by means of 8 bored shifts) a dug out of outside Shaft L 102 feet long having 3 entrances 25 steps deep is in course of erection 25 feet underground. Further smaller dug-outs have been erected at the A.D.S. & 2 relay posts, all of which have been constructed & 2 relay posts, all of which have been constructed. Lately technical advice & a few extra workers have been given to no 19 to R.E. C.R.P. of similar dug-out and is further rotated at (Map 57.C Q.27.C.3.6) as an ADS for men in evening Division. C.P.O.	WORK Making of Dug out Hospital.
JUNE 21. 1917	100 feet of trench in trays having 3 entrances. Split slash 2 feet wide have been dug at NEUVILLE -BON JOURNAL for the protection of residents personnel in event of shelling etc.	

Army Form C. 2118.

WAR DIARY
or
INTELLIGENCE SUMMARY.
(Erase heading not required.)

Instructions regarding War Diaries and Intelligence Summaries are contained in F. S. Regs., Part II. and the Staff Manual respectively. Title pages will be prepared in manuscript.

Hour, Date, Place	Summary of Events and Information	Remarks and references to Appendices
JUNE. 30. 1917 NEUVILLE - BONJOURVAL	Completion of large dug-out at METZ.	Dug-outs
JUNE. 30. 1917	Captain Johnston evacuated to No. 48. C.C.S. with R.U.O. C.P.O.	Evacuation of M.O.
JUNE. 30. 1917	During the month the following cases have been evacuated from A.D.S. at METZ:— Sick 490 Wounded 120 —— Total 610	Sick + wounded evacuated

O.D. Nicholls
Lieut Col. R.A.M.C. (T.F.)
O/C 2/3 W. Rid. Fd. Amb.
54 Division

War Diary
2/3 N. Mid. Field Amb.

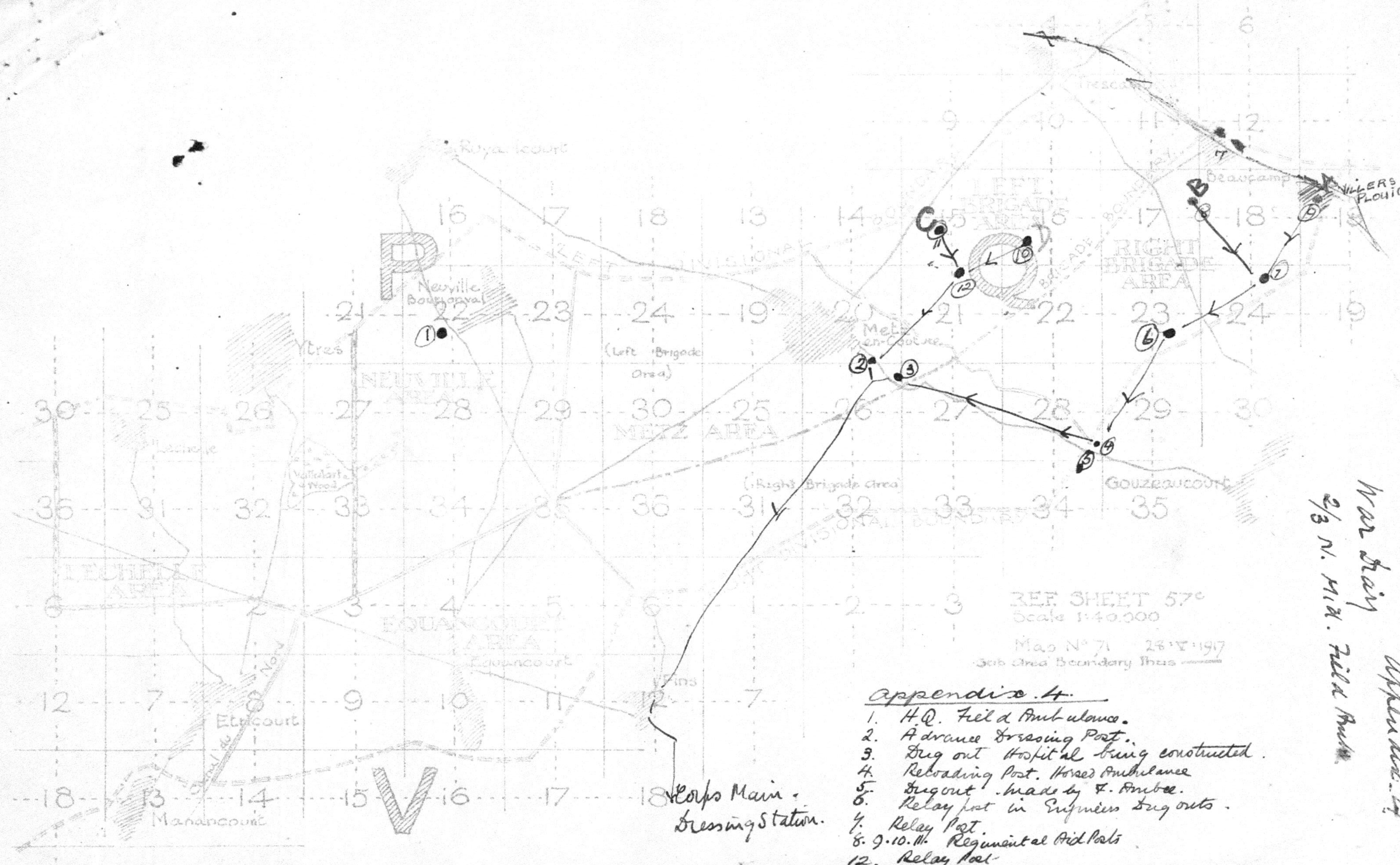

Appendix 4

Appendix 4.
1. H.Q. Field Ambulance.
2. Advance Dressing Post.
3. Dug out Hospital being constructed.
4. Rebinding Post. Horsed Ambulance.
5. Dug out. Head of F. Ambce.
6. Relay Post in Infantry Dug outs.
7. Relay Post.
8, 9, 10, 11. Regimental Aid Posts.
12. Relay Post.

REF SHEET 57c
Map No 71   28·V·1917
Scale 1:40,000
3rd Inca Boundary lines

CONFIDENTIAL

140/298

Vol 6

COMMITTEE FOR THE
MEDICAL HISTORY OF THE WAR
Date   10 SEP. 1917

WAR DIARY

OF

2/3 NM Fd Amb

July 1917

Army Form C. 2118.

WAR DIARY
or
INTELLIGENCE SUMMARY.
(Erase heading not required.)

Instructions regarding War Diaries and Intelligence Summaries are contained in F.S. Regs., Part II. and the Staff Manual respectively. Title pages will be prepared in manuscript.

Hour, Date, Place	Summary of Events and Information	Remarks and references to Appendices
NEUVILLE = BOURJONVAL. 57.c.7.22. July 2. 1917.	At 10.30 p.m. a gas alarm. No actual gas experienced in units area, but gas casualties occurred one mile north. CMD	GAS.
" 3 " 1917	False gas alarm. 2 P.M. CMD	"
" 10 " "	No. 417009 Sgt Bevan) attended for 6 days gas course. No. 421333 Sgt. Harper) at Barastre. CMD	"
BARASTRE, MAP. 57C. Edition 2. France 1/40,000 O.15. d.7.2. and O.10. c.1.2.	Relief of existing area completed with 2/3 7. D.(H.C.) 5-8 for 7 men + 2 sections of this unit to camp O.10.c.12. kilomaterly of unit to Bevmit school, BARASTRE (where on base and Hostel was materiel) completed in accordance with operation order No. 2 this appendix. 5. CMD	RELIEF? MOVE.}} Appendix. 5
" July/15/17	1 officer + 30 O.R. report for duty to O.C. 2/5 H.C. 7 Rndre (58 Dn) at MARICOURT. CMD	DUTY.

Army Form C. 2118.

WAR DIARY
or
INTELLIGENCE SUMMARY.
(Erase heading not required.)

Instructions regarding War Diaries and Intelligence Summaries are contained in F.S. Regs., Part II. and the Staff Manual respectively. Title pages will be prepared in manuscript.

Hour, Date, Place	Summary of Events and Information	Remarks and references to Appendices
BARASTRE. 24/Jy/17	Capt. Stephen R. Malory-Kennedy, U.S. Reserve reports for duty. C.W.O	STRENGTH.
" " 27/July/17	Divisional Tactical Scheme. Orders for Collecting 1000 Casualties, in Appendix 6. C.W.O.	Tactical Scheme. Appendix 6
" " 29. Jy. 1917	2 N.C.O's & 3 men report & take over guard at the stores of No. 7. AUSTRALIAN FIELD AMB.E. (ALBERT) C.W.O	DUTY
" " 27 July 1917	Letter to A.D.M.S., 5g Div: on re cross of R.V. & Sick cars Appendix 7.	Appendix 7
" " 31 July 1917	Issuing the M.T. Horse Transport Orders & Time table for A.S.C. M.T. attached Appendix 8.	Horse Transport A.S.C. Appendix 8

C. R. Chapman
Lieut. Col. R.A.M.C.(T) O.C.
313 Fr. Mob. Div. Sanitary Sections

Appendix/5/
No 2.

OPERATION ORDERS

BY

Lieut. Colonel C.A. Stidston.. Commanding.

2/3rd North Midland Field Ambulance. 59th Divn.

1. Map Reference. FRANCE. Sheet 57c (Edition 2) 1/40,000.

2. On Wednesday July 5th. 1917 Lieut. Kingston and the Tent Sub-Division of "C" Section will proceed by Route March to the "Convent School" BARASTRE (O.16.a.2.2.) via ETRES and BUS, and there, prepare for a Hospital of 50 Stretchers to accomodate the Sick of the 176th Infantry Brigade Group.

3. O/C "B" Section will complete relief of the Collecting Area with the Advance Section of the 2/3rd Field Ambulance. 58th Division by 6-0 p.m. on Sunday July 8th. 1917, and will then march -- complete with Baggage -- to Headquarters at NEUVILLE BONJOURVAL.

4. The entire Ambulance -- less Hospital party at BARASTRE and less advance party to be detailed later -- will parade in full Marching Order, with Transport in the Brick Yard at NEUVILLE BONJOURVAL at 7-30 a.m. on Tuesday July 10th. 1917.

5. Headquarters of the Field Ambulance will close at NEUVILLE BONJOURVAL on Tuesday July 10th. 1917 at 8-0 a.m. and will open at the "Convent School" BARASTRE on Tuesday July 10th. 1917 at 8-0 a.m.

6. The site of occupation of Main Body will be issued later -- when ascertained.

7. The Field Ambulance will move with Mobilization Stores and Equipment only.

8. Detailed Orders will be issued to the Officers concerned later.

Lieut. Col. R.A.M.C. (TF)
O/C 2/3rd North Midland Field Ambulance.

DISTRIBUTION.

1. A.D.M.S., I.V. (2copies)
2. O/C Adv. Section. 2/3rd F.A.
        58th Division.
3. All Officers of 2/3rd N.M.F.A.
4. War Diary.   (2copies)
5. File   (2copies)

COPY NO....

Appendix 6 (no 2)

59th DIVISION TACTICAL EXERCISE NO 1.

OPERATION ORDER NO 1
BY
LIEUT.COL.C.A.STIDSTON.. COMMANDING 2/3RD NORTH MID. FIELD AMBLCE.

24/7/17.

REFERENCE MAPS.
1. FRANCE. Sheet 57c   Edition 2.
2. "   Sheet 62c   1/40,000
3. Map a.   (copy enclosed)
4. Map b.   do.

1. On Z day the 59th Division will attack the enemy's trenches between U.1.b.70.20 and K.36.d.40.20. (Map 1) at the same time the M th Division will attack on the right and the N th Division on the left of the 59th Division.

2. The attack of the 59th Division will be made by the 178th Infantry Brigade on the right and the 177th Infantry Brigade on the left. Dividing line is shewn on Map a.   Objectives are:-
    a. German Front line Trench.
    b. Star Trench.
    c. Treacle Trench.

3. After the capture of Treacle Trench, 176th Infantry Brigade will pass through 178th and 177th Brigades and consolidate a position in continuation of Prometheus Trench through (Map 1) 0.32 central and Windmill mound to the main PERONNE = BAPAUME Road.
176th Brigade will leave its assembly trenches at zero and will time its advance so as to be close up to the barrage at Zero plus 53.

    Simultaneously the 200th Infantry Brigade of the Mth Division is to attack Prometheus Trench and the 210th Brigade of the N th Division will gain the eastern end of LE TRANSLOY.

4. 178th and 177th Infantry Brigades will form up with the attack in the front, support and 2 reserve trenches.
176th Brigade will form up in intermediate line.

5. Artillery Barrage as in Map "B"

6. 2/3rd North Midland Field Ambulance will collect and evacuate up to 1000 wounded from the 178th Brigade.

7. EVACUATIONS. Casualties will be evacuated to Corps Main Dressing Station at BOUCHAVESNES (62c.. C.4.d.)

8. The 2/2nd N.M.Field Ambulance will be collecting for the 177th brigade on our left, and the X th Ambulance for the 200th Inf. Brigade on our right.

9. The Ambulance will be distributed as follows:-
H.Q.-COMBLES - 57c. T. 28.
A.D.S.- "THE HEBULE". - 57c U.13.a.4.6.
    O.C. "A" Section.
    2. Medical Officers.
    Tent sub-division "A" Section.
    24 Reserve Bearers from "A" Section.
    3. Horsed Ambulances.
    10 Miller-James Wheeled Stretchers.
    2. Water Carts.

COLLECTING POST.-- In dugouts -- 57c U.7.a.6.0.
    2 Medical Officers of "B" Section
    36 Bearers. of "B" Section.
    ½ Tent sub-division of B.Section.

Dug-outs b Hebule by Beeauville.

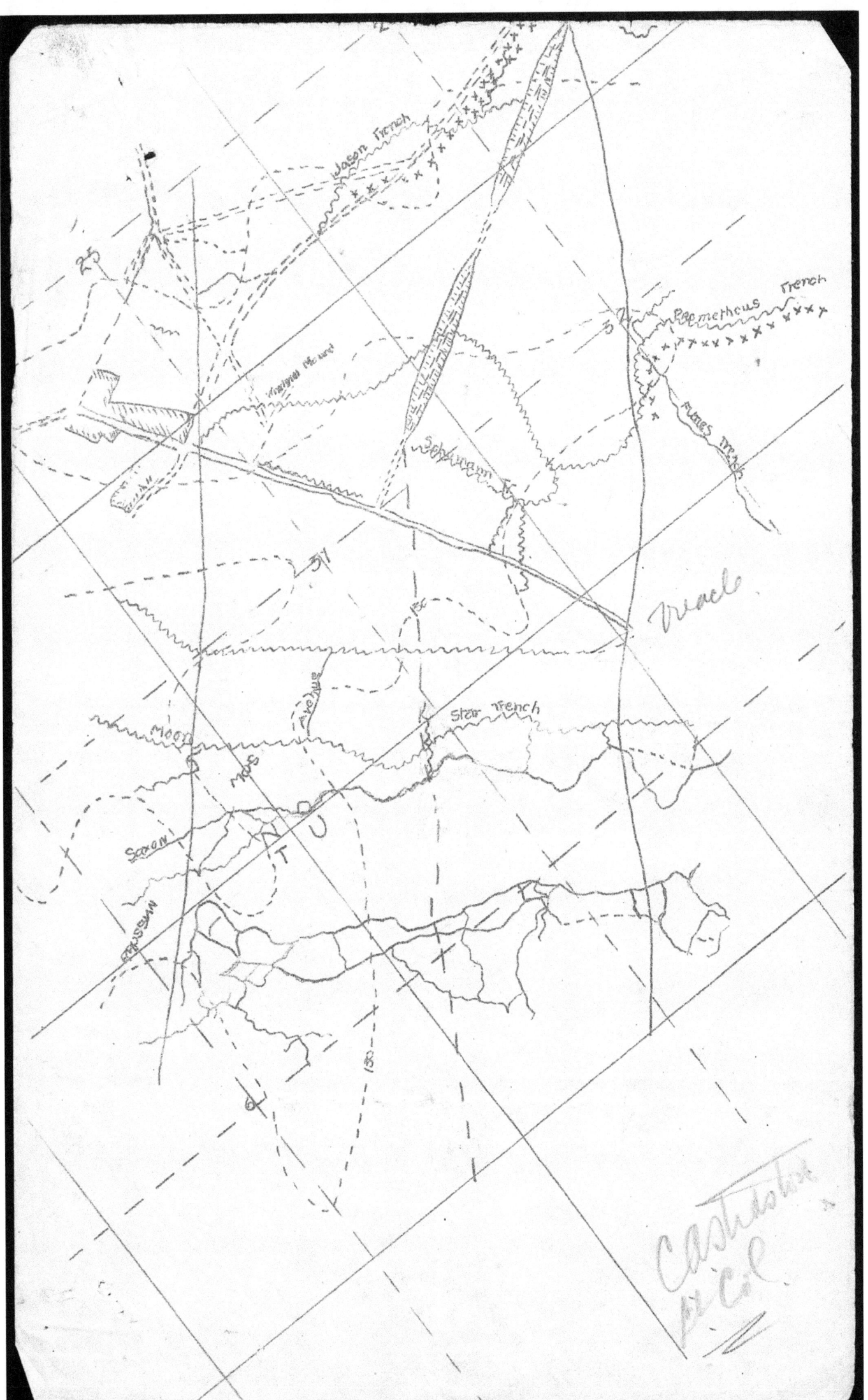

C O P Y.. P.U.O + LICE   Appendix 7

From:- O/C 2/3rd North Midland Field Ambulance..

To:- A.D.M.S.
    59th Division.

    During the past 20 days, 368 cases have been admitted from Troops in the 176th Brigade Group to this Hospital. Of these, 171 cases (that is just under 50%) have been P.U.O. cases, and of these 171, 119 (that is over 70%) have had to be evacuated to Convalescent or Casualty Clearing Hospitals. 26 cases have been discharged to duty (that is less than 7%).. 26 cases remain in Hospital (that is less than 7%) of which remaining cases 50% will have to be evacuated.

    I would beg to point out that if this rate of wastage persists, approx 1000 men of the Division will become Sick per Month, of which 500 will be lost to the Division at first for a period of 1 week, and later from 1 to 4 weeks, and the other 500 for a period of 3 to 5 weeks.

    Having in view the evidence as regards infection by lice, in the book of Dr Arthur Hurst (late Hertz) recently published, and such articles as that of Dr Grievson in the current issue of the "Lancet", and the recent works of German physicans, I would suggest that during the present period of intensive training, at least 3 days might be devoted to delousing the Division, and to elaborate a scheme of isolation of the contacts and co-sleepers.

    The figures indicate the man-day loss to the Division thus occupied, would be found much less than the man-day loss at present occurring from this contagious louse-born disease.

    All the patients who come to this Hospital with this disease are lousey. This preliminary suggestion is put forward for your consideration. I would beg to state that it is almost impossible for a man to remain louseless, whilst blanketless..

    (signed) C.A. STIDSTON.. Lieut.Col.R.A.M.C
  O/C 2/3rd North Midland Field Ambulance.. T.F.

July 27th. 1917.

STANDING ORDERS..

FOR TRANSPORT ATTACHED 2/3RD NORTH MIDLAND FIELD AMBULANCE..

Appendix 8.

1. The Officer appointed by the Lieut.Colonel Commanding the Field Ambulance will issue all orders and receive all orders, and be responsible to the Officer Commanding for the general efficiency of the Transport.

2. The office of the Officer so appointed will be his tent or quarters " in the Field ".

3. In the absence of the Officer i/c Transport, the Warrant Officer A.S.C. will receive and issue any necessary orders.

4. The Warrant Officer A.S.C. is directly responsible to the Oi/c Transport for the maintenance of discipline, duty roster, condition of vehicles and harness, and horses and mules.

5. The Warrant Officer will report to the Oi/c Transport at 9-0 a.m. daily for any orders or reports, and will furnish daily at the same time, a state shewing names of Orderly Sergeant and picquets, duty section, also Sick report of men and horses.

6. A statement will also be shewn daily of all horses shod, specifying which hoofs were dealt with.

7. ALL papers, lists of repairs or requisitions are, before being handed in, to be signed by the Oi/c Transport.

8. The allotment of sites for Horse lines, parks, incinerators, latrines Warrant Officer, Sergeants and men's quarters will be made by the Oi/c Transport, when on the march or in taking up new quarters.

9. When any Officerw wishes to inspect the Transport or Transport lines., e.g. O.C.59th Div.Train., A.D.V.S., the Warrant Officer is at once to report by messenger to the Oi/c Transport.

10. Should any N.C.O. or man be leaving the camp either for a course of instruction or leave, he will at first report to Oi/c Transport through his Section Sergeant.

11. As far as possible, all work will be conducted by Sections, and the responsibility of Section Sergeants encouraged, and if possible there will be a duty section for the day, to furnish wagons, picquets and fatigues.

12. Sergeants will adopt towards their subordinates such methods of command and treatment as will ensure respect for their authority.

13. Any soldier suffering from Venereal disease is to report such without delay. Concealment of such disease is a crime.

14. Para 560 Kings Regulations is to be understood by the N.C.O's and men. e.g., "A soldier of a stable guard or picquet is posted over horses, or otherwise a sentry, and is regularly relieved as such, he is to be regarded as a sentry, although without arms".

15. Horses will be watered four times daily, at arranged times, when circumstances permit, and every horse will be on parade for this purpose at arranged hours, before actual watering commences.

16. These orders will be initialled from time to time by the Warrant Officer, as having been read and understood.

17. The Warrant Officer must be present on all parades and stables, including early morning stables.

18. The Orderly Sergeant of the day is responsible for the cleanliness of the horse lines and quarters of men, posting of picquets: He is to report personally to the Officer i/c Transport " all correct" when relieved and be present at the Cookhouse distribution of meals. He is also responsible for the dispatching and safe return of all vehicles, and will at once report any injury to a horse or damage to a vehicle or equipment. On no account will he leave Camp.

19. No N.C.O. or man will leave the Camp without the knowledge of the Oi/c for any purpose except duty.

20. All issues of Green envelopes, tobacco or extras will be made by, or in the presence of the O i/c.

21. In case of any N.C.O. or man being admitted to Hospital, the W.O. will report to Officer i/c Transport at once.

22. As far as practicable there will be two horse lines each for Ride and Draught horses. The horses will always be tied up at their allotted place on these lines.

23. Nose-bags when not in use, will be hung up, and inspected once daily.

24. Sergeants are notified by ~~an Officer~~ that any order given by an Officer must be at once complied with, and without question, and if not instantly complied with, the consequences are serious.

25. The Oi/c of Transport is empowered to deal with minor offences, but should the man prefer it, he can elect to go in front of the Commanding Officer.

26. The W.B. will ascertain from the Oi/c whether horses are to be grazed, or when grazing is to be discontinued.

27. Hay nets will always be suspended from a wire along the tops of the Horse line posts, for feeding.

28. Nosebags and hay nets are to removed immediately feeding is completed by the horse picquets at once.

29. On no account must an Officers horse be ridden by any but the Officer on whose charge it is, except with special permission or when being exercised by his groom, under his (the Officers') instructions. This also applies to Mounted Horse picquets.

30. No Officers horse is on any account to be used for any purpose but riding, without reference to the Oi/c.

31. A Roll call will be read at Early morning, noon and evening stables and any N.C.O. or man absent will be reported without fail to the Officer i/c

32. A time-table will be posted in the harness room shewing times of Stables, watering and feeding of horses, mens meals etc., etc.,

33. Horse picquets will not absent themselves off the lines between stable hours, and will know always the number of horses under their charge.

34. All sick horses will be inspected at 10-0a.m. by the Oi/c.

35. Watering, feeding and grooming of horses will take place at the regular hours appointed, without fail, when in camp.

36. Any applications to the C.O. by W.O., N.C.O's or men will be made through the Officer i/c Transport.

37. Whenever an order for wagons or limbers is received, it must be ascertained if any loaders or fatigue party has been warned, and in order to save wasted journeys, the horses should not be hooked in until the loaders or fatigue party reports to the Orderly Sergt.

Sheet 2..

38. Horse respirators will be kept in Harness Shed and inspected weekly.

39. The Officer i/c will see all men reporting sick at his tent or quarters at 7-0 a.m.

40. There will be four Mounted Picquets posted when all the horses are out grazing. Two will stand by their horses and two remain mounted, hour about.

41. All men proceeding out of Camp to sports or Cinema etc., will parade and be inspected by the W.O. before leaving Camp. They must be properly dressed and equipped.

42. Every day at the beginning of stables, the Corporal farrier will, with the shoeing smith, examine every horse in the Stables. He will report to the Officer i/c. He will also report any unhealthy condition of the feet.

43. A Roster will be posted shewing nominal roll of men available for picquets, and adhered to in order.

C. A. Stidston
Lieut. Col.R.A.M.C.(TF)
O/C 2/3rd North Midland Field Ambulance..

CONFIDENTIAL..

WAR DIARY OF

THE

2/3RD NORTH MIDLAND FIELD AMBLCE.

FOR

AUGUST... 1917.

:=:=:=:=:=:=:=:=:=:

Army Form C. 2118.

WAR DIARY
or
INTELLIGENCE SUMMARY.
(Erase heading not required.)

Instructions regarding War Diaries and Intelligence Summaries are contained in F.S. Regs., Part II. and the Staff Manual respectively. Title pages will be prepared in manuscript.

Hour, Date, Place	Summary of Events and Information	Remarks and references to Appendices
Aug. 2. 1917 BARASTRE	Capt. H.A. Butler R.A.M.C. reports for duty. C.A.S.	Strength
" 3 " "	Corporal Hodgkiss leaves for Cookery Class at Albert. C.A.O.	Duty
" " " "	Two O.R. A.S.C. attached report for duty. C.A.O.	Duty Strength
" 4 " "	Notification received that Capt. W. Johnston (P.U.O) was evacuated to England 27/6/17. C.A.O.	Strength
" 6 " "	Lt. Owens + 2.O.R. report for duty BELLE-VUE FARM ALBERT. evacuated by 7th Australian Field Ambulance C.A.S.	Duty
" " " "	Three O.R. join Lt. E.E. Owens C.W.O.	Duty
" 8 " "	Notification received of Capt. G.F. Dennings evacuation (P.U.O) England. C.A.O.	Strength

Army Form C. 2118.

WAR DIARY
or
INTELLIGENCE SUMMARY.
(Erase heading not required.)

Instructions regarding War Diaries and Intelligence Summaries are contained in F.S. Regs., Part II. and the Staff Manual respectively. Title pages will be prepared in manuscript.

Hour, Date, Place	Summary of Events and Information	Remarks and references to Appendices
Aug. 11. 17. BARASTRE	F.G.C.M. held on Q.M.S.T. WOOD under III ARMY R.O. "having alcohol in his billet". The accused was found guilty men tinent Coys. to reduction to rank of Sgt. but the G.O.C. 59 Division did not confirm the finding app.	F.G.C.M
" 13. 17. " "	At the present time the following are away from the unit on duty :-	

					STRENGTH
					DUTY

Officer	O.R.	UNIT	PLACE	DUTY	
	2	4½ & 3rd ARMIES VILLERS-BRETTONEUX		Care of army troops, civilians & German Prisoners	
1	30	III C.R.S.	MARICOURT	MEDICAL	
1	20	48 C.C.S.	YTRES	"	
	1	21. C.C.S.	YTRES.	DENTAL	
1	7	7. AUST. F.A.	ALBERT	GUARDING & CHECKING STORES	
	5	?	THILLOY	DIGGING LATRINES	
1	1	21 C.C.S.	YTRES	MEDICAL	
Total 5	65				

WAR DIARY
or
INTELLIGENCE SUMMARY.

(Erase heading not required.)

Army Form C. 2118.

2/3 N.M.F. Ambce. 59 Sqn

Hour, Date, Place	Summary of Events and Information	Remarks and references to Appendices
Aug. 13. 17. BARASTRE	CAPT. H.A. CUTLER reports for duty to O.C. 21 C.C.S. C/O	Duty
	1 N.C.O. & 3. O.R. reported sick from Abbt. C/O	Strength
	1 N.C.O. & 6 Grners – reinforcements to A.S.C attached reported for duty. C/O	Reinforcements.
" 18.17 " "	Captain S.R. M CENNEDY. U.S.R. struck off strength on attachment to no 48 C.C.S. Authority ADMS 59 DIV. C/O 29	Strength
" 20.17 " "	CAPT. HENDERSON EVERIL evacuated to 21 C.C.S. with P.U.O. C/O	Strength
" 22.17 " "	1. O. & 29 O.R. returned from duty at 2 C.R.S MARICOURT.	" "
	LT. S.H. KINGSTON reports for duty to 75 Lanes Reg.	DUTY
	1. O. & 5. O.R return from duty at ALBERT. C/O	Strength

WAR DIARY
or
INTELLIGENCE SUMMARY.

(Erase heading not required.)

Army Form C. 2118
2/3 N.M.F. AMBCE. 57 DIV

Place	Hour, Date	Summary of Events and Information	Remarks and references to Appendices
BARASTRE	22/Aug/17	The UNIT proceeded to HELLENCOURT MAP. LENS. 11 in accordance with Operation Order No 3.	MOVE Afton Rec 9. + there Appendix 9.
MILLENCOURT (LENS. 11. H.6.1.1.)	23/Aug/17	Opened a hospital of 20 stretchers. 20. O.R. returned from duty at 48. C.C.S.	STRENGTH C.A.O. " "
		CAPT. H.A. CUTLER returned to duty from 21 C.C.S.	C.A.O. " "
		CAPT. F.R.M. HEGGS + 2 O.R. returned from duty at VILLERS = BRETONNEUX.	C.A.O.
"	"	The unit moved to SENLIS. MAP 57 D V.17.C.5.7 + occupied a camp over used as a hospital + opened a 20 stretcher hospital for 176 Bdge, inspecting light cars to III C.K.S at MARICOURT + serious to no 9. C.C.S AVELUY.	MOVE C.A.O.
		At BARASTRE the Unit had a detention hospital from Aug 10.17 to Aug 22 17, during which period the following epitomism the case - details	

Army Form C. 2118.

WAR DIARY
or
INTELLIGENCE SUMMARY

2/3 N.M.T. AMB.C.E. 59 DIV.

(Erase heading not required.)

Place	Date	Hour	Summary of Events and Information	Remarks and references to Appendices
SENLIS. 57 D.V.17e.57.	Aug 26. 1917		Total admissions 845. Discharged to duty 172. Evacuated A.C.S. 279. Transferred F.C.P.S. 394. Sub. 845	The prevailing disease being P.U.O.
"	27		Arrival of Lt-Col C.H. LINDSAY. C.M.G. as A.D.M.S. C.M.O. Inspection of Unit, Transport, Hospital & tent by G.O.C. 59 Division. Major General C.T. ROMER. C.B. C.M.G. A.D.C., who wished all ranks to be informed of his "satisfaction pleasure at the orderly Turn-out of all ranks & excellence of transport" C.M.O.	A.D.M.S. INSPECTION
"	28. 1917		Advance Party, Lieut E.E. OWENS & S.O.R. proceed by car to WINNIZEELE. HAZEBROUCK. S.A.S.D. 2. 1/100,000. 2.9. 60. 15. C.M.O. CAPT. C.S. LEE Reports for duty A.D.M.S. 59 Div. C.M.O.	ADVANCE PARTY STRENGTH

Army Form C. 2118.

WAR DIARY
or
INTELLIGENCE SUMMARY

(Erase heading not required.)

Instructions regarding War Diaries and Intelligence Summaries are contained in F. S. Regs., Part II. and the Staff Manual respectively. Title Pages will be prepared in manuscript.

Place	Date	Hour	Summary of Events and Information	Remarks and references to Appendices
SENLIS 67 D V.17.c.6.7.	Aug. 31. 1917		Unit prepared tomor as by my Operation Order No. 4. (Appendice 10). Mon postponed at to-day for 24 hours, vide War Diary Sep. 1917. C.W.C. C.O. instructor: Colonel R.A.M.C. Field Ambulance Lieut Colonel N. Midland 59 for over O/c 3/3 N. Aug/31/1917	Appendix 10 MOVE

OPERATION ORDER NO.
BY
LIEUT. COLONEL C.A.STIDSTON.. COMMANDING
2/3RD NORTH MIDLAND FIELD AMBULANCE..R.A.M.C.TF.

appendix 10.

August 27th 1917.

1. The Unit will entrain at ALBERT at 5.21 a.m. on Friday August 31st.

2. Lieut. E.E.Owens. Serjt Benson T. and 1 Other rank will proceed by Motor car on the 29th instant and report to the Area Commandant WINNEZEELE. The route is detailed separately.

3. A complete "Marching out state" shewing the numbers of Officers, men, Horses, G.S.Wagons, Limbered G.S.Wagons, 2 wheeled wagons and Bicycles, will be prepared by Captain Heggs and handed to the R.T.O. three hours before the hour of entraining.   Limbered G.S.Wagons will be counted as two-wheel vehicles.

4. Supply and Baggage Wagon will accompany the Unit.

5. The entraining of the Unit will be completed 1 hour before the hour of the departure of the Train, when it will be moved from the loading platform into a siding.

6. Transport will be loaded on the EAST side of the Station, and the personnel on the WEST side.

7. Breast ropes for the Horse Trucks will be supplied by the Unit. Ropes for lashing vehicles on the trucks will be supplied by the Railway Company.

8. Serial Number of Unit Unit is :- 86
   Numbers of Trains :- Transport No 18. Personnel. No 22.

9. The Senior Officer on each train will act as O/C Train, and will provide picquets at all stops, at each end of the Train to prevent troops leaving.

10. SUPPLIES. Rations for consumption August 31st will be carried on the man. and for the 1st September in the Wagon.

11. MOTOR AMBULANCES. The Motor Ambulances -less one - which will remain behind, will proceed by road to WINNEZEELE on the 30th inst, under the command of a Medical Officer of the 2/2nd North Mid Field Ambulance.   The Ambulances will be loaded by the night of the 29th instant, and parked according to this Medical Officer's orders. The convoy will move off at 8-0 a.m. on the 30th instant, via -- DOULLENS -- ST POL -- LILLERS -- HAZEBROUCK -- STEENWOORDE -- WINNEZEELE. The Officer i/c Convoy will arrange for the Motor Ambulances to be at the Station of detrainment, to pick up any Sick of the Brigade Group.

12. The Ambulance that is left behind, will be used, under the command of an Officer of the 2/1st North Mid Field Ambulance to evacuate any sick of the 177th Infantry Brigade, and will proceed to new Station under his orders, on or after the 31st instant.

13. DRESS.   All Ranks will march to the Station, and entrain in Full Marching Order.

14. The Headquarters of the Unit will close at midnight on the 30th instant at SENLIS and re-open at midnight on the 30th instant, in the new area.

Castidston
Lieut.Colonel.R.A.M.C..TF.
O/C 2/3rd North Midland Field Ambulance..

2/3RD NORTH MIDLAND FIELD AMBULANCE..
R.A.M.C..TF.

ORDERS BY LIEUT. COL.C.A.STIDSTON.. COMMANDING.

:=:=:=:=:=:=:=:=:=:=:=:=:=:=:=:=:=:

THURSDAY..AUGUST 30TH.
    Orderly Officer...... Capt Cutler.
    Next for Duty........ Capt Smith.

    Orderly Sergeant..... Sergeant Gregory.

     Reveille........ 5-30 a.m.
     Parade.......... 5-45 a.m. Roll Call.
     Breakfast....... 7-0 a.m.
     Sick Parade..... 8-30 a.m.
     Parade.......... 9-0 a.m. Loading Wagons.
     Dinner.......... 12-0
     Tea............. 5-0 p.m.
     MUSTER PARADE... 6-0 p.m.
     Lights out...... 6-30 p.m.

     REVEILLE........ 11-45 p.m.

FRIDAY..AUGUST 31st. Issue of Rations.. 12-15 a.m.
        Fall In........... 1-0 a.m. FULL MARCHING ORDER.

LOADING PARTIES.
   Loading Party (if required) under the Command of Captain Cutler will consist of Section "A", at the Station of entrainment. Section "B" will constitute the un-loading party at the Station of de-trainment.

REAR PARTY.
   Captain Cutler and a rear party of 4 Other ranks of B.Section, will remain behind ½ an hour, to act as rear party. One Horsed Ambulance will remain with this party.

         C.Stidston

        Lieut.Col.R.A.M.C..TF.
    C/C 2/3rd North Midland Field Ambulance.

DISTRIBUTION.

1. A.D.M.S. 59th Division.
2. Headquarters. 177th Brigade.
3. War Diary. (3copies)
4. All Officers of the Unit.
5. File

CONFIDENTIAL WAR DIARY OF THE 2/3 RD NORTH MIDLAND FIELD AMBULANCE...

SEPTEMBER.. 1917.

(Vol. 9).

Army Form C. 2118.

WAR DIARY
or
INTELLIGENCE SUMMARY

(Erase heading not required.)

Instructions regarding War Diaries and Intelligence Summaries are contained in F. S. Regs., Part II. and the Staff Manual respectively. Title Pages will be prepared in manuscript.

Place	Date	Hour	Summary of Events and Information	Remarks and references to Appendices
LUNA = PARK	SEP.1. 1917		Unit entrained at Albert 2.21 A.M. Left at 5.21 A.M. Route march from SENLIS & all details having been completed assembly to Op. Order no. 4. Appendix I. Proceeded via Doullens, ST POL, LILLERS, BERGUETTE to HAZEBROUCK & House I PROVEN. Arrival PROVEN 5 P.M. No Casualties. Route March to LUNA PARK (I.I. which place is later order allotted us) Mul. 27. Ed. 2. 1/40,000. L.9.C.2.1. Sitouts O.S. OR 185. Wagons 18. Cycles 2. Horses 45. O.O.R.	MOVE C.O.R.
"	SEP.3. 1917		Took over 19 Corps Auxiliary Rest Station at LUNA PARK from 3. F.AMB.C.E. { 20 MARQUEES + 79 HOSPITAL Division. { 4 Bell Tents A.M.O. Patients 16.	HOSPITAL
"	SEP.4. 1917		1 Officer & complete Tent Subdivision of 'C' Section proceed to 5th ARMY REST STATION, M.R.P. HAZEBROUCK STA 2.D. 20.12. C.A.P. Transport of Section 'C' followed. C.A.P.	DUTY
"	S. 1917		Inspection of Rest Station & Billets & Horse Lines etc by D.D.M.S. 19 Corps. Inspection	

WAR DIARY or INTELLIGENCE SUMMARY

Army Form C. 2118.

(Erase heading not required.)

Place	Date	Hour	Summary of Events and Information	Remarks and references to Appendices
LUNA PARK MAR. 27. L.9.L.2.1.	8/9/17		CAPT. C.S. LEE reports for duty, A.D.M.S. 59 DIV, in place of Major McA. Hastings D.A.D.M.S. absent on leave. QMO	DUTY
"	10/9/17		CAPTAIN BAILEY THOMPSON R.A.M.C. reported sick with Scarlet fever has unit. Proceeded forthwith to V Army Post Station Aurosat H.E. 59 S. QMO	STRENGTH DUTY CARRS
"	11/9/17		CAPT. F.R.M.H. EGGS. Classified from ZZR Corps to I Corps AMS QMO	DUTY CARRS
"	"		LIEUT E.E. OWENS reports as M.O. 8/4 Lincs. 8" 59 DIV QMO (L.4.O.R)	"
"	12/9/17		CAPT. H.A. CUTLER reports as M.O. ★ DEPOT BK MERKESSEM "	
"		Sept 27. A. 27 LWS		
"	15/9/17		As only one M.O. (+ lt C.O.) remained to work the Post Station, Capt. H. EGGS returned to unit for duty. QMO	STRENGTH
"	17/9/17		Erection of 6. Marquees extra in Station Grounds QMO Arrival of 36 Plos, Reinforcements. QMO	Preservation Reinforcement

Army Form C. 2118.

WAR DIARY
or
INTELLIGENCE SUMMARY

(Erase heading not required.)

Place	Date	Hour	Summary of Events and Information	Remarks and references to Appendices
LUNA PARK Sheet 27. L.9.d.2.11.	September 1917 18/9/1917		CAPT. F.R.M. HEGGS & A. section proceed to Vth Corps Scabies Station POPERINGHE to arrange party to relieve 11 E. LANCS. F. AMBCE. O.M.O.	DUTY
POPERINGHE Sheet 27. F.B.C.94.	19/9/17		CAPT. J.E.S. SMITH & 23 O.R. report for duty to O.C. 11th Corps M.W.C.P. at THENNILL VLAMERTINGHE. Sheet 28. H.5.a.9.9. O.M.O.	DUTY
			The remainder of the unit proceeded from LUNA PARK & POPERINGHE & completed the relief of 11 E. LANCS. FIELD AMBCE, taking over Vth C.S.S. & 325 A/tents 18. 230 Scabies & 75 Medical (Surgical cases) O.M.O.	MOVE DUTY
			This unit now return today at LUNA PARK (VTH AUXILIARY C.R.S.) & the 142 N? F. AMB. O.M.O.	RELIEF
			The present disposal of the unit is:—	
			3.O. 160 O.R. Vth C.S.S. POPERINGHE	
			1.O. 23. O.R. Vth C.M.W.C.P. VLAMERTINGHE.	
			1.O. 30 O.R. Vth Army, Rest Station. Sheet 27.q.15.a.	
			1.O. 4. O.R. DEPOT Bⁿ MERCKEGHEM. Sheet 27. A.27. O.M.O.	
			1.O. Pat went from Hospital	England
			2.O. Lewis R.H.D. O/2/5 LEICESTER REGT	of
			1.O.M. Lewis R.H.D. in 11th LINC. REGT	unit

2449 Wt. W14957/M90 750,000 1/16 J.B.C. & A. Forms/C.2118/12.

Army Form C. 2118.

WAR DIARY or INTELLIGENCE SUMMARY

(Erase heading not required.)

Place	Date	Hour	Summary of Events and Information	Remarks and references to Appendices
POPERINGHE Sheet 27 SEP. 1917 F.6.c.9.4.	22		2 Motor Ambulances mobilised & drove } duty at 9/1 N.M.(S) 7 Bushe England 2 Horsed Ambulances to Lille " " " " } (returned) 1 Section Transport I Army Rest Station and (Sheet 28 N.2.d.b.1.) Advance party I.M.O. + 20 O.R. proceed to "MOATED FARM" to take over V.A.C. Sick Collecting Post, by 10 P.M. SEP. 23, 1917. Capt HEGGS relieving Capt SMITH, Capt SMITH relieving Capt BAILEY — THORNTON CAP	England Out Duty (returned) RELIEFS
POPERINGHE	23		Relieved at the Cluster by 26 FIELD AMB. to HADLEY report for duty ADMS office CAP Proceeded to VLAMERTINGHE to take over I.F.C.S.S. Lobdey Post	RELIEF DUTY
VLAMERTINGHE 28 Sheet 28/7/1/N H.2.d.b.1			from 1/3 W. LANCS F.AMB. S.S. DIV. Completion of relief has been finalised. 24 hours. CAP (returned)	DUTY
MOATED FARM VLAMERTINGHE H.2.d.6.1. 24/9/17.			Relief completed. 51 patients here, 31 evacuated to CCS, 20 left to visits. Accommodation for 200 left case. Cases are treated here for maximum of 48 hours. CAP Motor cycle ride round to MDMs for duty. Remaining 3 DIVIER cars report for duty to MAC. Rod' from CAP	SICK STATION DUTIES

2449 Wt. W14957/Mp0 750,000 1/16 J.B.C. & A. Forms/C.2118/12.

WAR DIARY
or
INTELLIGENCE SUMMARY

(Erase heading not required.)

Army Form C. 2118.

Instructions regarding War Diaries and Intelligence Summaries are contained in F. S. Regs., Part II. and the Staff Manual respectively. Title Pages will be prepared in manuscript.

Place	Date	Hour	Summary of Events and Information	Remarks and references to Appendices
VLAMERTINGHE H₂ N 6.1 (Sheet 28)	24/9/17		1. M.O. (Captain BAILEY-THOMPSON) + 9.5 O.R. proceed to Reserve Stretcher Bear Post "Scud End" Sheet 28. 1.2. C.2.5 for duty, motor ambulance at D.C. 2/1 N.M.7 Amb: Any available men were sent. Leaving O.R. 1 M.O. + 21 O.R. (including Convalescent personnel of the unit) to man the sick collecting post until no one turned "Sickwinkel" B.P.	duty
"	2.15 pm		1. O.R. reports sick eye 2nd proximity to A.D.M.S. 51 Div CWO	duty
"			2. Two cars report for duty to A.D.M.S. 59 Div CWO	(two duty)
"			3. Drivers A.S.C. + 3 Horse Ambulances report here for duty from O.C. 2/1 N.M.7 Amb. B.W.	Report of A Parties
"	29/9/17		Snowing last 4 days approx 300 sick have passed through the post & with handoth 150 to 200 held daily. One Motor Ambulance has returned ? duty from V.A.C. Captain Cuttle has been withdrawn (by ADMS) from V Army R.S. + sent with line. 3.O.R. from crew truck sick + sent — as yet insufficiently — reported killed	General
"	30/9/17		Capt: air Butler returned to duty with the unit.	

2449 Wt. W14957/M90 750,000 1/16 J.B.C. & A. Forms/C.2118/12.

Army Form C. 2118.

WAR DIARY
or
INTELLIGENCE SUMMARY.
(Erase heading not required.)

Instructions regarding War Diaries and Intelligence Summaries are contained in F. S. Regs., Part II. and the Staff Manual respectively. Title pages will be prepared in manuscript.

Hour, Date, Place	Summary of Events and Information	Remarks and references to Appendices
VLAMERTINGHE SHEET 28. H.4.6.1. SEP. 30. '17.	The following have been killed in action (25/9/1917) and 421191 Pte NORRIS, T.B. 421339 " PAGE. A. AND CAPTAIN BAILEY THOMPSON reports heavy hostile 2nd Front before No 07. 95 D.R. of RD. west Zillebeke wounded CMB	(CASUALTIES STRENGTH

CONFIDENTIAL...

WAR DIARY

OF THE

2/3RD NORTH MIDLAND FIELD AMBULANCE.. R.A.M.C..TF.

FOR THE MONTH OF OCTOBER.. 1917..

(Vol. 10.)

Army Form C. 2118.

2/3RD (N.B.)
FIELD AMBULANCE,
50TH DIVISION.
No............
Date............

WAR DIARY
or
INTELLIGENCE SUMMARY.
(Erase heading not required.)

Instructions regarding War Diaries and Intelligence
Summaries are contained in F. S. Regs, Part II.
and the Staff Manual respectively. Title pages
will be prepared in manuscript.

Hour, Date, Place	Summary of Events and Information	Remarks and references to Appendices
VLAMERTINGHE. OCT.1.17 Sheet 28. H₂ d.6.1.	Relieved at the "Divisional Coll Collecting Post" at the MOATED FARM by FIRST NEW ZEALAND FIELD AMBULANCE. MOTOR CAR :1. proceed to STEEN BECQUE & ADVANCE PARTY. Horse Transport proceed to STEENBECQUE, Maj. Hagebrouck S.R.A.F. 7.15, but on arrival there first that unit is to proceed to St Martin, same Map, S.E. 7.8 proceed there. C/O The remainder of the unit entrain 19.05 VLAMERTINGHE klear 21.05 & reach STEENBECQUE 23/30 on same date. C.P.O. During the 2 hours & a half that this unit rested viz in the train at VLAMERTINGHE many enemy aeroplanes dropped bombs in the vicinity of the train. I would suggest that need aeroplane over reach a period entails unnecessary risks reins no military purpose. C.P.O.	RELIEF. MOVE. MOVE. MOVE. NOTE.

Army Form C. 2118.

WAR DIARY
or
INTELLIGENCE SUMMARY.
(Erase heading not required.)

Instructions regarding War Diaries and Intelligence Summaries are contained in F.S. Regs., Part II. and the Staff Manual respectively. Title pages will be prepared in manuscript.

Hour, Date, Place	Summary of Events and Information	Remarks and references to Appendices
STEENBECQUE. Oct/2/17 Nr. Hazebrouck S.A. 4.7.7.15.	Arrival of train STEENBECQUE 6.30 A.M. March & billet up. Opened tent unit in R.K. Stationed at ST MARTIN S.E.7.7.8 (Hazebrouck S.P.) CMD	MOVE
ST. MARTIN. Oct/3/17 Hazebrouck SA. S.E.7.7.8	ROUTE MARCH to ST. MARTIN / Breakfast at BOESEGHEM CMD	MOVE
" " Oct. 4.17	Opened small tent hospital at ST MARTIN CMD	HOSPITAL
" "	CAPT HEGGS reports for duty to C.R.E. S/Sir as M.O. Billetting party to DELETTE who moved later to COYECQUES. Met Hazebrouck STA. S.E. 2.2.5 CMD	DUTY
" "		MOVE
CONECQUE. Oct. 5 Hazebrouck STA. S.E. 2.2.5	Mvr from ST MARTIN to COYECQUE completed according to Operation order No 7 (Appendix #11) CMD	MOVE (Appendix 16)
	Opened small hospital at COYECQUE apo. CMD	HOSPITAL
	Today this unit is 3 years old CMD	3rd ANNIVERSARY OF FORMATION OF UNIT

Army Form C. 2118.

WAR DIARY
or
INTELLIGENCE SUMMARY.
(Erase heading not required.)

Hour, Date, Place	Summary of Events and Information	Remarks and references to Appendices
Oct. 5, 1917	During the recent fighting E. of YPRES 24 Sep to 30 Sep. this unit has sustained the following casualties :-	CASUALTIES
	KILLED IN ACTION. 421191 Pte NORRIS, J.B. 25/9/17	
	419041 " PATRICK, S. " " "	
	421329 " PAGE, A " " "	
	421194 " BELCHER, J.H. 27/9/17	
	The 1943 are buried in WIELTJE CEMETERY. (MAP) C.28.a.4.7 28.	
	DIED OF WOUNDS 421338 Pte ELLIOTT, F.H. 27/9/17	
	WOUNDED 20219 " " BRIDGE, J. 26/9/17	
	47357 " " RODAN. H. " " "	
	(G.S.W.+ Fracture) → 3979 " " STACEY, T. 25/9/17	
	Femur 421631 " " MORRINGTON. H. " " "	
	47712 " " LAW. S. " " "	
	(M.C.)	
	(Continued)	

Army Form C. 2118.

WAR DIARY
or
INTELLIGENCE SUMMARY.
(Erase heading not required.)

Hour, Date, Place	Summary of Events and Information	Remarks and references to Appendices
	GASSED (MUSTARD)	CASUALTIES (continued)
	421177 — S. Sgt. — PRICE, H. — — 29/9/17	
	421270 — CPL — FAULKNER, H — " "	
	344059 — " — KENNING, W.H. — " "	
	421181 — L/CPL — SAYFRITZ, F — " "	
	421176 — PTE — PRITCHARD, F. — " "	
	421186 — " — RUTTER, F.W — " "	
	421373 — " — WILLIAMS, W.J. — " "	
	6753 — " — READ, J. — " "	
	421050 — " — JACKSON, G.J. — " "	
	421484 — " — HILL, W.J. — " "	
	421410 — " — PERKS, R — " "	
	421265 — " — REECE, W. — " "	
	421379 cms — " — MEREDITH, M. — " "	
	421392 — " — HOLDEN, A. — " "	
	421300 — " — HOLLIS, G.H. — " "	
	6437l — " — SMITH, J. — " "	
	368410 — " — FOWLER, R.H. — " "	
	366403 — " — HOLLINGSWORTH, T.E. — " "	
	421279 — " — HULME, H. — " "	
	421069 — " — FREEMAN, S.G. — " "	
	421397 — " — BATES, W — " "	
	421229 — " — SHEEN, A. — " "	
	421326 — " — SWATMAN, S. — — 29/9/17	
	(Continued)	

Army Form C. 2118.

WAR DIARY
or
INTELLIGENCE SUMMARY.
(Erase heading not required.)

Hour, Date, Place	Summary of Events and Information	Remarks and references to Appendices
	GASSED (continued)	CASUALTIES (continued)
	421162 — PTE — PAGE, G.E. — — 29/9/17	
	421164 — " — KENDERDINE, E.W. — — " "	
	421357 — " — PRICE, G.A. — — " "	
	421482 — " — WATKINS, H — — " "	
	421207 — " — BOTWOOD, H. — — 30/9/17	
	421383 — " — CHICK, F.J. — — 26/9/17	
	C.W.P.	
	The following are buried in WIELTJE Cemetery. Map Reference C. 28. a. 4. 7.	BURIAL SITE
	No 421191 Pte J.B. NORRIS	
	" 421329 " A. PAGE	
	" 419041 " S. PATRICK	
	C.W.P.	

WAR DIARY
or
INTELLIGENCE SUMMARY

Army Form C. 2118.

Place	Date	Hour	Summary of Events and Information	Remarks and references to Appendices
COYECQUES (HAZEBROUCK) (S.A.S.E.2.2.5)	3/10/17		4. O.R. returned from L.R.S. (C.W.)	STRENGTH
"	8/10/17		3. R.B. men have arrived to replace 3. A.S. men of R.S.C. H.T. The latter report this eve. C.W.O	"
TANGRY 11/10/17 (Some II. E.I.2.5)			Route march of Unit from COYECQUES to TANGRY. 14½ miles. Unit completed as per operation order No. 8. September 12. C.W.O	MOVE Appendix 12
MAREST. 12/10/17 (Sans. M.E.I.9.6)			Route march of Unit to MAREST from TANGRY. 4 miles. Unit completed as per operation order No. 9. September 13. Daily.	MOVE Appendix 13
BARLIN. 13/10/17 (Sans.M.E.13.5)			Route march of Unit to BARLIN from MAREST. 11½ miles. Unit completed as per operation order No. 10. September 14. C.W.O	MOVE Appendix 14
			2) Various parties to SOUCHEZ. I.O. I.O.R. C.W.O. Various work completed under Orders 17&17.Bdys. The work of Unit	

WAR DIARY or INTELLIGENCE SUMMARY

(Erase heading not required.)

Place	Date	Hour	Summary of Events and Information	Remarks and references to Appendices
SOUCHEZ			In Area allotted to Unit with H.	MOVE
Souchez 11,12, & 7			Route march of Unit from BRUAY to SOUCHEZ. A most comprehensive arrangement of Evacuation made. No H. appendix "A"	Appendix "15"
36.a. S,6,a,3,6.			By 10. A.M. completed all details of taking over H.D.S. etc	
	13/10/17		SOUCHEZ. A.D.S. @ at AYGRES. A.D.S. @ at LA COULOTTE &	
	14/10/17		Sundry R.A.P's Held by Unit, as shewn in Maj. Appendix 15	Appendix 15
			Relieved No.1. CANADIAN FIELD AMBULANCE. O.C.	
			Evacuation from L. BN. & by road from R. By. Evacuation	McKerhty formation
			Relay on road. This will have the Effect of relief also	
			on our left the 25 F.M. & Motor collect wounded Posts, on	
			our right 48th Division O.C.	
	16/10/17		Capt J. Timms to Laval to take Unit to meet at M.D.S. O.C.	STRENGTH
	17/10/17		Return of Corporal Walker & 2 O.R from 59 Divn Sept 13 at MERCKEGHEM. O.C.	DUTY

Army Form C. 2118.

WAR DIARY
or
INTELLIGENCE SUMMARY.
(Erase heading not required.)

Hour, Date, Place	Summary of Events and Information	Remarks and references to Appendices
SOUCHEZ 19/10/17 (56.C.S.6.a.2.3)	The Divisional General, Major General C.F. ROMER. C.B. CMG. addressed the M.O's of the Division at the M.D.S. CWP.	Address by G.O.C Division
	The Divisional General presented to the Football Team of this Unit the Medals presented by the late A.D.M.S. to the winners of the Inter Ambulance Competition CWP	Football Medals
	24 O.R. Reinforcements arrived Army CWP	Reinforcements
21/10/17	Capt J.E.S. Smith with C Section tent subdivision rejoined the Unit from V Army Rest Station CWP	
22/10/17	Lt Col C.A. SLATER proceeded on leave. CWP	
24/10/17	Capt CLUTHY LEE evacuated to Hospital Capt J.E.S. SMITH left in command. CWP	
27/10/17	A conference of Regimental Medical Officers and Instructors now held at Mondicourt Station Tuesday	Conference [illegible] [illegible]

Appendix 12

OPERATION ORDER NO 8.
BY
LIEUT. COL. C.A. STIDSTON.. COMMANDING.. 2/3RD N.M. FIELD AMB..

October 10th 1917.

REFERENCE MAPS. Hazebrouck 5a.
Lens Q1.

1. The Unit will leave COYECQUE at 11-0 a.m. and proceed by Route March, transport following, to TANGRY W of PERNES.

2. ROUTE.. COYECQUE -- RECLINGHAM -- Bometz --Fiefs -- SAINS LES PERNES -- TANGRY. Distance 14 miles.

3. Bugler Tonks will report at COYECQUE Railway Station at 7-0 a.m. and will guide a Motor Lorry to the Q.M. Stores.

4. The 178th Infantry Bde Group will be constituted as follows:-
178th Infantry Brigade..	TANGRY.
5th Sherwood Foresters.	BAILLEUL. & AUMERVAL
6th do.	FIEFS.
7th do.	BOVAVAL & HEUCHIN.
8th do.	SAINS -LES-Pernes.
2/4th Lincolns.	GUERNONVAL. HESTRUS. EPS.
470th Field Co.R.E.	BAILLEUL & AUMERVAL.
175th M.G.Co.	SACHIN.
178th Light T.M.B.	SACHIN.
516 CO. A.S.C.	TANGRY.
2/3rd NorthxMid Field Amb.	TANGRY.

5. The O/C 2/3rd North Midland Field Ambulance will forward to Brigade Headquarters by 9-0 a.m. on the 11th inst. a Return of men received into the Ambulances, with his remarks thereon.

6. 500 yards will be maintained between Transport of one Unit and the head of the next Unit.

7. Sick unable to march will parade as under:-
2/5th Sherwood Foresters.	DELETTE Church.
2/6th do.	COYECQUE Church.
2/7th do.	ReCLINGHAM Church.
2/8th do.	DENNESBROEUCQ. Church.
2/4th Lincolns.	ERMY.

8. Sergt Hunter will collect the above Sick at the hour named in Motor Ambulances, and transfer same immediately to TANGRY also any sick remaining in the Hospital.
By Brigade Orders any sick men who cannot be Carried on the Ambulances, will be returned to their Units and be marched as a slow party under a N.C.O.

9. A Horsed Ambulance will report by 10-30 a.m. complete with orderly etc to follow Units as detailed in para 7 from RECLINGHAM -- DELETTE -- DENNEBROEUCQ.
A Motor Ambulance will follow the 2/6th Sherwood Foresters from COYECQUE.

10. A rear party consisting of Sergt J.J.Evans. Ptes Courts F. Court J. and Chick F.L. will remain behind with 3 days rations in charge of Stores.

11. Train Wagon when off loaded will rejoin No 4 CO. 59th Div. Train on the 10th inst atBAILLEUL.

12. Rations for the mid-day meal will be distributed at 9-0 a.m. and carried on the soldier.

13. Re-filling point will be notified later.

2.

14. Capt Lee. L/Cpl Sayfritz. Sergt Tinkler and Pte Rodan will leave by 9-30 a.m. and report to Staff Captain at SAINS LES PERNES at 12-30 p.m. to-day.

15. WAGONS. All Wagons will be loaded and all Officers Kit loaded thereon by 10-0 a.m.

16. The second Blanket will be handed in to the Q.M. Stores in rolls of 10, by 9-0 a.m.

17. Lieut Cullen will see that all Fire Orders and Fire Buckets are recovered, and that all billets are left in a satisfactory condition.

18. Headquarters of the Field Ambulance will ~~out~~ close at 11-0 a.m. at COYECQE and re-open at TANGRY at 11-0 a.m. October 10th 1917.

Lieut. Col. R.A.M.C.T.F.
O/C 2/3rd North Midland Field Ambulance..

Distribution.

1. All Officers of the Unit.
2. H.Q. 178th Brigade.
3. War Diary (2 copies)
4. File.

Copy No....

appendix 13

OPERATION ORDER NO 9.
BY
LIEUT. COLONEL C.A. STIDSTON.. COMMANDING. 2/3RD NORTH MID. F. AMB.

October 10/1917.

Map Ref. LENS 1 1.

1. The Unit will fall in at the Church TANGRY at 9-15 a.m. October 11th. Thursday.

2. The Unit will proceed to MAREST   Total distance 3½ miles.

3. Transport will follow in rear of Unit.

4. 3 Horsed Ambulances and 1 Motor Ambulance will report as follows for the conveyance of Sick, who cannot march, to new billets Report at Units at 9-0 a.m. on Thursday the 11th inst.
   175 M.G.Co.   From SACHIN   to HUCLIER
   178 T.M.B.   "   SACHIN   to ANTIN & ANTIGNEUL
   470 Field Co. R.E.   "   BAILLEUL & AUMERVAL to CONTEVILLE.
   2/6th Sherwood Foresters " FIEFS   to VALHUON & LEHAMEL.
   2/7th   do..   "   BOVAVALL HEUCHIN to PRESSY-LES-PERNE
   2/8th   do..   "   SAINS-LES-PERNES to PERNES
   2/5th   do..   "   BAILLEUL & AUMERVAL to CHAMBLAINS CH
   516 CO A.S.C.   "   TANGRY   to BRITTEL & GROSSART
   2/4th Lincolns.   "   HESTRUS. EPS &   to DIEVAL
   One Horsed Ambulance to each of the following:- 2/5th. 2/7th 2/8th Sherwood Foresters. One Motor Amb. to 2/6th Sherwoods.

5. Brigade Headquarters opens at CHAMBLAINS CHATELAIN at 11 a.m. on 11th instant.

6. Lieut. Cullen., Sergt Tinkler, L/Cpl Sayfritz and Pte Rodan will proceed at 7-25 a.m. to FAUX & MAREST to complete billeting.

7. Refilling Point.. Junction of road due S. of N. in SACHIN . Refill on Thursday 11th inst at 9-0 a.m. and 5-0 p.m. Train Wagons will off-load in Units new area and return to re-filling point. Baggage wagons will remain with Units until completion of move.

8. The O/C 2/3rd North Midland Field Amblce will forward to Bde H.Q. by 9-0 a.m. 12th inst. A return of patients carried by Ambulances, with his remarks thereon.

9. Mid day Ration will be issued at FAUX & MAREST.

10. 2nd Blanket to be handed in to the Q.M.Stores by 8-0 a.m.

11. Reveille. Breakfast etc as for the 10th inst.

12. H.Q. Field Ambulance close at TANGRY 9-25a.m.. and open the same hour at MAREST.

Lieut.Col.R.A.M.C..TF.
O/C 2/3rd North Midland Field Ambulance.

DISTRIBUTION.
1. A.D.M.S. 59th Div.
2. H.Q. 178th Brigade.
3. All Officers of Unit.
4. War Diary)(Two copies)
5. File

Copy No...   Appendix B

OPERATION ORDERS   NUMBER 10.
BY
LIEUT. COL. C.A. STIDSTON.. COMMANDING. 2/3RD NORTH MID. FIELD AMB.

Map Ref. LENS 11.   October 12th 1917.

1. Captain C.S. Lee and 10 Other Ranks, detailed by him, will leave MAREST in two Daimler cars at 9-0 a.m. and proceed to SOUCHEZ, and there report to the O/C 1st Canadian Field Amblce. 3 days Rations will be taken.
   These two cars will report back to BARLIN on completion, to O/C Unit.

2. The Unit, with Transport complete will be ready to move off at 9-30 a.m. towards PERNES. Fall in 9-15 a.m. outside Q.M. Stores.

3. Captain H.A. Cutler will send 3 Horsed and 1 Motor Ambulances to report at 10-0 a.m. to follow Units as follows, and take their Sick to destinations, reporting on completion to H.Q. of this Unit..
   - 2/5th Sherwood Foresters..   CHAMBLAINS - CHATELAIN.
   - 2/6th   do.   VALHUON.
   - 2/7th   do.   PRESSY-LES-PERNES.
   - 2/8th   do.   PERNES

4. Brigade Headquarters will open at BARLIN at 12-0 noon 13th inst.

5. Mid-day Ration will be issued at 9-0 a.m. at Q.M. Stores.

6. Rear party with 3 days Rations L/Corpl Bryan. Pte Caswell. Pte Courts F.

7. Lieut. Cullen. Sergt Tinkler & Pte Rodan will proceed to BARLIN as billeting party at 9-0 a.m.

8. Units proceed as follows:-
   - 178 Bde Headquarters..   to   BARLIN.
   - 2/5th Sher. Foresters..   to   HERSIN
   - 2/6th   do..   to   BARLIN.
   - 2/7th   do..   to   GAUCHIN - LEGAL.
   - 2/8th   do..   to   VERDREL.
   - 175 M.G. Co.   to   GUOY-SERVINS
   - 178 T.M.B.   to   BARLIN.
   - 470th Field Co. R.E.   to   BARLIN.
   - 516 Co. A.S.C.   to   BARLIN.
   - 2/4th Lincoln Regt.   to   OLHAIN.

9. All Officers Kits. Mess stores, etc will be loaded without fail by 9-0 a.m.

10. Re-filling point... not yet notified..

C A Stidston
Lieut. Col. R.A.M.C.. TF.
O/C 2/3rd North Midland Field Ambulance..

DISTRIBUTION..
1. A.D.M.S. 59th Div.
2. H.Q. 178th Bde.
3. All Officers of Unit.
4. War Diary. (two copies)
5. File.

Appendix 15

OPERATION ORDER NO 11.
BY
LIEUT. COL. C.A.STIDSTON&. COMMANDING. 2/3RD NORTH MID. FIELD AMB.

October 13th 1917.

Map Ref.. LENS 11.

1. The Unit will fall in at 8-40 a.m. in the Square (Motor Car Stand)

2. The Unit complete with Transport, under the Command of Lieut Cullen will march to SOUCHEZ, passing the level crossing due S. of B in BARLIN. at 9-0 a.m.
Route.. BARLIN. HERSIN. GT SERVINS. GOUY SERVINS. ABLAIN. SOUCHEZ.
Distance. 10½ miles.

3. The Packs of "gassed cases" will be carried.

4. Captain Cutler will on receipt of information from Units, collect their Sick and transfer them:-

178 Brigade Headquarters..	CHATEAU DE LA HAIE
2/5th Sherwood Foresters.)	GOUY - SERVINS.
2/6th do.)	
2/7th do.	VANCOUVER CAMP.
2/8th do.	PETIT-SERVINS.
175 M.G.Co.	CARENCY.
178 T.M.B.	PETIT-SERVINS
516 Co. A.S.C.	GOUY-SERVINS.

5. One Daimler Motor Ambulance will report for duty at Headquarters at 9-0 a.m. with Sergt Smith.

6. Mid-day Ration will be issued at 8-30 a.m. at Q.M.Stores.

C A Stidston
Lieut.Col.R.A.M.C..TF.
O/C 2/3rd North Midland Field Ambulance.

DISTRIBUTION.
1. A.D.M.S. 59th Division.
2. Headquarters 178th Bde.
3. All Officers of Unit.
4. War Diary (two copies)
5. File.

⊞ A.D.S.
La boulette.

Glucas R.A.P.
△ R.P
ANXIOUS

CYRIL
P. MOORES R.P.

BURKES HOLE

NAPOO R.P.

ADS FOSSE 6
ANDRES

CIVENCHY

12·8 1917

DM.D.S.H.Q.
SOUCHEZ

RAP

Cambrai - 17

SCALE 1:20,000

Confidential

War Diary
of
O.C. 2/3rd North Midland Fd Amb?

From 1/11/17 to 30/11/17

Vol. 11

Army Form C. 2118.

WAR DIARY
or
INTELLIGENCE SUMMARY.

NOV. 1917

(Erase heading not required.)

Instructions regarding War Diaries and Intelligence Summaries are contained in F.S. Regs., Part II and the Staff Manual respectively. Title pages will be prepared in manuscript.

Hour, Date, Place	Summary of Events and Information	Remarks and references to Appendices
SOUCHEZ. Nov.4.17 (36.C.S.8.a.28)	A.D.M.S. 39 Division presented on parade Complimentary Cards to 325769 Pte WORSLEY.H.H. + 31889 Pte WILLIAMS.O. for devotion to duty on Oct 26/1917 CMD	HONOURS AND AWARDS
Nov.4.17.	Captain F.R.M.HEGGS. posted temporarily as M.O. to 69 Div. R.E. (Authority ADMS. 39 Div) CMD	STRENGTH
Nov.7.17	4. O.R. proceed to a course of sanitation at 13 Corps School of Sanitation CMD	SCHOOL
SOUCHEZ. 8/10/17	Visit by D.D.M.S. V TH CORPS CMD Inspection by Major General C.J. ROMER. C.B.,C.M.G. A.D.C. G.O.C. 39 DIV. CMD	INSPECTION
9/10/17	Conversation to Lieut V.J.Cullen re alcoholism CMD	CONFIDENTIAL CONVERSATION
"	Conference Lt. F. Anker 39 Div. AD.M.S.H.Q. CMD	CONFERENCE
	Lt V.J. CULLEN posted temporarily to 2/5 S.F.MO	DUTY

Army Form C. 2118.

WAR DIARY
or
INTELLIGENCE SUMMARY
(Erase heading not required.)

NOV. 1917 (2)

Hour, Date, Place	Summary of Events and Information	Remarks and references to Appendices
SOUCHEZ (36.c.S.6.a.2.9) 10/11/17 12/11/17	Sgt. W.G. COOKSEY granted a Lieutenancy on probation R.O.C. Struck off the strength of the unit.	PROMOTION
	Inspection of Sanitation of M.D.S. by O.C. No 75 Sanitary Section	INSPECTION
13/11/17	Took over from the M.D.S., R.A.Po.I, R.P.o of left sector from 2/2 N.M.F. Ambce, pending relief by CANADIAN F.A.C.A.S	DUTY.
	Received warning notice re move of DIVISION from A.D.M.S. + 176 INFY BDE	R.E. MOVE
13/11/17	During the past month of occupation of the M.D.S at JENKS SIDING + JACQUESTOWN the following alterations have been effected and work done: →	WORK DONE

WAR DIARY
or
INTELLIGENCE SUMMARY
(Erase heading not required.)

Army Form C. 2118.

Place	Date	Hour	Summary of Events and Information	Remarks and references to Appendices
SOUCHEZ (CONTINUED)	NOV. 1917 (3)		For Maps shewing alterations etc VIDE APPENDIX 12	APPENDIX 12
			1. SANITATION	
			a. In both stations the deep latrine system has been converted to the bucket system and incineration effected of all faecal matter.	
			b. Two attention trenches have been erected & ten new sump pits & pits 4ft. to 6ft. square dug.	
			c. A circular pit has been dug for disposal of incinerated material.	
			d. Completion of bath-house & erection of French army bath.	
			e. Erection of Patients latrine at Inspection.	
			f. Institution of a manure-dump.	
			g. Erection of latrine trees on new pits at all A.D.S.'s, R.A.P.'s & Relay Posts, also urine pits.	
			(continued)	

WAR DIARY
INTELLIGENCE SUMMARY.
(Erase heading not required.)

NOV, 1917 (4)

Army Form C. 2118.

Place	Date	Hour	Summary of Events and Information	Remarks and references to Appendices
SOUHEZ (continued)			h. A drying Room has been arranged.	
			i. A Butchers shop has been fixed.	
			J. Turning the tops of all butchers' table.	
			2. GENERAL	
			A. A large NISSEN HUT at JACQUESTOWN has been fitted up to staffed as an officers center.	
			B. A large NISSEN HUT has been taken down at Jacques town & erected (vide Appendix 12) at Tenth Riding.	
			C. A small NISSEN HUT has been taken from Jacques Town & erected as an Officers' hut at M.D.S.	
			D. The centre joining the huts at M.D.S. has been taken down & a large gabled, iron-roofed building erected connecting as under a hut to 6 bay Nissen Huts. 3 Nissen Huts have been joined laterally by wide passages. (continued)	

WAR DIARY
INTELLIGENCE SUMMARY.   NOV. 1917

Army Form C. 2118.

Place	Date	Hour	Summary of Events and Information	Remarks and references to Appendices
SOUCHEZ (CONTINUED)			E. 2 New roads have been made, one near Affendix in the roads the repairs informs of 100 tons of clay has been obtained local.	12
			F. Corners of roads have been rounded (not heap) dabbled stones placed & white painted railing erected for guidance of cars at night at cross cut Bouy. A railed ramp has with white railings has been built for the gun centre at Lorepus Farm.	
			G. All buildings have been provided in full with fire-orders, water round trellis, & tools.	
			H. The orderly Room has been transferred from Chenoncy Theatre id indentates to complete a/schette.	

CWP

Army Form C. 2118.

WAR DIARY
or
INTELLIGENCE SUMMARY.
(Erase heading not required.)

Nov (6) 1917

Place	Date	Hour	Summary of Events and Information	Remarks and references to Appendices
SOUCHEZ (continued)			I. The Horse-Lines have been erected in on W-E circles.	
			J. Steps to Officers Mess the building of 4 rooms in Officers quarters completed. Re-erection of Officers cookhouse.	
			K. Drainage has been altered reinforced & a 20ft pit sunk for trade waste water.	
			L. A great no. of signs & red lights for day & night has been made & erected at all the DDS posts etc. & trieating signs. Two M.O. Slack huts have been erected.	
			N. A cellar across the road has been adapted into hut as Clothing Store.	

(signature)

WAR DIARY
INTELLIGENCE SUMMARY

Army Form C. 2118.

NOV. 1917. (7)

Place	Date	Hour	Summary of Events and Information	Remarks and references to Appendices
SOUCHEZ (CONTINUED)				
	13/11/17		During the past week 4 No R.E. 1 Sgt + 12 O.R. from 9/ of N.M.F. Ambce have assisted in these alterations. CMO	GASSED CASES
			61 Gassed cases arrived at the No R.E. from the 1st Army loaned by 9/ N.M.F. Ambce returned to their unit. CMO	Appendix XIII
	15/11/17		1 NCO + 12 O.R. loaned by 9/ N.M.F. Ambce returned to their unit. CMO	
	16/11/17		Conference of O's C Ambulances 59 (N.M.) Division at H.Q. ADMS 59 Div. CMO	CONFERENCE
	16/11/17		Five Officers + one section No. 3. Canadian Field Ambce arrived in advance relief party. These Officers + 56 O.R. are proceeded tonight to take over ADS 1+2 + all RAPs + RPs at present of Breed manned by this unit. CMO	RELIEF BY 3rd CANADIAN F. AMBCE
			MDS's	
	17/11/17		Relief of all ADS's, RAPs, RPs in the area has been completed by the 3rd Canadian Field Ambulance from the front line. RELIEF CMO	

Army Form C. 2118.

WAR DIARY
or
INTELLIGENCE SUMMARY.
(Erase heading not required.)

Place	Date	Hour	Summary of Events and Information	Remarks and references to Appendices
SOUCHEZ	17/4/17		Forty Five (45) "Gased Cases" remaining in M.D.S. from 13/4/17 today evacuated to No. 22. C.C.S. Nos 11/12 Appendix XIII A.M.O.	Appendix XIII
	18/4/17		See the absence of others the Unit has remained at SOUCHEZ. C.M.O. Captains Whitehead, Neenan, Lennon report for duty C.M.O.	LOCALITY STRENGTH
BERNAVILLE 19/4/17. (LENS. 11. 1/100,000. 3.(I).O.2)	19/4/17		Under orders 176 Inf. Bdge. the unit marched from SOUCHEZ to BERNAVILLE (LENS.11.1/100,000. 3.(I).O.2) + there billeted. Move was completed according to operation orders No. 12. Appendix XIV	MOVE Appendix XIV
"	20/4/17		Under ½ hour notice from A.M.O. Captains Whitehead + Neenan sent to o/c 2/2 W.M. F. Ambce for duty. Authority A.D.M.S. 59. DIV. A.M.O.	STRENGTH
"	21/4/17		Conference of O.'s.C. F.Ambces. at A.D.M.S. HQ 59 DIV. A.M.O. Conference of M.O.'s the Ambce + R.M.O.S 176 Inf. Bgs at 2/3 F.A. HQ. C.M.O. Under 1 hour notice from C.M.O. Deposited all "unessential equipment stores" at 176 Inf. Bdg's dump Capt Neenan sent (authority A.D.M.S. 59Dn) to cert wo No. 24 lunion Regt. M.M.O.	MOVE CONFERENCES DUMP DUTY

WAR DIARY
or
INTELLIGENCE SUMMARY
(Erase heading not required.)

Army Form C. 2118.

Place	Date	Hour	Summary of Events and Information	Remarks and references to Appendices
COURCELLES-LE-COMTE LENS 11. S.J. 20.90	21/10/17 19th		At 40 minutes notice the unit Route-Marched to COURCELLES-LE-COMTE & there were billeted. Left BERNAVILLE 10 P.M.	MOVE
"	22/10/17		through a route-march of unit also turned in BERLES-AU-BOIS, BIENVILLERS, HENNESCAMPS, DUDOYT, COURCELLES, 17½ miles. Arrived 5:30 A.M. without incident. OMO	
			Owing to 700 galls petrol having turned in D.S. & S. stn, the unit is without petrol, owe 1 ton A.M.O	PETROL
			75 Stretchers & 100 Blankets sent for from OC. No 3. Cas: GREVILLERS (authority XIII Corps) OMO	STORES
"	23/10/17		75 Stretchers 100 Blankets dumped at COURCELLES, (authority of ADMS 59 Div) under a L/Cpl. OMO	STORES

Army Form C. 2118.

WAR DIARY
or
INTELLIGENCE SUMMARY.
(Erase heading not required.)

Instructions regarding War Diaries and Intelligence Summaries are contained in F. S. Regs., Part II. and the Staff Manual respectively. Title pages will be prepared in manuscript.

Place	Date	Hour	Summary of Events and Information	Remarks and references to Appendices
HEUDICOURT 57.C.W21.A.9.	24/11/17		Under O.O. 66. 176 INFY BDE:— Personnel of the Unit entrained at BIHUCOURT (LENS.11.S.J.50.45) & detrained at FINS 9.30 P.M. & marched to HEUDICOURT. Transport men brigaded & went via ERVILLERS, BAPAUME, ROCQUIGNY, MOTOR TRANSPORT had been left behind to charge of 176 INFY BDE Sick & travelling sick in the morning arrived at HEUDICOURT at 9.30 A.M.	MOVE
	25/11/17		Confidential report re Lieut V.J. Cullen and BERNAVILLE one day-load of excess stores details from annexes.	REPORT
				STORES
	26/11/17		1.1.R.O.O. + 30 O.R. report to OC. C.S.C.P. FINS to DUTY half day roads. C.A.C. one Lorry load (the 2nd) of Stores arrived from BERNAVILLE	DUTY STORE
	27/11/17		Captain ——— (at 1. PM) — L.W.M. from this Unit relieve Capt B of 8 green 2d sect 176 Staff MO. Today at a moments notice the unit moved by route on	RELIEF MO MOVE
RIBECOURT 57.C.L.25.7.6.	28/11/17		march to RIBECOURT. On arrival no rations	
	29/11/17		march to RIBECOURT with 176 Infy Bde.	

WAR DIARY
or
INTELLIGENCE SUMMARY.
(Erase heading not required.)

Army Form C. 2118.

Place	Date	Hour	Summary of Events and Information	Remarks and references to Appendices
RIBECOURT 57c.L.25.c.7.6			being available the Unit pitched its own camp & billed thereunder. Shelled during the night, no casualties	MOVE C.M.D
"	28/11/16		Visited 4th GUARDS F.A at FLESQUIERES. 57.C.L.24.c.3.7 from whom (by order G.O.C. 176 Inf.Bde.) Mr "Take over". Visited A.D.S. LA JUSTICE (57.C.L.1. a.9.6), all this area to under direct observation tree shell fire. Actual A.D.S. not approachable within 100 yards, also at request of neighbouring artillery. C.O. visited M.D.S. FLESQUIERES. With R.A.M.C. 59 Div. visited M.D.S. FLESQUIERES & arranged completed details re change. C.O.	A.D.S
"	"		D.M.Y. Clerk, Storekeeper proceed to M.D.S. FLESQUIERES to "take over".	M.D.S.
"	"			M.D.S.
"	"		1. N.C.O. & 30 O.R detailed for "Road laying" C.M.D.S. Sick Collecting Post Station Two-horse Road received CAS.	DUTY
"	"		Lt. V.J. CULLEN sent to interview G.O.C. 59 Div. CAS	DISCIPLINE

WAR DIARY
or
INTELLIGENCE SUMMARY.
(Erase heading not required.)

Army Form C. 2118.

Place	Date	Hour	Summary of Events and Information	Remarks and references to Appendices
FLESQUIERES 57.C.K.24.B.3.7.	29/11/17		The unit spent the night 28/29.11.17 at RIBECOURT and at 6 A.M. to FLESQUIERES & 1/2 relieved the 4th & 7th F. AMB. GUARDS MOVE Div, completing the relief by 10 A.M. C/O. The Main Dressing Station in occupied also by :-	MOVE
			① Advance office ADMS. 57 Div.	
			② Part (14 OR) 9th Tent Subdivision of 2/2 N.M.F. Amb.	M.D.S
			③ A Party from No 2. Cavalry F. Amb.	
			④ A Party (L.O. J.O.R. of a. 7. Amb.) 4.7 Div.	
			⑤ 2 Motor Ambces 91 M.M.7. Ambce. 2 M. Ambces 2/2 N.M.F.A.	
			3 H. Ambces 2/2 N.M.F. Ambce. a/o	
			10 A.M. — 6 P.M. 161 Wounded have been evacuated. C/O	NO. OF WOUNDED
			Today I found LT. V. J. CULLEN intoxicated in stble of a written order acknowledged by him that he was to come to alcohol, I placed him under close arrest notified A.D.M.S C/O	RE LT V J CULLEN

Army Form C. 2118.

WAR DIARY
or
INTELLIGENCE SUMMARY.
(Erase heading not required.)

Place	Date	Hour	Summary of Events and Information	Remarks and references to Appendices
FLESQUIERES	30/11/17	1 P.M.	At 1 P.M. wounded & gassed cases began t'arriv from BOURLON in rapidly increasing numbers; all available Motor Ambulances of the 3, F. Amb., 59 Div., were sent to M.D.S., LA JUSTICE. A.C.C. arranged sup. of 27 M.A.C. were had	
57.C.C.K.	29.6.3.7		Fresnoy (16): 40 Cases sent t'railhead RIBECOURT 57(L.36.2.4.4. SDS railhead TRESCAULT otters night 3.11.45 C.C.S. Urgent messages had been sent to O.C. 27 M.A.C. for 30 more cars. But work was difficult under fire	
			Our own cars (permanent relief taken place was very steady). Cars evacuated by 3 Horse Ambulances & 3 Motor Ambulances Hy & 9.5 wagon with teams of 3 Horse & Fyr cut. An indicating head transport of No. 2, 7 Ambe. any moment Hun in the meantime withdrawn 2 Motor Buses from France were very the Evacuate cases. Great care was developing rather tardy + steadily. Present position 6 P.M:— Fresnoy 4.6.2. Total 665 12. Midnight Cases continue to arrive in great numbers. Walking Three Horse M. Ambces S & London F.Ambes have arrived to assist in evacuation. The unit horse transport is making its 2nd Journey & returning empty Limbers H.S. wagons and army estd. 6 P.M → 12 P.M. Henry Sklled Casualties 2 men Killed, 28 wounded, 2 horses killed, 5 wounded. Fresnoy 480 Remaining 407 Total Position at 12 Midnight	

C.D. Whitaker Lieut Colonel RAMC(TF)
O/C 2/3 N. Mid. F. Amb TF
5/9/Sm

PLAN - M.D.S.

Appendix 13.

COPY.

From. O.C. 2/3rd. North Midland Field Ambulance.

To. A.D.M.S. 59th. Division.

A BRIEF REPORT ON SOME GASSED CASES.

1..... At 4.30.a.m. to-day 61 gassed cases were received at the Main Dressing Station from the front line.
2..... Apparently, early this morning a rapid bombardment by High Explosive, Mustard shells and other Gas Shells occurred in the neighbourhood of Clucas and Avion trenches. Some Special Company Royal Engineers working on Gas Projectors, some men of the 469th Company R.Es and some men of the North Staffs. Regiment became casualties.
3..... Only two cases of slight wounds occurred.
4..... Eight patients are perfectly well and are returning up the line. The rest shew very slight symptoms and I propose detaining them here until tomorrow (unless I receive instructions from you to the contrary) when I think they will be well enough to return to their Units.
5..... The GAS..... Some patients, including Gas N.C.Ps state that definite Mustard shells were used and also a gas they had not smelt before, variously described as minty, like weeds and herbal, and like a Herbalist shop. Others state that Mustard oil, Phosgene and Lachramatory were being used, as stated by their Officer/
6..... Symptoms.... All very slight. (a)Catarrh in the eyes, throat and chest yielding no sign to stethoscope.
   (b). Much abdominal pain of a colicy nature and pain in left Hypochondrium. Very frequent desire to micturate and free micturition.
   (c). Very slight external erythema suggesting early stages of burns.
   (d). Two cases of slight vomiting.
   (e). General feeling of tiredness and appearance of post anaesthetic state.
   (f). No Cardiac symptoms at all, no increase of pulse rate and respirations, no rise in temperature.
   (g). In some cases the reflexes are increased; in others, lessened.
   (h). Specimens of Urine are being examined.
7..... I have lately heard of a new gas of which cases are said to have occurred in the 11th.Division, in which extensor paralysis of wrist and ankle speedily occur.

November 13th. 1917. ....Lt-Col.R.A.M.C.T.
                                                O.C. 2/3rd. N.M.Field Ambulance.

SECRET.

Appendix XIV

OPERATION ORDER NO 12.

BY

LIEUT. COLONEL C.A. STIDSTON.. COMMANDING. 2/3RD NORTH MID. FIELD AMB.

MAP REF. LENS 11. 1/100,000.   November 17th 1917.

1. The Unit will be transferred to the 3rd Army, Vth Corps on November 19th 1917.

2. The Unit will move on the 19th instant with the 176th Inf. Brigade Group to BERNAVILLE.   Distance 12 miles.

3. The entire Unit, complete with Transport will parade at "JACQUESTOWN" at 1-30 p.m. on Monday the 19th instant, in Full Marching Order, carrying one Blanket.   The 2nd blanket will be handed in to the Quartermasters Stores at "Jacquestown" at 9-0 a.m. in rolls of 10, tied with string.

4. The Unit will arrive at the Cross Roads in VILLERS-AU-BOIS, via CAMBLIGNY at 3-30 p.m. and will proceed in Brigade Column via AOQ -- HAUTE-AVESNES -- ACHEZ-LES-BUISANS, to BERNAVILLE.

5. A Ration for consumption at the half-way halt will be issued at 1-0 p.m. to all ranks.

6. SUPPLIES.   Supplies will be delivered to Unit's Quartermasters Stores daily, for consumption next day, on and after the 19th instant, and until further Orders.   On arrival at destinations, Units will detail a guide from Advance parties, to look out for the Supply Wagons, during evening, and guide same to Quartermasters Stores.

7. ADVANCE PARTY.   An Advance party consisting of Captain Timms, Sergeant Winkler and Pte Courts F. will proceed to CAMBLIGNY CAMP by 8-45 a.m. November 18th, and will proceed by Motor Lorry, to prepare the Units' camp at its destination.

8. SANITATION.   There is a manure dump at BERNAVILLE.

9. MEDICAL.   Advanced Depot, Medical Stores is at SAVY.

10. Canteen and Entertainment Hut to hold 1200 at BERNAVILLE.

11. 176th Brigade Headquarters will close at CHATEAU-DE-LA-HAIE at 10-0 a.m. on the 19th inst. and will re-open at BERNAVILLE on arrival.

12. All Area Stores will be handed over to in-coming Unit, together with all B.R.C.S. Stores and a copy of the receipt obtained, will be forwarded to A.D.M.S. 59th Division.

13. Office of the A.D.M.S. will close at CHATEAU-DE-LA-HAIE at 10-0 a.m. on the 17th inst. and re-open at BERNAVILLE at the same hour.

14. Headquarters of the Field Ambulance will close at BOUCHEZ at mid-day 19th inst. and re-open at BERNAVILLE at the same hour.

C A Stidston
Lieut. Col. R.A.M.C.
O/C 2/3rd North Midland Field Ambulance.

DISTRIBUTION..

1. Headquarters, 176th Brigade.
2. A.D.M.S. 59th Division.
3. All Officers of Unit.
4. War Diary. (two copies)
5. File.

COMMITTEE FOR THE
MEDICAL HISTORY OF THE WAR
Date -4 MAR. 1918

Army Form C. 2118.

2/3 NM [signature]

Vol 11

WAR DIARY
or
INTELLIGENCE SUMMARY.
(Erase heading not required.)

Instructions regarding War Diaries and Intelligence Summaries are contained in F.S. Regs., Part II. and the Staff Manual respectively. Title pages will be prepared in manuscript.

Place	Date	Hour	Summary of Events and Information	Remarks and references to Appendices
FLESQUIERES 57C.R.24.6.3.7	DEC.1.17		Evacuations are being satisfactorily conducted xxxxx to M.R.C. Cars at rear and	HOSPITAL MDS.
		7.P.M.	all cases have been evacuated CMO	
	DEC.2.17	12 Mid-Day.	Cooks ad united, Groomed, Fed, clothed, evacuated during last 3 days, total 2149. CMO	
			2nd Lt. T. ALLEN, Austrink ADMS, 57 DIV, 6 day took charge of Lt. V.J. CULLEN for transport to 57 DIV Reinforcement Camp. CMO	Lt V.J. CULLEN
" "	DEC.4.17		Established a Dressing Station at RIBECOURT + function in the event of a withdrawal of front line. Withdrew lorries in 2 relay posts. Evacuated 19 wagon loads of Stretchers, Blankets + Medical Stores to M.D.S. TRESCAULT + 2/2 N.M.F.A. H.Q METZ. Sent 62 O.R. to report for duty to O/C 2/1 N.M.F.A. TRESCAULT CMO	MOVE
RUYAULCOURT 57C.P.10.C.2.2	DEC.5.17	5.30 P.M.	Here took over M.D.S. FLESQUIERES + proceeded to RUYAULCOURT MORE Here took over M.D.S. from 9th Andre Guards Division, + established M.D.S. for with 2 Tent-Sub divisions 47 Div (L Bruce) a combined M.D.S. for 57th + 47th Divisions. Sick and army evacuated to BOS + wounded to YTRES + later to GREVILLERS CMO	DUTY

T2134. Wt. W708-776. 500000. 4/15. Sir J.C. & S.

Army Form C. 2118.

WAR DIARY
or
INTELLIGENCE SUMMARY.
(Erase heading not required.)

Instructions regarding War Diaries and Intelligence Summaries are contained in F. S. Regs., Part II. and the Staff Manual respectively. Title pages will be prepared in manuscript.

Place	Date	Hour	Summary of Events and Information	Remarks and references to Appendices
RONVILLE COURT 57.c. P.10.c.22	Dec/8/1917		Work of M.D.S. to 47th & 59th Divisions continues. No evacuated are:-	
		11.A.M. 5/12/17 - 5/30 P.M 9/12/17		
		5.P.M. 7/12/17 to 5 P.M. 8/12/17		
			WOUNDED SICK	
			59 Div Other Btns 59 Div Other Btns Grand Total WORK	
			24 17 74 195 587	
			36 13 59 59 524	
				GAS
			During the past 2 days it has become clear that several officers & men have been suffering from definite symptoms - chiefly pulmonary - of gas, contracted in the main stony landing. Resting fatigue parties guard cases being rendered the unit temporarily weak. Today however the general condition has largely improved.	HEALTH
			After 3 days frost a thaw has set in viewed the road b/n lines up all road lots in our heg blanked to trucks.	WEATHER
	Dec/9/17		Cases 5P.M. 8/12/17 - 5P.M. 9/12/17 59 Div Wounded 39. Sick 35 other Div. " 1" " 76 " 105	STRENGTH
			Grand total since 5/12/17 = 1081	
			Lieut E. S. Sellis RAMC evacuated with bronchitis to BUS	WORK
	Dec/10/17		CAPT. R. G. OWEN, U.S. MPRC reports for duty with the unit	STRENGTH

Army Form C. 2118.

WAR DIARY
or
INTELLIGENCE SUMMARY.
(Erase heading not required.)

Place	Date	Hour	Summary of Events and Information	Remarks and references to Appendices
RUYAUCOURT 57.C.P.10.L.2.2.				
	Dec/19/17		During the period Nov 30 to Dec 10. 63 Sixty three Officers O.R. of the unit have been definite "gas" symptoms 5 Others have been evacuated, but the 63 have remained on duty and	GAS
	Dec/20/17		During the past 10 days, total admission to this Corp Main Evacg Station has reached the following numbers:— Sick. 1943. WOUNDED. 930. TOTAL 2873	Patients
			The following Divisions have evacuated to this C.M.D.S. Seven Divisions 14th 63rd, 59th, 61st, 2nd, 1, 19th	Divisions
			During the last 10 days 3 M.O's 47th Div (1st/3rd Lond FA) have left the M.D.S. have been replaced by 3 M.O's U.S.R M.O.R.C of M.O.S.	CHANGES OF M.Os
			Numerous small parties for shelling. Several units damaged, for not returning have been attached to the unit for a maximum of 116 per all relief for trains of various ambulance cars. Few controlled from here	ATTACHED

WAR DIARY or INTELLIGENCE SUMMARY

Army Form C. 2118.

Place	Date	Hour	Summary of Events and Information	Remarks and references to Appendices
RONAULCOURT 57.C. R.10. L.22.	Dec/20/17		1.N.C.O. & 6 O.R. to MOB. STORES A & C Sections sent to take over F. Ambce units BARASTRE 57.0.10.a.11. for this unit. From units in 2.3rd 1.N.C.O. & 6.O.R. sent to F.A. Ste ROCQUIGNY to take over 7 hr 1 M.M. 7 Ambce + M.M. 7 Ambce XMAS SHOPPING Completed 1 Day in AMIENS Received from 59 Div "CRUMPS" 220 Frames " " " Unit Recreation Fund	PENABLE NOTES
MOVE 2/19/1 BARASTRE 57.C.O.16.d.73			Units order ADMS 59 the unit handed over V CORPS M.D.S at ROYAULCOURT to 53 F. Amb & 17th Div & proceeded by route ment to BARASTRE. 2 Clerks left behind to complete 59 Div. Returns & Advance party withdrawn from ROCQUIGNY. C/V. During occupation of V.C. MDS 3500 cases run through in 16 days C/V.	MOVE
"	Dec/23/17		To day Lt V.G. CULLEN was Tried at H.Q. 178 Infy Bde by F.G.C.M.	No OF CASES F.G.C.M. C/V

Army Form C. 2118.

WAR DIARY
or
INTELLIGENCE SUMMARY.
(Erase heading not required.)

Place	Date	Hour	Summary of Events and Information	Remarks and references to Appendices
BARASTRE	24/12/1917		The Transport, Hos 3 G.S. Wagons + 1 water cart left BARASTRE at 7 A.M. MOVE under orders of the Brigadier Transport 176785 fr. OKS	MOVE
BERLENCOURT (LENS.N.3.F. 10.30) 25/12/17			The Personnel of the Unit / water cart & 176 Infy Bde moved 10.30 A.M. BARASTRE to BAPAUME entrained 10.30 A.M. & arrived at FREVENT at 4.45 P.M. & marched to BERLENCOURT a distance of 2½ miles & were billeted 7-8 P.M. in Horse transport arranged by advance party. Snow fell at intervals during the day. Nearly thirty the night preceding the transports arrival until 11.30 A.M. 1. Horse Artcle. + 2 G.S. Wagons had to be left by the roadside 8 kilometres out. The 3 G.S. Wagons/1 W.C. entrained BAPAUME 11.30 P.M. 25/12/17 & arrived BERLENCOURT	JOURNEY
	26/12/17		-having detrained at FREVENT - 5. A.M. 26/12/17, having been greatly delayed en route by snow drifts. CAS The extended H. Horses & G.S. Wagons are being fitted with CAS under authority granted by His Majesty The King to Field-Marshall Commanding-in-Chief. His awarded the following decorations:-	HONOURS + AWARDS
	26/12/17		Sir Tim Genl. Sir Hunter Mac Major (7. & Cot.) C.A. Stenston R.A.M.C. O/3 North Midland Field Ambulance. CAS	

Major (T. & Col.) C.A. Stenston R.A.M.C.
O/3 North Midland Field Ambulance.

WAR DIARY
INTELLIGENCE SUMMARY
(Erase heading not required.)

Army Form C. 2118.

Place	Date	Hour	Summary of Events and Information	Remarks and references to Appendices
BERLENCOURT	28/12/17		The following M.O.'s have been received posted on strength:- CAPT. I.D. KELLEY. M.O.R.C. U.S.A. LT. A.L. WASHBURN. M.O.R.C. U.S.A.	STRENGTH
"	29/12/17		A small reception hospital has been opened. Cases are sent to No.6. Stationary Hospital PREVENT. No orders re special cases are to hand. C.A.D.	HOSPITAL
"	"		The Unit as a whole, is in fact waiting for Pay horn trains & after evtending personal & units equipment has gone into training. C.A.D.	REST + WORK.
"	"		Remounts received today:- 2. H.D.: 2.L.D., 2.R. C.D.	R.S.C.

C.A.Whitaker (?)
Lieut Col. R.A.M.C. Anls
O/C 93 N. Mid. 59 Div

2/1st North Midland F. A.

COMMITTEE FOR THE
MEDICAL HISTORY OF THE WAR
Date -4 MAR. 1918

Army Form C. 2118.

WAR DIARY
or
INTELLIGENCE SUMMARY.
(Erase heading not required.)

Instructions regarding War Diaries and Intelligence Summaries are contained in F.S. Regs., Part II. and the Staff Manual respectively. Title pages will be prepared in manuscript.

2/3 NMI Field Amb
D
Vol 12

Place	Date	Hour	Summary of Events and Information	Remarks and references to Appendices
BERLENCOURT (LENS 11, 3, F, 10.30)	JAN. 4/1916		176 Six officers of the Brigade attend VI Corps lectures at 104 Z. Mules at MOYENVILLES. Ten lectures, 2 daily for 5 days.	COURSE OF LECTURES
	Jan. 6. 1918		C.O. Unit presented Cards of Commendation to No T/4 230717 P/S.S.M. BOOM B.S.C. No. 421218 S. Sgt. EVANS JOSEPH No 421446 Sgt. SMITH JOHN WILLIAM. (vide appendix 17)	HONOURS AND AWARDS VIDE APPENDIX 17 CMS
	JAN 9 – 12. 1918		CAPT. T. KELLEY M.O.R.C. U.S.A. attended a Course on Sanitation at 3rd ARMY SCHOOL OF SANITATION, ARRAS.	COURSE OF SANITATION CMS
	JAN. 8. 1918		Inspection of Horse Transport by O.C. Sq. D.T. DSC	INSPECTION CMS
	JAN. 12. 1918		No 421003 A/D.M.S. WOOD T. awarded the D.C.M.	HONOURS AND AWARDS CMS
	JAN 8. 1918		LT. WASHBURN M.O.R.C. U.S.A. reports to 2/2 N.M.F. Amb. for duty and in orders A.D.M.S. 59 Div. CMS	STRENGTH CMS
	JAN 14/13		At a parade at PENIN, MAJOR GENERAL C.T. ROMER C.B. C.M.G. A.D.C. presented D.S.O. LT. COL. L.A. STIDSTON, R.A.M.C. T/C 23rd N.M.F.A the following ribbons:- D.C.M. No 421003 A/D.M.S. WOOD T. 2/3 N.M.F.A CMS	HONOURS AND AWARDS CMS

T2134. Wt. W708—776. 500000. 4/15. Sir J. C. & 8.

WAR DIARY
or
INTELLIGENCE SUMMARY.
(Erase heading not required.)

Army Form C. 2118.

(2)

Place	Date	Hour	Summary of Events and Information	Remarks and references to Appendices
BERLENCOURT LENS 11.3.F.0.30	JAN. 20.18	3.	H.D. Kivas received to day, completing establishment, 980	P.S.C. #7
	JAN 21. 18.		MAJOR GENERAL C.F. ROMER. C.B., C.M.G. A.D.C. inspected the Unit in Column of Route & enquired a hot tat a congratulatory message from himself to issued to all ranks on the excellence of the parade. CWD	INSPECTION BY G.O.C. 59 DIV
	27/1/18		No. 913 C.M. SIMPSON. T.E. reports for duty he taken on the strength CWD	REINFORCEMENT COURTS MARTIAL
"	29/1/1918		To day the following are being tried by F.G.C.M. at H.Q. 2/5 N.S. Reg. LIENCOURT No. 421531 PTE H. MIRRINGTON No. 707 PTE F. BULTITUDE CWD	
			General The Unit merits has been devoted to resting, recovery re-equipping, training. The village on arrival required a great deal of work in repairing towns, improving sanitation,	

T2134. Wt. W708—776. 500000. 4/15. Sir J.C. & S.

Place	Date	Hour	Summary of Events and Information	Remarks and references to Appendices
(continued) 29/1/16			& cleaning, this Coy. 1 with the help of the R.E. put the most part General Column effected. CWD. Weekly programmes of training have been drawn down for football competition with #1 + #2 F.A. to be drawn up. The unit (name) out of the Divisional Football Competition in the first round. The General Service Health of the unit has greatly improved during the month. All ranks have done satisfactorily at physical work. CWD	GENERAL
31/1/16			A.D.M.S Conference of F.A. C.O.'s CWD	CONFERENCE

C Ashton
Lieut Col. R.A.M.C (T.F.)
O/C 2/3 N.M. 5 Ambce
50 Div
31/1/1916

APPENDIX... NO. 17

COMMENDATION CARDS AS UNDER HAVE BEEN RECEIVED FROM THE G.O.C.
59TH DIVISION. AND WERE PRESENTED ON PARADE ON JANUARY 6TH, 1918.

No T4/23 9717.   A/S.S.M. COOMBS C.
          Your Commanding Officer and Brigade Commander have informed
me that you have distinguished yourself by conspicuous bravery in the
field.
          I have read their reports with much pleasure.

                              (signed) C.F. Romer.
                                       Major-General.
                                       Commanding 59th Division.

British Army in France.
Date. Dec 2nd. 1917.

" For 48 hours continuously this Warrant Officer worked incessantly
under frequent shell fire.

He emptied his transport and with great ability used it for the
evacuation of gassed cases; he exposed himself fearlessly and
superintended several convoys with great courage and marked
efficiency and devotion to duty.   He very greatly assisted the
evacuation of patients and later the recovery of Stores during a
most critical and anxious time, and in the intervals of his transport
duties he devoted himself to the assistance of the gassed and
wounded.

421216. S.Sergt Joseph Evans.   Introduction similar..

Under frequent shell fire this N.C.O. worked continuously for 48
hours at the treatment and evacuation of gassed and wounded, and
by his coolness and excellent example he was invaluable at a
critical time.

421446. Sergeant John William Smith.   Introduction similar.

This N.C.O. cooked continuously for 48 hours under shell fire.
His cookhouse received direct hits, and two stoves were destroyed.
In all, he provided for 2500 patients.   On this and several
similar occasions, his fearlessness and devotion to duty has greatly
increased the comfort and safety of wounded and gassed and made it
possible for all ranks to carry on..

Army Form W.3091.

Cover for Documents.

Natures of Enclosures.

CONFIDENTIAL.

WAR DIARY

OF

2/3rd. NORTH MIDLAND FIELD AMBULANCE.

From. February 1st. 1918 to February 28th. 1918.

(Volume. II).

COMMITTEE FOR THE MEDICAL HISTORY OF THE WAR — Date 9 APR. 1918

Notes, or Letters written.

Army Form C. 2118.

WAR DIARY
or
INTELLIGENCE SUMMARY.
(Erase heading not required.)

Instructions regarding War Diaries and Intelligence Summaries are contained in F.S. Regs., Part II. and the Staff Manual respectively. Title pages will be prepared in manuscript.

① 7 FEB. 1918

Place	Date	Hour	Summary of Events and Information	Remarks and references to Appendices
BERLENCOURT (MAPLENS,N.)	3.F.1918	10.30	No. 707. PTE. BULTITUDE. T. Tried by F.G.C.M. 27/1/18. Offence "When on active service absenting himself without leave" in that he "in the field absented himself without leave from Roll-call 8/12/17 at the expiration of his leave until Dec. 24. 1917." Found Guilty. Sentenced to "25 days F.P. No. 2." Confirmed by J.C. Cope, Brigadier General, Comdg 176 Infy Bde.	PROMULGATION OF SENTENCES OF TWO COURTS-MARTIAL APPENDIX No 1.
	7.2.1918.		No. 421631 PTE MIRRINGTON. H. Tried by F.G.C.M 27/1/18. Offence "Army Act Sec. 6.1.5. "When on active service committing an offence if against the property of a resident in the country in which he was serving" in that he, in the field, on the 27/12/17 stole "90 (ninety) francs in notes the property of Madame Berthe Huot "a resident of France" from) Guilty. Sentenced to 18 months Imprisonment to Hard Labour. Sentence confirmed by J.C. Cope, Brigadier General, Comdg 176 Infy Bde C.M.G.	Appendix No 1.

Army Form C. 2118.

WAR DIARY
or
INTELLIGENCE SUMMARY.
(Erase heading not required.)

Instructions regarding War Diaries and Intelligence Summaries are contained in F. S. Regs., Part II. and the Staff Manual respectively. Title pages will be prepared in manuscript.

Place	Date	Hour	Summary of Events and Information	Remarks and references to Appendices
BERLENCOURT (LENS.11.3.F.10.30)			The sentence passed on No.421631 Pte MIRRINGTON. H. has been commuted to 90 days F.P.No.1 by Brigadier General C.M JAMES	SENTENCE OF F.P.G.M. COMMUTED 
	FEB. 7. 1918		C.B. C.M.G. a/ Divisional Commander 69 DIV. CRO	
BERLES-AUX-BOIS			To day the unit under Operation Order NO 13 marched from BERLENCOURT to BERLES-AUX-BOIS + there bivilled. Orders has been published that the operation order quoted will not come into action for the 2nd day owing to the unit coming to move under orders of the 176 Inf Bde instead of the DIVISION (Op.Order 13)	MOVE
	FEB. 8. 1918			
" "			The unit proceeded by route march from BERLES-AUX-BOIS to HAMELINCOURT—there, after 10 mile march, took over at 10.30am F.A.17. at 136 F.Ambce. 40 Div. CRO	MOVE
	FEB.12.1918		Main Dressing Station vacated by 136 F.Ambce. 40 Div. CRO (OP.ORDER.14)	DUTY
HAMELINCOURT Rfa. s. 7			The scope + function of the M.D.S is as from arrival at :- All other ranks are employed in fortifying the huts against bombs. CRO	APPENDIX 4 DUTY
	FEB. 13." 1918			

WAR DIARY
or
INTELLIGENCE SUMMARY.

Army Form C. 2118.

Place	Date	Hour	Summary of Events and Information	Remarks and references to Appendices
HAMELINCOURT (A.4.a.8.7)	Feb 14th 1918		Lt.Col. STIDSTON. A.C. D.S.O. officer commanding this Fd. Amb. proceeded on leave de usuis. Capt W. BAILEY-THOMSON as acting. O.C. Lt & Quartermaster RICHARDS. returned from leave & reported in this Unit. Pte. Rivington H. no 421531 was transferred over to the A.P.M. 59th Div. for disposal. Four water cart duty men from 2/6 S. Staffs returned to their Unit after a course of instruction in this Unit. MRT.	M Stanstig No 5. M.p. No 6.
HAMELINCOURT Feb 15th 1918		10 A.M	A conference of Field Ambulance Commanders were held at the A.D.M.S office, the subject being method of evacuation in case of an enemy attack & general medical organisation. Thirty Six (36) bearers reported to O/C 2/1. North Mid. Fd. Amb. for duty from this Unit. Sgt. Major S.M. BRITAIN proceeded to Hosp. sick, 2 m. a.m. on 14/2/15. 12 mid. Capt. A. MEARNS returned upon leave & I handed over the command of the Fd. Amb. to him. MRThomson	M Bailey No 6 M.p. No 6(a) M.p. No 6(b) M.p. No 6(c)

WAR DIARY
or
INTELLIGENCE SUMMARY

Army Form C. 2118.

Place	Date	Hour	Summary of Events and Information	Remarks and references to Appendices
HAMELINCOURT	1918 Feb 16th		CAPT. A. MEARNS RAMC took over A/Command the unit from A/Lt W. BAILEY. THOMSON	
			Nth div of hospital to me: which making adequate advance personal increment to	
			personal & horses in case of trouble.	Am
	Feb 17	3pm	After attended meeting of Divisional Medical Br held at sixteen	
			Subject - R.M.O's experiences in hard frost.	
		11am	Inspection of three transport waggons now (making improved arrangement	
			for personal & horses in case of trouble — resulted in	
			(1) Dug outs for personnel to be commenced	
			(2) Roofing of three standings 5 ft 4 feet higher	
			(3) Separation Kitchens & ambulances emption can so for loading	
			alarm — 50 yds apart as at present much gravel was available	Gm
			He suggests was ready 50 yds apart	
		10pm	E.A. dropped 2 bombs just outside the huts (camp — No damage	
			to type or personnel cant known in a far as done one on two	
			from thought a lamp if while cheek showe acted as sentinels these	
			were rumored to be Camm fought the filling memory	
				Am

WAR DIARY
or
INTELLIGENCE SUMMARY.
(Erase heading not required.)

Army Form C. 2118.

⑤

Place	Date	Hour	Summary of Events and Information	Remarks and references to Appendices
MAMETZ WOOD 57c S.W. A.4.9.5+7.B.	1915 Feb 16		From this date [?] form [?] of the unit was changed from an M.D.S. to a Divisional Rest Station. This entailed several alterations in distribution of the Camp as changes occurred which necessitated some of the baths accommodation [?] [?] at present fed being - opening two Regimental Recn. to give bath to large [?] put - enough 15 of [?] with [?] [?] 57c A.4.6. 57c A.3.a. The Committee for [?] HAMEL WINCOURT + MAMETZ WINCOURT + MOYENVILLE. A Corporal and a [?] worked out in detail + all precautions have been carefully [?]. Up to apparatus. All available waggons were put out to collect wood available [?] so could we till further orders. Lieut WASHBURN MORC detailed for supervision of all sanitary arrangements of the camp. (Local [?]) Horse + [?] [?] [?] this day by A/OR this unit. Report [?] satisfactory. It is evident that the transport work is kept up to expectations of this unit as in [?].	✗ App. No. 7 App. No. 5

W.

WAR DIARY
or
INTELLIGENCE SUMMARY
(Erase heading not required.)

Army Form C. 2118.

Place	Date	Hour	Summary of Events and Information	Remarks and references to Appendices
HANNESCOURT 	Feb 19 1916		Work on the passage mentioned above was continued yesterday and it revealed a series of 16 chambers cut out in the chalk leading from the main passage. Work of exploration, the rest in the fallen [?] portion commenced with parties of 200 or more people and be placed there. What couldn't spend up the debris fallen cleared up. There is evidence [?] that the stone passage leads from a second building. Chunks to another removed hole for both these entrances are chalked up. It has not been used for many many years.	✓ SKETCH I
	20.		Two men from 2/Lt Kircher arrived for watch shift instruction with the rest "NCOs". Coy Major S.M. BRITAIN proceeded to Blackpool.	App. No S.(3)
	21.		Aerial activity in the morning over this district. E.A. flew [?] over - heavier firing - Nothing of importance occurred in addition	
	22.	5.30 Rode on	S.C. RICHARDS QM & T. WOODS CM QA FAULKNER attached to be "B" Company in ORDNANCE STORES	App. No 9.
		11. a	at BEHAGNIES A.D.M.S. inspected the anti-lethal feature of Grenemon passage	
	23.		Usual work was carried on on completing the posterior flat clearing the debris and allowing the emergency exits where necessary. Order ADMS 5x+16in 20/2/15 complied with.	App 9(9)

WAR DIARY
INTELLIGENCE SUMMARY

Place	Date	Hour	Summary of Events and Information	Remarks and references to Appendices
HAMELINCOURT	1918			
	23		Col. KINGSTON RAMC & Capt TORRENS left & attended a series of lectures at VII Corps School of Instruction	App. 10.
	24		In a few days a week. The letter relieved by Capt KERSEY I.D. MORC and the rest of staff at MORY	"10(a)"
			The two extra cast duty men & 2 Hotchkiss recruits of the Employ Coy course found officers & returned to their unit	
	25		Extra work was commenced in Prison Camp for operation on Tuesday role. The days act to proceed. Transport was completed but only several in buckets for potation apart of functions. Ricinity from officers have stabling in completes of is a heap of is feel	App. 11
	26 9am		Col. P.H. Webb accompanied Infection Officers & returned to nine DRO 1005	
			DMS III Army inspected was Camp to see its working condition 9 RO 3351. Going into the working of the work as a BPS and .... of hidden sanitary arrangements, all in fact, both, to everything. Thanked (ADMS III/28/159) he did not inspect the transport lines.	App 12

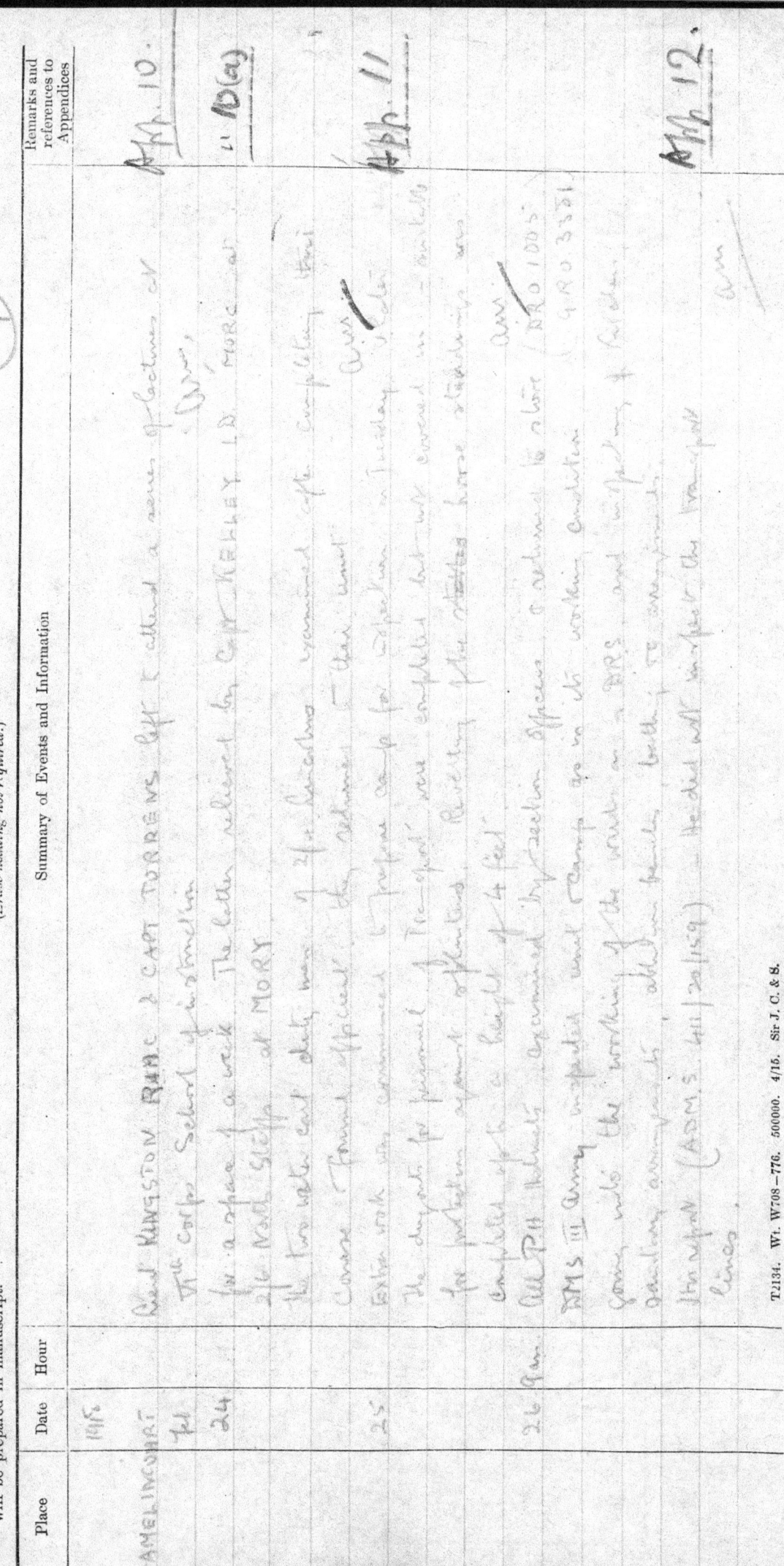

Army Form C. 2118.

WAR DIARY
or
INTELLIGENCE SUMMARY.
(Erase heading not required.)

Instructions regarding War Diaries and Intelligence Summaries are contained in F. S. Regs., Part II. and the Staff Manual respectively. Title pages will be prepared in manuscript.

Place	Date	Hour	Summary of Events and Information	Remarks and references to Appendices
HAMEL/ICOURT	1916		General work on entrenchment	
	Feb 26	2 pm	Orders received for Bns (1. Remarks) to prepare for a move at short notice. Work other than in appearance to a more covered path work and path way was proceeded with; exemption of all ranks controls so made to enable to the unit	App No 13.
	27		104 Field Ambulance to take particulars to send to an M.D.S. CAPT HERMAN & LIEUT RUGGASS visited the new camp to be taken over from 21 N.M.A Field Ambulance. May Rgt H.Q. detail My 97 C. but found that the move could be completed by 1st March only	ditto.
	28		work in connexion with the move was pressed with midnight all party stores material re were handed over in accordance with General Cleaning up with regard to known camp sanitary scheme & Occupation occupied the rest of the date. (an hour earlier)	
			M.T.	

Extracts from Daily Orders. 2/3rd. North Midland Field Ambulance.
Appendix No. 1.

Feb. 1st. 1918.
PROMULGATION OF SENTENCE.
No. 707. Pte Bultitude F.   Tried by Field General Court Martial 27/1/18 for:- "When on Active Service" absenting himself without leave, in that he, in the Field absented himself without leave from roll call 8/12/17 at the expiration of his leave until 24/12/17. Found guilty and sentenced to 28 days Field Punishment No.2. Confirmed by J.C.Cope. Brigadier-General Comndg.176th. Infantry Brigade. Promulgated this day Feb.1st. 1918.

No. 421531. Pte Mirrington. H.   Tried by Field General Court Martial 27/1/18 under Army Act, Section 6.(1)(f) for "When on active Service" committing an offence against the property of a resident in the country in which he was serving, in that he, in the Field, on the 27/12/18 stole 90 (ninety) francs in notes, the property of Madame B Husson, a resident in France. Found guilty and sentenced to 18 months Imprisonment with Hard Labour. Sentence confirmed by J.C.Cope. Brigadier-General Comndg. 176th. Infantry Brigade. Promulgated this day Feb. 1 1918.

Feb. 7th. 1918.   Appendix No. 2.
SENTENCE OF F.G.C.M. COMMUTED.
No. 421531 Pte Mirrington. H.   The sentence passed on No. 421531 Pte Mirrington has been commuted to 90 days Field Punishment No.1. by Brigadier-General C.M. James. C.B., C.M.G., A/Divisional Commander 59th. Division. Promulgated this Day 7/2/18.

Feb. 14th. 1918.   Appendix No. 5.
LEAVE.
Lieut-Colonel C.A. Stidston. D.S.O.   Proceeded on leave to England this day....14/2/18.
Lieut: Qmr. S.C. Richards.   Returned from Leave to England this day. 14/2/18

Feb. 15th. 1918.   Appendix No. 6.
CONFERENCE.
Capt. W. Bailey-Thomson.   Is detailed to attend Conference of Field Ambulance Commanders at A.D.M.S. Office at 10.0. a.m.

Feb. 15th. 1918.   Appendix No. 6(a)
MOVE.   The Sergeant Major will detail 36 Bearers to report to O.C. 2/1st North Midland Field Ambulance for duty.

APPOINTMENT.   Appendix No. 6(b)
421150 T/S/M. Brittain, S.   appointed Temporary Lieut & Quartermaster from 14.2.18.
Capt. A. Mearns   takes over duties of Acting Officer Commanding this Unit from this day.   Appendix No. 6(c)

Feb. 18th. 1918.   Appendix No. 7.
DIVISIONAL REST STATION.   It is notified for information that this Camp is now 59th Divisional Rest Station.

Feb. 20th. 1918.   Appendix No. 8(a)
421150. T/S/M. Brittain, S.   proceeded to England this day to take up Commission.

Feb. 22nd. 1918.   Appendix No. 9
Lieut & Qmr. S.C. Richards
Q.M.S. Wood, T.
Cpl. Faulkner, G.A.   will attend lecture at VI Corps Cinema at 5.30 p.m. today. Subject "Economy in Ordnance Stores."

Feb. 24th. 1918.   Appendix No. 10
SCHOOL of INSTRUCTION.   will proceed to VI Corps School of
Lieut. S.H. Kingston   Instruction today for a course of lectures.
RELIEF.   Appendix No. 10(a)
Capt. J.D. Kelley, MORC.   will proceed to relieve Capt. Torrens at 2/6 N. Staffs Regt. for one week

MOVE ORDER.   APPENDIX. 3.

SECRET.

OPERATION ORDER NO. 17
by
Lieut. Colonel C.A.Stidston, D.S.O. Officer Commanding
2/3 North Midland Field Ambulance.

Ref. Maps. Lens 1/100,000.
Blc. 1/40,000.

---

1. The Unit will move by Route March on Feb.8th from Berlencourt to Berles-au-Bois, 13 miles; and on Feb.9th from Berles-au-Bois to Hamelincourt (Clonmel Camp), 12½ miles.

2. **Friday, February 8th.**
   Reveille .... 5.30 a.m.
   Breakfast .... 6.15 a.m.
   Fall in .... 7.15 a.m.
   March Off .... 7.30 a.m.

   Route:- Leincourt - Grand Rullecourt - Sombrin - Saulty - East of Arras-Doullens Road - N.of Bailleulment - Bailleulment - Berles au Bois. The starting point of the Column at 8.30 a.m. at the cross roads where the road to Sombrin leaves Grand Rullecourt.

3. **Saturday, February 9th, at Berles au Bois.**
   Reveille .... 5.30 a.m.
   Breakfast .... 6. 0 a.m.
   Fall in .... 7. 0 a.m.
   March off .... 7.15 a.m.

   Route:- Berles au Bois - Bienvillers - Hannescamps - Bucquoy - Courcelles le Comte - Hamelincourt.
   The starting point of the column at 8.15 a.m. at the point where the Hannescamps Road leaves Bienvillers-au-Bois.

4. Intervals of 300 yards will be maintained between Units and the Regulation Transport intervals will be maintained.

5. Headquarters 176 Infantry Brigade will close at Leincourt on February 8th and open at Pommier on the same date.

6. Headquarters A.D.M.S. remains at Le Cauroy until Feb.10th and then opens at Gomiecourt.

7. **ADVANCE PARTIES.** Capt. Bailey Thomson and Sgt. Tinkler will rendezvous at the Cross Roads LEINCOURT at 7 a.m. on Friday 8th and will be conveyed by motor lorry to Town Major's Office at BERLES AU BOIS to arrange billets. The same Officer and N.C.O. will rendezvous at Town Major's Office BIENVILLERS AU BOIS at 7 a.m. on Saturday 9th to proceed to HAMELINCOURT.

8. **SUPPLIES.** On the 7th at 9 a.m. at Etree-Wamin for the 8th by own first line Transport.
   On the 7th at 12 noon at Etree-Wamin by train wagon for the 9th. This wagon returns to Headquarters A.S.C.Co. and reports with supplies at Berles au Bois on arrival of the Unit.

9. **TRANSPORT.** The transport will be loaded on ~~Friday~~ THURSDAY 7th before sunset, including spare Officers' kits. Officers' kits will be loaded on the transport not later than 6 a.m. on Friday 8th.

10. **BLANKETS.** All surplus blankets over one per man will be handed in at the Barbers Shop by Section N.C.O's before teatime on Thursday 7th inst in rolls of 10 stringed and labelled.

11. **Dress for the March.** Full March Order. Helmets will be worn and one blanket carried. Ground Sheets will be carried if weather is fine and worn if it rains.

12. **REAR PARTY.** A Rear Party consisting of L/Cpl. Bryan, Pte. Court, J. and Pte. Holmes, W.G. will remain with three days' rations in the Barber's Shop in which all the excess of stores are to be dumped before sunset on the 7th.

13. **EQUIPMENT.** Any stores or equipment of the Unit or Personnel that may be left behind on the lines and in the Billets will be handed over to Salvage Company and the ranks responsible will be issued with corresponding equipment on repayment in the new Area.

12.0 noon
7/2/18
Copy No 8

...............................Lt. Col. R.A.M.C.T.
O.C. 2/3rd North Midland Fld. Amblce.

DISTRIBUTION.

1. A.D.M.S. 59th Division.
2. Headquarters 176th Infantry Brigade.
3.)
4.) To the Two Medical Officers in the Unit.
5.)
6.) To the Warrant Officers of the Unit.
7.)
8.) To War Diary.
9.)
10.) File.

SECRET

Appendix No. 4

Operation Order No.14
by
Lieut. Col. C.A.Stidston, D.S.O., Comdg.

(1) The Unit will move to HAMELINCOURT by Route March via MONCHY and ADINFER on February 12th 1918.

(2)   Reveille ...... 3.0 a.m. for Transport.
                           5.0 a.m. for R.M.C.
      Breakfast......5.30 a.m.
Packs will be handed into
Stores by ....6.0 a.m.
      Fall in ....6.30 a.m.

Dress:- Skeleton order. Service caps will be worn and steel helmets will be carried on the shoulder.

(3) **Rations** The mid-day ration will be carried on the Cooks' Limber and issued on arrival.

(4) **Advance Party.** The Advance Party will consist of Lieut. S.H.Kingston and 20 Other Ranks of "B" Section and will leave by 4 Motor Cars at 7.0 a.m.

(5) **REAR PARTY.** The Rear Party will consist of Sgt.J.J.Evans Ptes.Court,J., Cox, Caswell, Roylance, who will be responsible for the loading of the Motor Lorry. All surplus stores will be handed into the Quartermasters' Stores by 6.0 a.m.

(6) **Sanitation.** A Sanitary Squad will be detailed by the Sergeant Major to see that all Latrines, Urinals and Billets are left in a Sanitary condition.

(7) **Officers' Kits.** All Officers' Kits will be loaded on Section Wagons by 6.0 a. m.

C A Stidston
Lt. Col. R.A.M.C.T.
O.C.2/3rd Nth. Mid. Fld. Amblce.

7.0 p.m.
11.2.17.

Distribution.
No. 1 Capt. W. Bailey-Thomson.
    2 Lieut. S.H.Kingston.
    3 Lieut. A.L.Washburn, M.O.R.C.
    4 Sgt. Major Coombs.
    5 A/Sgt. Major Wood, T.
    6 File.

2/3rd. North Midland Field Ambulance.

FIRE PRECAUTIONS.

Appendix No. 5

1. **Fire Alarm.**
   Four sharp blasts of the whistle.

2. **Fire Picquet.** to consist of
   (a) Sanitary Squad. N.C.O. in charge.
   (b) Gas Picquet. N.C.O. in charge.

3. **Rules governing Fire Picquet.**
   (a) Each man returned from Gas Picquet is to make entire rounds of the Camp and report to his N.C.O. any irregularity in fire equipment or possible fire outbreak.
   (b) Such irregularities are to be reported by Gas Picquet N.C.O. to Sanitary N.C.O. and all responsibility for rectification of same is placed upon Sanitary N.C.O.
   (c) Sanitary Squad are responsible for carrying out all Fire Precaution Regulations and for fire prevention and apparatus during interval of fire rounds of Gas Picquet.

4. **Fire Fighting.**
   (a) Upon a case of fire, N.C.O. of Sanitary and Gas Picquet is to notify at once the Orderly Officer, Sergt-Major and Orderly Sergeant.
   (b) Sanitary and Gas Picquet men are to constitute fire-fighting squad, "stand to" immediately at board containing fire-fighting apparatus located in front of Orderly Room, there to await orders.
   (c) All other men of the Unit are to "stand to" on circular road in front of Orderly Room under command of Fire Officer.

REGULATIONS FOR PREVENTION OF FIRE.

1. Fire inspection to be made of entire camp following relief of each Gas Picquet.
2. In case of fire four sharp blasts of the whistle are to be blown.
3. All huts are to be provided with two fire buckets containing water (not sand) at each door (except in case of Motor Transport).
4. During frost all buckets are to be kept inside huts to prevent water freezing.
5. No tin marked "Fire" is to be used for any other purpose.
6. No water is to be put in four gallon petrol tins unless tin is painted red and marked fire.
7. All stove pipes are to be kept at a sufficient distance from woodwork or other inflammable material to prevent scorching of same.
8. Where any danger of scorching of wood by pipes exists wood is to be covered with tin or asbestos.
9. All stoves and pipes are to be regularly cleaned and are to be kept clean.
10. Nothing is to be placed near a fire that will constitute a source of danger from fire as cocoanut matting etc.
11. Protection before fire places and stove openings must be so constructed as to make it impossible for falling live coals or ashes to start a fire.
12. No fire is to be made except in places permanently provided for the purpose.
13. Fires, Stoves, Braziers, naked lights and smoking are forbidden in any room or barn which contains hay, straw or other inflammable material.
14. No open lighted brazier or naked light is to be left unattended in any hut or billet.
15. Smoking or striking of matches is strictly forbidden in huts or dug-outs where inflammable material is kept or stored.
16. At "Lights Out" all fires must be extinguished and live coals and ashes be deposited at a safe distance from hut or dug-out.
17. All petrol driven conveyances must be parked and refilled at least ten yards from refilling points, huts or dug-outs where petrol or oil is stored.
18. Only in case of huts or dug-outs of the Motor Transport containing oil or petrol are fire buckets to be filled with sand.

19. Cookhouses, Field Cookers, Forges and incinerators will not be placed against the walls of any buildings, or in the vicinity of ricks or stacks of inflammable material. Their precise position will be fixed by an officer.
20. Petrol must not be used in any heating or cooking stoves. Petrol, paraffin, oil and candles must not be stored near any stove, brazier, fireplace or lamp.
21. Tent lanterns when available, will always be used in billets, huts or tents; when these are not available and candles are used they must be fixed in an empty tin to protect them on three sides, and top and bottom, and placed as far as possible from any canvas or tarred material in the billet.
22. Fire fighting apparatus found on board in front of Orderly Room under no circumstances is to be touched except for fire fighting.

(signed) J. A. NYLUM. Jnr.
CAPT M.O.R.C
Fire Officer.
2/3rd. North Midland Field Ambulance.

SKETCH I

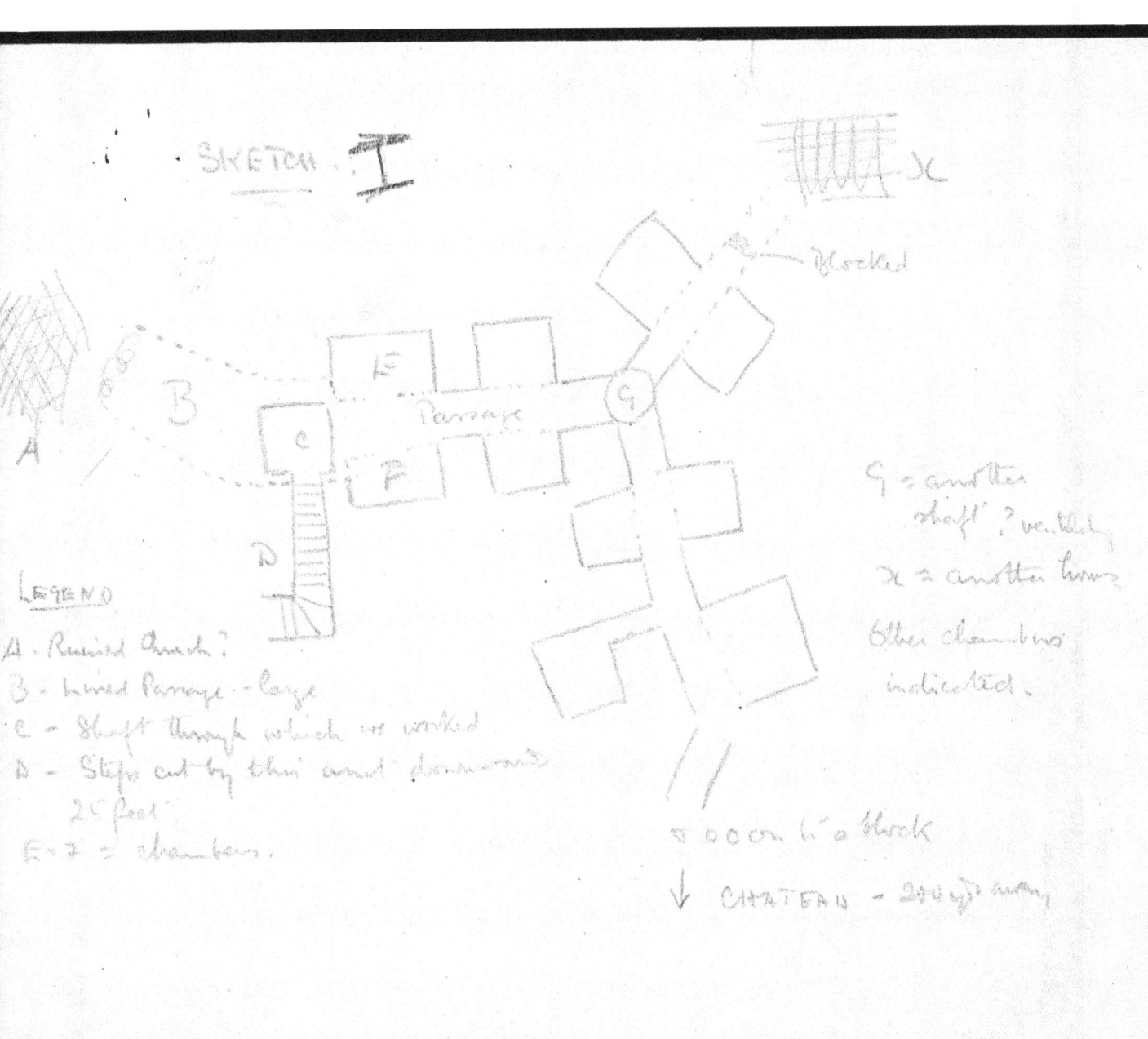

- Blocked

G = another shaft? ventilation
x = another house
Other chambers indicated.

LEGEND
A - Ruined Church?
B - Lined Passage - large
C - Shaft through which we worked
D - Steps cut by thin annul downward 25 feet
E-F = chambers.

room b/a block
↓ CHATEAU - 200 yds away

Extracts from Daily Orders 2/3rd. North Midl and Field Ambulance.

Appendix No....6.(4).

DUTY. 22/2/18.
S/Sergt-Major Coombs. Will detail sufficient wagons to proceed to Beaumetz to draw ten tons of wood fuel.
Auth. A.D.M.S. 59th. Division. 20/2/18.

Duty. 23/2/18.
S/Sergt-Major. Coombs. Will detail sufficient wagons to draw ten tons of wood fuel from Mory.
Auth. A.D.M.S. 59th. Division.

Appendix No. 11

Extract.

Inspection of Medical Arrangements
of the
59th. Division.
By
D. M. S. Third Army.

Tuesday, February 26th. 1918.

11.20.a.m. Leave ERVILLERS.

11.30.a.m. Arrive HAMELINCOURT. - (2/3rd. N.M.Field Ambulance)
Lt. Col. Stidston.

12.0.noon. Leave HAMELINCOURT.

H.Q. VI. Corps.
22nd. Feb. 1918.

Colonel.
A/D.D.M.S.
VI Corps.

Appendix No. 12

Extract.

O.C. 2/3rd. N.M.Field Ambulance.

The D.M.S. Third Army expresses himself as being highly satisfied with the Field Ambulances of this Division at his inspection this morning and wishes his approval to be conveyed to all ranks.

26/2/18.

(sd). C.H.Lindsay. Colonel A.M.S.
A.D.M.S. 59th. Division.

App. No 13.

<u>SECRET.</u>   OPERATION ORDER NO 15 by. Captain Alexander Mearns.
             A/Officer Commanding. 2/3rd. N.M.Field Ambulance.
                                                    March 1st. 1918.
1.. The Unit will move to the site occupied by 2/1st. N.M.Field Ambulance at BEHAGNIES.   Map reference H.1.central. 57c.
       Reveille........6.30.a.m.   Breakfast. 7.30.a.m.
2.. All blankets surplus of one per man will be rolled into bundles of ten and handed into the Quartermasters Stores by 8.0.a.m.
3.. Sergt-Major Coombs will see that all wagons are on the circular road in from of the Hospital by 8.0.a.m. for loading.   Wagons are to be loaded by 10.0.a.m.
4.. Corpl Latham and three men will proceed on the afternoon of the 28th. February to the new camp and prepare to take over.
5.. The Sergt-Major will detail a sanitary party to see that the Camp at Hamelincourt is left in a clean and sanitary condition.   All rubbish to burned etc.
6.. Actual time of moving off will be notified later to all concerned.

Issued at.7.p.m.
28/2/18.
                        ....Capt. R.A.M.C.
                        A/OC. 2/3rd. Nth. Mid. Field Ambulance.
Distribution:-
Copy No. 1. A.D.M.S. 59th. Division.
  "   " 2. For all Officers of the Unit.
  "   "   3. War Diary.
  "   "   4. War Diary.
  "   "   5. File.
  "   "   6. File.

140/2900

-6 JUN 1918

Confidential

WAR DIARY.

~ OF ~

2/3RD (N.M.)
FIELD AMBULANCE,
59TH DIVISION.

MARCH 1918.

(Volume. 3).

WAR DIARY
or
INTELLIGENCE SUMMARY

Army Form C. 2118.

2/3 N M [?]

Place	Date	Hour	Summary of Events and Information	Remarks and references to Appendices
	1918			
HAMELINCOURT	March 1		As indicated in War Diary 28/2/18 with its appearing - Move order. Move was handed over to 104th FIELD AMBULANCE the necessary certificate signed by the Vet. Officer. It doubt specific situation was declared by the Vet. Officer to be not a danger to the other's eye weathers. It is presumed damaged. This in the end case of epidemic N ophthalmic situation in the transport	
"	"	2.30 p.m	The whole unit paraded for inspection. The took the road - travelling first across country to ERVILLERS, thence by road to BEHAGNIES arriving at the latter place at 4 p.m. - On halt made on the road. The camp marked by Lieut: 2/L N md 3 Amb. was taken over as left - consisting for most days NISSEN HUTS and a Tarkinin.	
BEHAGNIES H1. Cauton	2		The CoM changing the camp from a trestle of an ambulance with a small bivouac and ResetPitchin was at once commenced. Plans laid down accordingly. The function camp which were to be - a rest station for about 50 patient where ailments would not necessitate their remaining more than a week - by I.C.T Cases diarrhoea slight fever an uplever french for an	

WAR DIARY
INTELLIGENCE SUMMARY.

Army Form C. 2118.

Place	Date	Hour	Summary of Events and Information	Remarks and references to Appendices
BEHAGNIES H.1 c h.1	1918 March 3		Plan Main Idea of the Camp will be as follows:- SD patients - accommodated in huts ; personnel in tents ; a drive for ambulances in a semi open area. Work in pitching tents, cleaning & tidying huts commenced. The water drain commenced. All ways in and out established suitable for this battle. As for the O/officer on there are half past & cracked huts ready to be converted for the house & enough room on the top of the hill so every appeared - nothing to start & fact has been commenced. Plan for enlarging commencing area - explain have been issued. The weather is been inclement. 	
"	4		Capt Towers & Lieut Kingdon returned from VII Corps School (v. attd week) Lieut baid out involving about 3 acre. Plan for a vegetable garden on being dug into the ground. Manure has been collected & is the present dug-out - a German one - is not large enough for patients. Another new have been put in to enlarge. Orders for preparing huts for timber. OR/Rev Poore arrived for the week. Gm	

WAR DIARY
or
INTELLIGENCE SUMMARY.

Army Form C. 2118.

Place	Date	Hour	Summary of Events and Information	Remarks and references to Appendices
BENAINE	March 5		Nothing [of importance?] occurred. The date general work of [utility?] day performed. Command dug up land with a view to replenishing [plot?] of land to [...]	
"	6	10.30 am	Conference of O.C. [...] held at H.Q.H.S. Officers [...] Scheme of the defence scheme [...] in case no [...] arrangements were [...] took place. [...] was of the [...] and [...] personnel in their relation to [...] in detail.	
"	7	2 pm	Inspection of all [...] letters by Lt. Col. [...] Cpt. Kelly inspected medical equipment of the two infantry Btn attached. [...] Rifle[...] General work on [...] Camp continued.	
"	8		Nothing [of importance?] occurred. [...] movement in [...] and [...] [...] to strike. [...]	

Army Form C. 2118.

WAR DIARY
or
INTELLIGENCE SUMMARY.
(Erase heading not required.)

Instructions regarding War Diaries and Intelligence Summaries are contained in F. S. Regs., Part II. and the Staff Manual respectively. Title pages will be prepared in manuscript.

Place	Date	Hour	Summary of Events and Information	Remarks and references to Appendices
BENHAMIES	1918 March 9	10 am	The Wadpell was inspected and found to be in excellent condition. Since the fine weather came in & with the work on which the horses are employed (V March 3) the condition of all transport horses is very fine - none being looked after. There is an & pm & am any addition to the sponge analysis. Carrier Pigeons of the Brits with a maximum found suitable to research it, colour of the coat to commence. The enemies, when this was done, showed its value when passed from a distance.	
	10	10 am	About a dozen gas shells dropped [at] the outskirts camp about 150 yd distance. The wind being away from us - no unwell could be detected. Various attacks in the cookhouse & staff horses have been completed. Plan for obtaining order from time evolved. Arms visited camp.	
	11		Have shells - gas - dropped about 10 o'clock same place as 10/3/15	

Army Form C. 2118.

WAR DIARY
or
INTELLIGENCE SUMMARY.
(Erase heading not required.)

Place	Date	Hour	Summary of Events and Information	Remarks and references to Appendices
BETHUNE	11		Additional Screens – stretcher bearers – distributed to ADSs under 2/1 N.M. & 3/1 in accordance with what was received: No more available owing to difficulties made during Feb. There are now arising difficulties with regard to now the station for SO cases – with 60 of which somewhat greater than there held – machines for the E.C.S. when called for.	Apps. I.
"	"	11 am	More registration needed for our men as practice is not favoured.	
"	"	2 pm	One of the German aeroplanes hovered over this camp at about 10,000 feet. It was thought that in one case the lower wing had a smaller chord than the upper; though this may have been due to its being just too high; the machine (with "Somme") to resemble one on which the Mallace troops were indeed in a ride on — the case in these machines. Several work of the camp has carried on as per plan.	

Army Form C. 2118.

WAR DIARY
or
INTELLIGENCE SUMMARY.
(Erase heading not required.)

(6)

Instructions regarding War Diaries and Intelligence Summaries are contained in F. S. Regs., Part II. and the Staff Manual respectively. Title pages will be prepared in manuscript.

Place	Date	Hour	Summary of Events and Information	Remarks and references to Appendices
PEZZWES	1916 March 12		Trench scheme detailed to NCOS MORGAN (2/L W. Rut Reg) in accordance with report from the O.C.	
			Circular print now completed. Work on the field continued. Aeroplanes made for a flight to aid the work.	am
			Nothing else to note	
	13		New huts for personnel - 24 completed. Push stop erected at various shells—rifle-rocks. All available transport wagons employed in clearing routes for a special French corn for casual purposes.	am
	14		Capt KELLEY I.O. left this unit for [?] work as M.O. with 2/4 Leicesters in accordance with instructions.	
			Nothing else to report.	am
	15		Information [?] instructions by Div Commander of the has been employed [?]	
			All fire buckets & syphons at this explosion [?] renewed	am

T2134. Wt. W708—776. 500000. 4/15. Sir J. C. & S.

Army Form C. 2118.

WAR DIARY
or
INTELLIGENCE SUMMARY.
(Erase heading not required.)

Instructions regarding War Diaries and Intelligence Summaries are contained in F. S. Regs., Part II. and the Staff Manual respectively. Title pages will be prepared in manuscript.

Place	Date	Hour	Summary of Events and Information	Remarks and references to Appendices
BEAUVAL (H.Q. 1st C. Fd Amb)	March 16		The Div Commander did not wait for D.A.D.M.S. visit to amb. D.D. M.S. was with him while he 3 wards were viewed	
		2 p.	All Ranks suppen Summer [illegible] was ordered by C.O/1st. Coy 1st Div Train [illegible] by G.A./D.S. Safety to be [illegible] from [illegible] earthworks, cover to horses during the day and [illegible] at night and [illegible] Ammt of work for horse lines in [illegible] with order for [illegible] [illegible]	
	17		12 horses from this unit reported to H.O. 2/1 N.Mid.Fd Amb to [illegible] H.Q. 3rd Corps [illegible] ten 10.3.15	
			Capt BERGIN left to proceed to V.C.o/d. School of Instruction for a week's course in musculoskeletal will arrive on	April 2
	18		Plans for new huts made. First arrangements for this [illegible] gum.1 made with A/ord.C officer, [illegible] [illegible] 1 week [illegible] General meant [illegible] [illegible] [illegible] [illegible] Ambulance establishing [illegible] We about to report. L/Colonel STIBBON R.E. attend for line Covered Rd & trek [illegible] opening	

[signed] Anold Lee

Lrc M/OT Capt McBRIDE

T2134. Wt. W708-776. 500000. 4/15. Sir J.C.&S.

WAR DIARY or INTELLIGENCE SUMMARY

Army Form C. 2118.

(8)

Place	Date	Hour	Summary of Events and Information	Remarks and references to Appendices
BEHAGNIES 57.C.H.I. Contd	1918 MAR 19		The usual pioneer work on the camp site has been interrupted by heavy 2 a.m. Improvement of dug-out is unsatisfactory for lack of timber. A motor-cart has been badly knocked about owing to a collision with a post, the horse having bolted at sight of lorries unloading road metal. A letter was written to O.C. 9/M. MID F. DYBCE asking him to return to five stock issued to him by arrangement prior to order to Contrary.	WORK GAS ACCIDENT FIRE SHEETS
"	" 20		A Board is sitting in re went rentoned yesterday. The A.D.V.S VI Corps inspected the horses of the unit & expressed himself as very pleased with their condition. General pioneer work of the camp-site has continued. Entire forage has occurred since 2 p.m. & is maintained 10 p.m.	BOARD OF ENQUIRY INSPECTION WORK
"	" 21	10 AM	At which hour a wire has been received from ADMS. to "carry on". In accordance with instructions in re active operation Captain Baily Thompson, Lieut S. Hardy Kingston, 3 N.C.Os & 24 O.R. have been dispatched to No 45 C.C.S. POMMIER-LE-GRAND	ACTIVE OPERATIONS

T.2134. Wt. W708-776. 500000. 4/15. Sir J. C. & S.

WAR DIARY
or
INTELLIGENCE SUMMARY

Army Form C. 2118.

Place	Date	Hour	Summary of Events and Information	Remarks and references to Appendices
BEHAGNIES 57.C.H.H. (British)	MAR 21.		Barrage eased mid-day. All patients have been evacuated. Cap? In compliance with 59 Div Defence Scheme all available Gunner Cars have been sent to O/c 2/2 N.M.F. Ambce at ERVILLERS + the 3 Horse Ambulances; all available horses (12)+ 2 Fwd cars to O/c 5/1 N.M.F. Ambce at DYSART WOOD CAS	PATIENTS The Defence Scheme
COURCELLES-LE COMTE 57K.A.21.2.8.	21/3/18 9PM		On verbal written instructions from A.D.M.S. 59 DIV at 4.30 P.M. (hours) MOVE t COURCELLES - marched with 20 men + a lorry of equipment to COURCELLES - LE-COMTE. At 9.PM the count of Major to returning for the remainder of stores etc left at BEHAGNIES in charge of CAPT. ALEX. MEARNS who is also in charge of any sick patients who may arrive. 3 Horse Ambces has been returned under order A.D.M.S. 59 Div to facilitate transport. Rumours of a great German advance continues to reach us + a German Barrage was obvious whilst we passed from BEHAGNIES to COURCELLES-LE-COMTE which village is the rendezvous of the with Drawing division ('59) Cap?	MOVE

WAR DIARY or INTELLIGENCE SUMMARY.

Army Form C. 2118.

(10.)

Place	Date	Hour	Summary of Events and Information	Remarks and references to Appendices
COURCELLES-LE-COMTE			(from divn HQ)	
		at 11 P.M.	Orders were received to move "to area immediately west of	MOVE.
S.C. A. 21.a.28			"AYETTE - ABLAINZEVILLE road (contained in Sqq 7.10, 7.11, 7.16.")	
	21/3/18	11 P.M.	Movement complience with which order was completed at 1.30 A.M. 22/3/18 Cas.	
ABLAINZEVILLE	22/3/18 3.30 A.M.		Arrival of 1st convoy of transport from BEHAGNIES. Cas.	TRANSPORT
		11. A.M.	Head Pushr sent for load [stores at COURCELLES-LE-COMTE. Cas.	"
			Return 3. P.M. Cas.	"
57.D.F.16.&62		7.30 P.M.	Orders were received to shift the camp to an open site in Sqq F.16. Moved Map 57.D. The camp was struck & working in relays of transport the entire equipment was transported to new site & tents pitched. This was completed 6.30 P.M. 23/3/18. Cas.	MOVE
"	MAR 23.1918 9.10 A.M.		Orders were received at 9.10 A.M. to take positions in a column moving off at 9.15 A.M. from the Rd trystrgg Camp was at once struck began from Bicas stone transfers were wording when storm tower in the road tothing in position (other voids being equidistently late) at 10.10 A.M. dresser, the day before leaving, the following arrangement	MOVE

WAR DIARY
INTELLIGENCE SUMMARY.
(Erase heading not required.)

Army Form C. 2118.

Place	Date	Hour	Summary of Events and Information	Remarks and references to Appendices
	23/3/1916		no steps have been made.	TRANSPORT AND STORES
57.D.F.16.0.8.2.			(1) After consultation with D.A.D.O.S. 57.D.in. instructed Tfor. Major AUQUO that A.D.S. Major knows a first rate had him left at als in morfin (having been finished stage by stage) but a note taken from Austrian regt. asked him to notify nearest d'France & notified w. re CAP	
			(2) made arrangements with O/C Prisoner Hospital FAYETTE (57.D.F.11) After our BRGS into Mattresses & general stores removed Polioed from BEHENCIES CAS F	
			(3) Obtained 4 Porters through A.D.M.S. & to serve from BOUZINCOURT. CAS oils & petrol stoves left under charge of I.M.O. + 3.O.R. CAS hrs only transfer made 2 journeys carrying stores to BOUZINCOURT. CAS	
			Route:- mended to BOUZINCOURT via BUCQUOY - PUSIEUX=AU=MONT - SERRE - MAILLY = MOVE =MAILLET - HEDDAUVILLE - BOUZINCOURT - BRUSHOTS S.O.Point BOUZINCOURT to AVELUY. (just W of AVELUY. Distance 15 miles. And lor S/ar this night. CAS	
23.3.1916/ 57.D.W.16.L.5.2. (AVELUY)				
AVELUY 57.D.W.16.L.5.2.	24.3.1916		Wagons are being reloaded & a convoy of 4 mule cars despatched for remainder of mobilization equipment stores etc	

Army Form C. 2118.

WAR DIARY
or
INTELLIGENCE SUMMARY.
(Erase heading not required.)

Place	Date	Hour	Summary of Events and Information	Remarks and references to Appendices
AVELUY STD.W.1b.J.S.S.2.	24/3/18	8.P.M.	Warning order received that ready to move with Infantry Brgde if necessary. O.R.O.	MOVE
		11.P.M.	Definite order received 1 Zero Hr. Probably 3.30 A.M. 257 B/M Coy	
25/3/18 BEHENCOURT (AMIENS.17.I.F 35.70.)		2.30 A.M.	Under orders of O.C. 59 Fd M.G. B.Z. The unit joined the column at BOUZINCOURT at 3.10 A.M. marched via SENLIS, HENENCOURT, HERISSART, Arrived 6 A.M.	MOVE SENLIS, HENENCOURT MOVE
			Hills. Arrived 6 A.M. Return Journey made by our 2 water trucks stores from AVELUY. old site had been bombed in the interval. Unit had rest from 6am. An advance Officer had followed BAISIEUX to BEHENCOURT.	
BION TRELET 26/3/18 RUBEMPRE LENS.IX (S.E.75.10)		6.45 A.M.	Under orders 128 Infy. Brigh H.Q. the personnel of the unit marched to CANDAS (+ later to MONTRELET) via RUBEMPRE - LEVAL - DE MASON - FMS DU ROSEL. Distance 16 miles. Canton being full the unit proceeded & marched there billetted. Though marched separately via VILLERS BOCAGE & TALMAS.	MOVE
MONTRELET (LENS.M.S.C.75.10) 27/3/18			The unit is employed disinfecting, investigating nothing when otherwise. O.R.O. As far as can be ascertained 40 O.R. of the unit are missing men in connection with advance posts in recent operations. O.R.O.	MEN MISSING

WAR DIARY or INTELLIGENCE SUMMARY

Army Form C. 2118.

Place	Date	Hour	Summary of Events and Information	Remarks and references to Appendices
MONTRELET (LENS 1K 52.7.S.W)	27/3/18		Lt. WASHBURN M.O.R.C. U.S.A. & 157 O.R. Lt. returned to the unit from 48 C.C.S. having proceeded to DOULLENS (after leaving ACHIET-LE-GRAND) via ALBERT. C.P.O. Invalided MICHEUVILLERS. Spent 4g C.C.S. the had light 26 3/4 to DOULLENS, invalided DOULLENS to Sand then Capt. BAYLEY-THOMPSON attached to 58 C.C.S. by transfer. Put on time of 49 C.C.S. On men attached C.P.O. Wagons wheeled off the utilizing mobilization store. C.P.O.	57.05=57R C.P.O. MOVE
"	28/3/18		Transport moved off under orders C.R.E. 57 DIV to proceed by 2 stages via to LAPUGNOY area to billet for night at HERLIN-LE-SEC (S.9/57 P.D.) Unit arrived at CANDAS station 1.0 P.M. (8,200 H.Q. 57.DIV.) & entrained. NOON (30th train) for LAPUGNOY. Actually entrained 12. — 2.45 P.M. & arrived at LA BUSNOY 12.30 A.M. 29 3/18 arrived at CAMBLIGNEUL at 5 A.M. C.P.O. (Men to disposal of Division having been relieved C.P.O.)	" MOVE " "
CAMBLIGNEUL 29/3/18 (LENS II.2.M. 40.55.5.)			Arrival of horse transport 10 P.M. One horse has been loaned to O/C 72 M.M.G. for 2/5 & 9/6 Sherman & Andre Keep en route. Kick parade arranged for 2/5 & 9/6 Sherman Hostile (minus M.O.'s) & 175 Duty B.S.n H.Q. Efforts to obtain Info. C.P.O.	MOVE C.P.O.

Army Form C. 2118.

WAR DIARY
or
INTELLIGENCE SUMMARY.
(Erase heading not required.)

Place	Date	Hour	Summary of Events and Information	Remarks and references to Appendices
CAMBLIGNEUL	30/3/18	10.30 A.M.	HIS MAJESTY THE KING visited the village, the unit paraded outside Town Hall. His Majesty spoke at length to the O.C. and about recent casualties & appeared greatly moved what refering to them.	VISIT OF H.M THE KING
"	31/3/18		Under orders C.R.E. 59 Div the horse transport proceed today C.M.P. to LILLERS, the day following tranch proven area under orders the sound. The unit is under orders from (Personnel) by tactical train on Monday April 1st to new area C.M.P	MOVE
			The following is a list of O.R. of this unit "missing, believed Prisoners of War" in operation 20-21st MAR. 1918	LIST OF CASUALTIES
			No. 106782 Corporal SMITH S.W.	
			421250 " WALKER. C.	
			23170 PTE ALSOPP. T	
			421444 " " ALDRIDGE H.F	
			86272 " " BLAKE. P	
			366396 " " BURTON F.J	

Army Form C. 2118.

WAR DIARY
or
INTELLIGENCE SUMMARY.
(Erase heading not required.)

15

Instructions regarding War Diaries and Intelligence Summaries are contained in F.S. Regs., Part II. and the Staff Manual respectively. Title pages will be prepared in manuscript.

Place	Date	Hour	Summary of Events and Information	Remarks and references to Appendices
			PTE	
			No. 421202 PTE BRADLEY, W.L.	*Continued list of Nasers*
			421271 — COOK, J.	
			3219 — CULLEN, L.	
			1057266 — DERHAM, S.	
			1044475 — CHADWICK, T.	
			435066 — FLOYD, E.	
			421406 — GIBBONS, J.	
			421197 — GOODWIN, E.	
			421248 — GOBOURN, A.	
			2450 — GARNER, G.R.	
			421293 — GARNER, C.	
			421268 — HILL, W.	
			421370 — HALES, A.	
			2564 — HOLMES, W.G.	
			368378 — THOMAS, G.T.	
			421231 — UNDERHILL, D.H.	
			421291 — JONES, B.	
			421039 — JACKSON, G.	
			73955 — KERR, H.	
			No. 421417, KEELING, B.	
			421411 PTE PADDING, J.	
			421505 — PARSONS, H.A.	
			421503 — PITTY, W.A.	
			421193 — POTHAN, W.	
			85619 — PERCY, J.W.	
			421164 — POWER, B.R.	
			421381 — RUSHTON, F.R.	
			90814 — ROBINSON, A.E.	
			354425 — RUSSELL, J.P.	
			473413 — RAY, F.	
			421419 — SMITH, H.	
			64371 — SMITH, J.	
			276.04 — STRIKE, T.R.	
			26827 — STORER, J.	
			421483 — THOMAS, E.E.	
			421483 — TONKS, W.	
			421426 — WATSON, G.W.	
			7713 — WEBBERLEY, G. CMD	
CAMBLIGNEUL	3/3/1915		Foot inspection of all troops in CAMBLIGNEUL. CAS	
			LT. R.C. WASHBURN, MPRC...USR reports for temporary duty (authority ADMS 59 DIV)	DUTY
			ao M.O. 2/5 LINES B^n at HOUDAIN. CAS	
			No. 37626 7/S.M. A.E. MEDDEN RAMC reports for duty. Authority :- RAMC letter	STRENGTH
			Base 59/97/18, 20 3/15 forwarded under DDMS VI Corps M3038/1/15 23 3/15	
				ONO
			12 Midnight. Mar 31. A/1. 10^15	
			W. Matcher Lt. Col. RAMC T.F.	
			O/C 2/3 W.M. T Make 5^Dr	

T.134. Wt. W708-776. 500000. 4/15. Sir J. C. & S.

Extracts from Daily Orders. 2/3rd. North Midland Field Ambulance.

Appendix.NO..1............

March 11th. 1918.
Stretcher Bearers.
   The Sergt-Major will detail 20 Stretcher Bearers to proceed to the 2/1st. North Midland Field Ambulance for duty, as per A.D.M.S. 59th. Division R.A.M.C.Orders.

Appendix. No.2............

March. 17th. 1918.
VI Corps Medical School.
Capt. C.J.D.BERGIN. Will proceed to VI Corps Medical School this evening for one week's course of instruction. Bedding, kit and batman must be taken. Further details will be communicated on arrival. (Authority). A.D.M.S. 59th. Div'm.355/20/152. dated 14/3/18.

160/2900.

COMMITTEE FOR THE
MEDICAL HISTORY OF THE WAR
Date -6 JUN. 1918

CONFIDENTIAL WAR DIARY

OF THE

2/3RD NORTH MIDLAND FIELD AMBLCE.

FOR THE MONTH OF.

APRIL 1918.

(Volume 4.)

Army Form C. 2118.

WAR DIARY
or
INTELLIGENCE SUMMARY.
(Erase heading not required.)

Instructions regarding War Diaries and Intelligence Summaries are contained in F.S. Regs., Part II. and the Staff Manual respectively. Title pages will be prepared in manuscript.

Place	Date	Hour	Summary of Events and Information	Remarks and references to Appendices
CAMBLIGNEUL	AP.1 1918		Route March of Personnel from Camp CAMBLIGNEUL to AUBIGNY. Entrained AUBIGNY 1.P.M. Arrived PROVEN 9.P.M. (via HAZEBROUCK) & marched to CLIFFORD CAMP. 27 Sheet F.19.3.7.	MOVE OK!
CLIFFORD CAMP (27.F.19.3.7)	AP.1.18.		En route to the camp a Saunder car "D" brought on fire owing to the wheels sinking in a deep rut, the cup on the under surface of the petrol tank was wrenched off the petrol caught at the near light. Phosphorus magnesia were immediately Taken to fire extinguishers on to car, water from the distd pond wellers to extinguish the fire which gutted the car. The Engine Chassis remained intact. C.A.S.	ACCIDENT
	AP.2.1918		Arrival of Hired Transport which left CAMBLIGNEUIL 31/3/18 proceed under orders of O.R.E. 57 Div. without casualties one that a wheel of lorry cast had collapsed, a wheel & spare tube from attained this afternoon from O.C. heavy w Somme in MADU Rd (from road between PROVEN & POPERINGHE C.A.S.	MOVE

WAR DIARY
INTELLIGENCE SUMMARY

Army Form C. 2118.

Title pages 2/3 N.M.7. AMBCE

Place	Date	Hour	Summary of Events and Information	Remarks and references to Appendices
CLIFFORD CAMP 27.F.19.3.	AP.2.18		CAPTAIN I.D. KELLY. M.O.R.C. U.S.A. posted to 2/4 LEICESTER B.". LIEUT. A.L. WASHBURN M.O.R.C. U.S.A. posted to 2/5 LINES B.Y. Authority A.D.M.S. 59 DIV. 357/54/43. 3/4/1918. CMS	STRENGTH
"	AP.3. 1918.		CAPTAIN ALEXANDER MEARNS promoted MAJOR from date 4/1/1918. CMS Witt Major A. MEARNS I visited & inspected the MILL VLAMERTINGHE, the Chateau POTIJZE & "FROST HOUSE", "JOY", "JURY" & THE BRICK-KILN" which RAP's s/c are b/h taken over by the unit from O/c 19 #7 AMBCE 33 DIV. CAP.	PROMOTION RELIEF App II.
			MAJOR A. MEARNS, CAPT. BAILEY-THOMPSON, LIEUT. HARDY-KINGSTON & "B" section proceeded to effect the relief which was completed under arrangements between the O/c.e. 7 Ambos by 3.P.M. AP.4.15 CMS	
			MAJOR THOS. STOKES ELLIOT, R.A.M.C. + CAPT H.D. CLEMENTI-SMITH. R.A.M.C. reported for duty. O.A.P.	STRENGTH
"	AP.4. 1918.		Remainder of unit proceeded to the MILL VLAMERTINGHE, sheet 28.H.8.a.9.9 the personnel entraining at QUENTIN (S. of POPERINGHS) after marching thither	MOVE
VLAMERTINGHE (28.H.8.a.9.9)			from CLIFFORD CAMP & detraining at ORILLE (VLAMERTINGHE) Completed taking over the hospital (overflow to DRS BRANDHOEK) by 3.P.M. Transport arrived by road. CMS	

WAR DIARY
or
INTELLIGENCE SUMMARY.

Army Form C. 2118.

Place	Date	Hour	Summary of Events and Information	Remarks and references to Appendices
VLAMERTINGHE 28. H.8.a.9.9.			MAP. Sheet. 28. S & 3 [sketch map with grid squares labelled C and D, showing YPRES, POTIJZE CHATEAU, W.W.C.P., A.D.S., S.C.P., A.D.S., FROST HO, TOT D, BRICK-KILN, JURY, PAGES POST, Collecting post, Mullers Hütten, Car stand, car routes]	SCHEME OF EVACUATION

Army Form C. 2118.

WAR DIARY
or
INTELLIGENCE SUMMARY.

(Erase heading not required.)

(4)

Instructions regarding War Diaries and Intelligence Summaries are contained in F. S. Regs., Part II. and the Staff Manual respectively. Title pages will be prepared in manuscript.

Place	Date	Hour	Summary of Events and Information	Remarks and references to Appendices
VLAMERTINGHE 28.H.a.9.9	Ap.5.1918		Following 2.O.R. reported "missing"/behind prisoners are today reported as Casualties.	CASUALTIES
			2364 Pte HOLMES W.F, No 102 F. Ambce	
			421248 Pte GOBOURN.A. No 43 C.C.S C.H.A	
	Ap.6.19.18.		Today I visited FROST who will C.R.E. 59 Div. + completed arrangements with him for refixing ceiling of the full-sized hut(?), roof of Mill VLAMERTINGHE.	AREA WORK
			From 6.15 - 7 a large shell fell into + around VLAMERTINGHE., Oxygen casualties resulted. These in turn dressed + evacuated to No 3 C.C.S. (AUSTRALIAN) at NINE ELMS. C.C.S	WORK
			Work of repair under C.R.E. 59 Div. has begun or to not C.C.S.	REPAIRS
			CAPT. T. HINCKS R.A.M.C reported for duty, + CAPT McMINN returned from temporary duty at 92 M.M. F, Ambce C.M.D. CAPT B. THOMSON left for England C.M.D. + CAPT HINCKS with a	STRENGTH
	Ap.7.1918		Capt CLEMENTI-SMITH contingent, one warrt + 3 H. Ambce east + 3 H. Ambce men have proceeded to the HOSPICE WATOU. There will start + 2 ORs. Pr 176 F.O.S duty Adjs is there doing F.O.M. duty	DUTY

Army Form C. 2118.

WAR DIARY
or
INTELLIGENCE SUMMARY.
(Erase heading not required.)

Place	Date	Hour	Summary of Events and Information	Remarks and references to Appendices
THE MILL VLAMERTINGHE	Apr 8. 1918		Routine work continues at all posts. O.O.	VL IPR R
	Apr 9. 1918		A meeting of the 59 Division Medical Society was held at the Mill. The members of the Committee having signed in recent election, a fresh committee was elected. Routine business completed & the question of funds for prisoners of war was discussed. O.O.	MEDICAL SOCIETY
	10.10.18		Before DAVENPORT of 13 R.M.T Aviles & 6 Sir Courtney Morris 46 Sir.) reports for duty, O.O. Decided to send medical orderlies of 500 francs & notify on of 250 francs to the furnished Prisoners of war Fund subscription, with list of names of prisoners of war from the unit. O.O. Orders have been received to take over the following posts 14/2	PRISONERS FUND
	11.1918		3. R.A.P:- TYNE COTTAGE D.17. a. 3. 2 RAMC POW INGOT HOUSE D.16. B. 8. 2. 1 N.C.O. 12 men " " JERSEY. 22. D. 16. C. 10. 3. 1 N.C.O 6 " Rem. " DARING CROSSING D.16. d. 6. 4. 1 N.C.O 6 " In this connection Hon. notified O.C. 2Ft R.M.T Avoles to send on three Sub-divisions to report to M.D.S. POTIJZE to help prevent these relief, from 135 F Avoles W/ Sir Off?	DUTY POSTS

WAR DIARY or INTELLIGENCE SUMMARY

Army Form C. 2118.

Place	Date	Hour	Summary of Events and Information	Remarks and references to Appendices
THE MILL VLAMERTINGHE	11/4/1916		176 & 177 Party at WATOU recalled (owing to Batt. going into the Line) & to 25 recd in hospital there - evacuated to D.R.S. at BRANDHOEK. Gas Inspiration for a hostile retirement of the line to No.9 Latrines at the Mill Rumerangle two men detailed to G.O. & a scheme formed to turn the Mill into a M.M.C. Station. Spec.	DUTY
	12/4/1916		No. of patients at the Mill further reduced & all arrangements made & land over the Mill Huts to 30th CCS.	DUTY
	13/4/1916		After standing by following a midnight warning orders the unit proceeded to the GODESWARMELDE as follows. The transport moved off at 3.30 under Lieut Sedwell 7/2 V.M. 7 Mules & arrd at 4 P.M. 14/4/1916 having been repeatedly lost in the dark. The unit entrained at BRANDHOEK at 5 P.M. arrived at	MOVE
GODESWARMELDE Sheet 27. K.29. c.7.b.			GODESWARMELDE at 7 P.M. & route marched it from two days Sheet 27 K.29. c.7.b. arriving about midnight. The motor transport preceded the unit & made a 2nd journey for stores then reported Muster Ordon of D.P.M.S. & 1/s 2/2 W.R.F.A. for duty.	MOVE

WAR DIARY or INTELLIGENCE SUMMARY

Army Form C. 2118.

Place	Date	Hour	Summary of Events and Information	Remarks and references to Appendices
GODESWAERVELDE Sheet 27.N.29.C.7.6. AP. 14. 1916			At 4.30 P.M. orders were received to move to LOCRE, & reconnoitre route over the evacuation of wounded in the Division. The C.O. & Major Elliot proceeded to LOCRE & got over fields out the HOSPICE for an ADS (M.D.S. being at the Gendarmerie, LOCRE), personnel & small amount of transport. Remainder of transport reported to O/C 92 N.M.7 Amb. proceeded to Sheet 27. R.7. f. central, to H.Q. of Ambulances of all 3.7 Andes came under orders of O/C 2/3 7A. Also the trans & 2M.O.S. of 2/1 7A. if wanted. The C.O. & Major Elliot visited 176 + 177 IB.D.S. H.Q. at Sheet 28. M.23.c.3.7. (179th) & sheet 28. M.25.c.8.7, & found that the areas the 2 Brigades were fought for taking on had changed, & hurriedly nearly would change. It being impossible to reconnoitre both sites before dark, we chose the more suitable & arranged for M.D.S. at 28.S.9.a.7.7. " 28.7.B.7.0. with R. Pots at S.8.d.4.3 S.4.d.5.6. & S.10.d.6.6. On returning to Batt Bdys HQ. we found that Bde H.Q. were moving forward at 10.30 P.M. to	MOVE
LOCRE Sheet 28. M.29 d.6.9 AP. 14. 1916				

WAR DIARY or INTELLIGENCE SUMMARY

Army Form C. 2118.

Hour, Date, Place	Summary of Events and Information	Remarks and references to Appendices
LOCRE Ref. 28. M.29.b.6.9 APR/14 1918 Cont	(176ᵇ) → Sh.28. S.8. d.2.5 (177ᶜ) → Sh.28. S.4. d.4.6. That 146 Brigade was going into action. Verbal arrangements were notified with Brigade H.Q. re promises to forward location of R.A.P.'s was received. Earlier in the day Lt.Col. H.Q.M. Sansom had sent me to Bury in LOCRE at the time — 40 stairs to assist Regimental Medical officers. As my own unit could not even until too late to arm the Brigade I sent Major ELLIOT & CAPT CLEMENTI SMITH with 2 M.O.s (CAPTS HENDERSON & CORNWALL) 7A to the M.D.S. when they returned on a Motor Ambulance to M.D.S. LOCRE at the site of our M.D.S. 2 other 7 Amber were also ... Place unknown to many days UNSEEN	

WAR DIARY
or
INTELLIGENCE SUMMARY

Army Form C. 2118.

Place	Date	Hour	Summary of Events and Information	Remarks and references to Appendices
(continued) LOCRE			rations huts & having previously from a hospital at 6 P.M. on M.A.S. t at 6 A.M. on M.O. & 24 O.R. from this unit proceeded to A.D.S.	
28. M.29 t. 6.9. AP.15.1918			(The unit having arrived midnight 14/15) & whered the 2 m.o. & 46 O.R. of the 2/1 W.M. F. Andree, who returned to their unit HQ LOCRE At 5 A.M. Major ALEX MEARNS with 19 O.R. & ambn with rations & medical stores proceeded to A.D.S. MONT NOIR Sheet 28. M.26. WORK a.8.1 from a F.A. of 34 Div. Two cars were sent to Run for evacuation. About 8.30 P.M. Mem Eglise being in flames a terrific bombardment of our front line squares T. 7.8.9. S. 19,20,21,22. 16,17,18 took place & continued until about the evening. The A.D.S. under charge of Major Elliot was so heavily shelled that it had to be withdrawn to a farm just north. The M.O. in turn who shelled to ruins & all records of patients known though lost. Rural material dressing) Major Mearns Elliot & after evacuating all the wounded by car, lorry, wagon finally by with trimming infantry trestle withdrew from the station to a trestly ambulance of casualties in hospital personnel etc	

WAR DIARY
INTELLIGENCE SUMMARY.

Place	Date	Hour	Summary of Events and Information	Remarks and references to Appendices
Continued (April 15)			The withdrawal had taken place via MONT NOIR & WESTOUTRE as the BAILLEUL - LOCRE ROAD was impassable owing to shellfire. For the same reason reinforcements of ammunition were hurried from Proven to the station we could expect messengers get through. About the same time self was sent 2 cars & 12 men at 4.20 to left on Route behind KEMMEL & several rounds of the 175 Infy Bde who had been attached to 19th Division. At the same time Major Mairis A.D.S at MONT NOIR was heavily shelled & shared the withdrawal. The shelling remains known to be successful in evacuating our 500 wounded & sitting cases to REMY SIDING throughout the night Helena without casualties. This personnel at 5 PM this morning (April 16)	in action
M.S.		At 4.5 o'clock LOCRE being shelled 1 incendiary (under relief of A.D.M.S.) found around M.17.c. central & recurring 5 huts in CURRAGH CAMP at M.17.c. 3.6 withdraw all my Officers, Personnel & Transport from LOCRE to HUTS[?] Have opened an A.D.S. A.D.	

Army Form C. 2118.

WAR DIARY
or
INTELLIGENCE SUMMARY.

(Erase heading not required.)

Place	Date	Hour	Summary of Events and Information	Remarks and references to Appendices
Sheet 28. M.17.C.3.b	Ap. 15. 1916.		During the night — 3 AM — under orders ADMS I sent Major Elliot, Capt Clementi Smith, Capt Hinks + 20 O.R. + reopened an M.D.S. at Hospice Locre. An attempt to find H.Q. 147 Bde at CROIX DE POPERINGHE proved futile. During the night 176, 177 duty types have been withdrawn and in Corps Reserve in + around M.17. The A.D.S. so trying my+ Cars are being evacuated to M.D.S. (21/2 H.M. 7 Poules) Sheet 27) R.17, L.5.4. A roll call of the unit at 12 noon gave the following as at present missing Sgt BENSON Ptes. BOYES — since reported back HOPPER McINTOSH MURDEN WARREN — wounded eye not a prisoner. As far as is known, RATH personnel of 3/1 are with units to which they were attached	Sheet in ACTION

WAR DIARY
or
INTELLIGENCE SUMMARY.

(Erase heading not required.)

Army Form C. 2118.

Place	Date	Hour	Summary of Events and Information	Remarks and references to Appendices
April 16th. (Continued)		4 p.m.	Unit has stood to all day, awaiting orders. A Report has been received from A.D.S, LOCRE that everything is working smoothly. 50 cases have been evacuated. 9 French Division has passed up in part & numerous remnants of odd English Division, mostly the same as have been fighting within the last 48 to 60 hours. A heavy bombardment of enemy area by guns around the A.D.S. is in progress. Streets of LOCRE have passed up, several batteries of 2A. H.Q. with Shrapnel & H.E. and the neighbourhood. LOCRE is being shelled with H.E. and the neighbourhood. Removal of casualties to 2/2. N.M. Dunk. T.17.b.6.27. Under orders A.D.M.S. the A.D.S at the Hospice LOCRE was again evacuated. All O.R. & material safely reaching A.D.S at CURRAGH CAMP by 9.p.m 150 cases were passed through in 24 hours.	IN ACTION. C.W.P C.W.P C.W.P C.W.P
April 17th. 1918.			Incessant bombardment of Enemy lines by Enemy guns has occured throughout the night. One R.A.M.C. man - He yeoman F - received a cut up from - probably an anti-aircraft shell. The two Brigades 176 & 177 remain as they were & the Ambulance functions as A.D.S, still during the night 75 cases were passed through.	C.W.P

WAR DIARY
INTELLIGENCE SUMMARY
(Erase heading not required.)

Army Form C. 2118.

Place	Date	Hour	Summary of Events and Information	Remarks and references to Appendices
R.P.D. (CONT)		11.30–12.30	Camp heavily shelled with H.E. & gas shells, about 30 H.E. falling. The lines & huts also had 40 or 50 gas shells. Considerable damage to shelter in some earthworks. 200 yds N.W. of camp. The infantry in neighbouring trenches attacked, wind not, but otherwise normal from R.D.M.S. 2 M.O. G.I. 19 O.R. & 1 M.D. horse were left in the camp. The remainder moved to Camp G 23.c.4.3.0. sat S.E. of R.11, & 7.3. Ring shelled intermittently on into to the ore orcad at — KOKEREELE FARM. all the horses shelled just previous were of ─ Midd reds 114 and the entire shelling continued until 4 a.m. Bright moonlight. Some air activity.	(?)
KOKEREELE FARM SHEET 27 R9 323 R.P.P. 19 1/.		4 a.m.	A loading post gramlet 29 191 7.9 at Sh.S.of. M. 26 B. 7.3 in front of LOERE was established, consisting of Motor Ambce. 1 M.O. 4 S.B.'s functioned immediately.	
	23.9.17		Orders issued M.D.M.S. arrived for 92 Freuse to take over B & camp at STEENVOORDE Lyn 23 Nov or the MDS at ELRUNGF CAMP vacated a wired MDS at the ORIE & to immediate mobilisation by "LORRIES" horses AHTE can and.	

WAR DIARY or INTELLIGENCE SUMMARY

Army Form C. 2118

Place	Date	Hour	Summary of Events and Information	Remarks and references to Appendices
KOKEREELE FARM Sht 29. R.9.L.3. AP/18/1918.			The French are steadily moving in front (St & S.W.) of this station & digging machine-gun pits around us. Our transport has sent under orders of 2/2 N.M.F.A. R.D.S. CURRAGH CAMP has been heavily shelled & the gun emplacements around it CMD Capt. Kingston reported to Major Elliot at R.D.S. CURRAGH Camp for duty CMD. To-night it froze & snowed. CMD night bombardment a full side run some CMD	GENERAL
R.P. 19. 10/16. 27. R.9 L 7.3			Capt HINGSTON reported back sick from reserved trite of 21 x 9/2 N.M.F.Ambce 6 kilometres W. of STEENVOORDE CMD Some exacuates have also been sent there. Stragglers have returned from ST JANS CAPELLE & other points. No orders (11PM) are to hand, but actually can be gathered most of the DIVISION have left the line. It's raining heavily, the roads are streaming & slushy, French O. & O.R. have taken over KOKEREELE farm. No M.A.C. cars have yet arrived to evacuation to "Hospitals" near POPERINGHE have been completed by our own M.T. & H.T. CMD Total evacuation during last few days will be embodied in a later letter CMD	GENERAL

WAR DIARY
or
INTELLIGENCE SUMMARY

Army Form C. 2118

Place	Date	Hour	Summary of Events and Information	Remarks and references to Appendices
Sheet 27. R.17. B.7.3. AP.19.1916 (cont)			To day I have notified the A.D.M.S. 39 Div. in re the impossibility of carrying across motorisation otherwise essential other than on motorisation (frequently cleansed) to complete in one journey. Vide copy of letter Appendix 18. CNP The camp site at CURRAGH CAMP. being heavily shelled preserving 8 great hits, the A.D.S. was withdrawn to 1st house or road to WESTOUTRE. During the night 3 casualties alone received CNP	DIFFICULTY OF TRANSPORT APPENDIX 18.
AP. 20.1/16			This morning I withdrew the A.D.S. to ROCKERZEELE farm, mid-day. The 17) Inf. BDE., for whom in have been collecting, removed to RENINGHELST without informing me, & all efforts to find their H.Q. though the night, without intervening we, CAPT. T.E.HINCKS reports for temporary duty to A.D.A. 59 Jr. SOURPTRE under orders A.D.M.S. to visit Sorts-removed to DOZINGHEM CNP	MOVE STRENGTH
AP. 20, 1916 HQ D.D.S. "DOZINGHEM"			Sheet 27. F.H. B.8.8 There spent the night. To day I returned Ambres to 9/1 & 2/2 N.M.F.A. CNP	MOVE

Army Form C. 2118

WAR DIARY
or
INTELLIGENCE SUMMARY
(Erase heading not required.)

Place	Date	Hour	Summary of Events and Information	Remarks and references to Appendices
HOUTKERQUE	AP. 21. 1918		Route March from DOZINGHEM to HOUTKERQUE, on arrival reported IX CORPS had taken over billets where upon we entered a camp site	MOVE
	27. £. 20. B. 3. 7		& there occupied 9 bell tents & one bivvie Hut C.O. Payed the unit	PAY
HOUTKERQUE	22. APRIL 1918		The Unit rests. Here I record the exceptional devotion to duty of all Officers N.C.O.'s & men under my command during the past few days (battle of BAILLEUL). The Motor Stores transport men I heard also with great gallantry. But for invariable good fortune I feel in my judgment we had of the unit would have occasional both slightly & rather seriously. All ranks have done splendidly. Archibald Red	ACTION
			CAPTAIN H.J. CLEMENTI-SMITH reports for duty to Off. 91. N. M. Force	STRENGTH
	23 APRIL 18		Inspection of all Mobilization Kettle Stores, Riddance of empty Med. Stores cases sent as Hoo last down to A.M.S., of salvage of Ordnance stores, to the great easing lightening of the Transport. C.P.O.	WORK

WAR DIARY
or
INTELLIGENCE SUMMARY
(Erase heading not required.)

Army Form C. 2118

Place	Date	Hour	Summary of Events and Information	Remarks and references to Appendices
	APR 19/18		Capt. R. M. McMINN reports for duty to 2/7th Bn SHERWOOD FORESTERS Bn vice CAPTAIN BOSTOCK who proceeds to No. 17. C.C.S.	DUTY CAS
	25 " "		Capt T.E. FUTCROFT reports for duty from 2/4 LINCS Bn	Strength CAS
	26 " "		Training & cleaning of personnel & trains. Return of S. Sgt Kentwell strength from 48 Ups. At 6.30 P.M on 1/2 hours notice the unit route-marched from HOUTKERQUE to CLIFFORD CAMP, Sheet 27.F.19.d. 5.5.	STRENGTH MOVE CAS
	27 " "			
CLIFFORD CAMP 27 Sht F19 d.25.55				
28 " "			Awaited orders CAS. Evacuated sick direct to No.3. Cav. C.C. Under orders 178 Inf Bgd. moved back to old billets at HOUTKERQUE	CAS CAS
HOUTKERQUE Sheet 27.E.90 B.2.7. APR.30.19/18.	29 " "			
			Capt. T.E. FUTCROFT reports, with 2 Daimler cars, for duty to O/c 2/2 N.M.7. Ambce RIMY SIDING.	DUTY CAS

Army Form C. 2118

WAR DIARY
or
INTELLIGENCE SUMMARY

(17)

Place	Date	Hour	Summary of Events and Information	Remarks and references to Appendices
MOVEMENTS OF A DETACHED PARTY			A party of 1 Staff Sergeant + 23 O.R. have been absent from the unit from 21 until April 25. The movements of this body during that period were as follows:— C.A.P.	DUTY
	Mar. 21.18.		BEHAGNIES to No 49. C.C.S. ACHIET-LE-GRAND. This C.C.S. was shelled, bombed + rumoured. Party moved to AVELUY in motor lorry. C.A.P.	
	Mar. 23.18.		Being bombed, moved by train from AVELUY to PUCHEVILLERS C.A.P.	
	" " "		At PUCHEVILLERS, erected tentage, received over 2000 wounded + evacuated same by ambulance train. Owing to bombing raids proceeded on:—	
	MAR. 26.18.		to PUXIE CHATEAU, part of the C.C.S. was left behind owing to hasty evacuation. Party arrived at ABBEVILLE on same day, + remained in the train until Mar. 29. C.A.P.	
	— 29—18		Proceeded to AUXI-LE-CHATEAU C.A.P.	
	— 30—18		Arrived at ST. RIQUIERS + helped to erect 49.C.C.S.	

Army Form C. 2118

WAR DIARY
or
INTELLIGENCE SUMMARY
(Erase heading not required.)

Instructions regarding War Diaries and Intelligence Summaries are contained in F.S. Regs., Part II. and the Staff Manual respectively. Title Pages will be prepared in manuscript.

18.

Place	Date	Hour	Summary of Events and Information	Remarks and references to Appendices
MOVEMENTS OF DETACHED PARTY (CONTINUED)	Ap. 17, 1918		Party sent by motor lorry to ABBEVILLE & proceeded by train to CASSEL. Marched to reinforcement camp ST MARIE-CAPELLE. Slept in the open for 2 nights.	C.V.O.
	Ap. 18. "		Returned to CASSEL, billeted at BAVINGHOVE C.V.O.	
	Ap. 24 "		Left CASSEL for ARNEKE. Arrived same date. Billeted by R.T.O.	Gas
	" 25 "		N.C.O in charge (S.Sgt KENDALL) saw 59 Div. Liaison & asked permission to en-lorry & find unit. Received permission & rejoined unit at HOOTKERQUE Ap. 25, 1918.	C.V.O.

C.O. Validator
Lieut Col R.A.M.C.(T.F.) FIELD AMBULANCE
O/c 2/3 N. MID. 59 DIV

SECRET.

OPERATION·ORDER NO. 17 by Lieut-Col:C.A.STIDSTON. D.S.O
Commanding. 2/3rd. North Midland Field Ambulance.

April 1st. 1918.

MOVE OF UNIT TO PROVEN VIA AUBIGNY.

1. The Unit will parade in full marching order at 10.45.a.m. on Monday, April 1st. at the Church.
2. The Unit will follow the 178th. Infantry Brigade Headquarters, (Head of Column passing Brigade Headquarters at 11.15.a.m.) to AUBIGNY and there entrain. 300 yards interval will be maintained between Units.
3. Any men sick or unable to march will report to the Orderly Officer at the Sick Hut at 9.30.a.m.
4. One Blanket will be carried by each man.
5. One Daimler Ambulance, Capt. A.Mearns will collect sick at HERMIN, at the Church, at 8.30.a.m. and transfer to AUBIGNY Station. One Daimlet Ambulance will transfer sick from CAMBLIGNEUL to AUBIGNY at 9.30.a.m.
6. The unexpended portion of the days rations will be issued from the Quartermasters Stores at 8.30.a.m. Water bottles will be filled.

Copy No. 8.
Issued at 9.0.p.m. 31/3/18.

................Lt-Col.R.A.M.C..TF.
O.C. 2/3rd. North Midland Field Ambulance.

Distribution:-
Copy No. 1. A.D.M.S. 59th. Division.
 " " 2. Headquarters. 178th.Infantry Brigade.
 " " 3.4.5.&6. All Officers of the Unit.
 " " 7. War Diary.
 " " 8. War Diary.
 " " 9. File.
 " "10. File.

App. II.

SECRET.   OPERATION ORDER NO 18 BY LIEUT-COL. C.A.STIDSTON. D.S.O.
          Commanding 2/3rd. North Midland Field Ambulance. 59th. Div.

Maps. Sheets 27 and 28. 1 in 40,000.   3/4/18.

1. The Unit will take over from the 19th. Field Ambulance 33rd. Division, on the 4th. inst., at the MILL, VLAMERTINGHE, at POTIJZE, and the area forward of this.

2. Major A Hearns will proceed at 8.0.p.m. 3rd April to the Mill, Vlamertinghe with "B" Section complete, plus transport, and will complete the taking over of the Sick Collecting Post at Potijze Chateau, the Advanced Dressing Station at Frost House, the Relay Posts at Joy and Jury, the Brickkiln and the new post in front of the Brickkiln. The relief to be completed by 12.0 noon on the lines arranged in to-days inspection. Two days rations will be taken.
          POTIJZE CHATEAU.............I.4.A.3.0.
          FROST HOUSE.................D.25.A.6.0.
          JOY.........................D.27.A.3.4.
          JURY........................D.21.D.6.3.
          BRICKKILN...................D.27.B.10.0.
          R.A.P.East of Brickkiln.....Map reference not known.

3. Sections "A" and "C" under the command of Capt. Clementi-Smith will parade in full marching order at 10.30.a.m. 4th.April 1918 and proceed to QUINTIN (POPERINGHE)) G.7.B.7.0. and there entrain at 12.30.p.m., detrain at ORISTE (H.2.b.1.1.) amd will proceed to the MILL at VLAMERTINGHE.
4. TRANSPORT.   The Transport will parade complete (less "B"Section) at 9.30.a.m. 4th. April 1918. and will proceed via POPERINGHE to the MILL, VLAMERTINGHE.
5. MOTOR TRANSPORT.   All available Motor Cars will be at the disposal of Major A Hearns from 8.0.p.m. April 3rd. 1918.
6. The 2/1st. North Midland Field Ambulance simultaneously relieve an Ambulance at the Prison and Arsenal at YPRES and the 2/2nd. North Midland Field Ambulance, one at BRANDHOEK.
7. Headquarters closes at Clifford Camp at 12.0.noon and opens at the MILL, VLAMERTINGHE at the same time 4th.April 1918.

Copy no: 8
Issued at 8.0.p.m. 3/4/18.   ....Lt-Colonel.R.A.M.C..TF.
                               Commndg. 2/3rd. North Midland Field Ambulance.

Distribution:-
     Copy No. 1. A.D.M.S. 59th. Division.
      "   "   2. Headquarters 176th. Infantry Brigade.
      "   "   3. Major A.Hearns.
      "   "   4. Capt. W.Bailey-Thomson.
      "   "   5. Lieut. S.H.Kingston.
      "   "   6. Capt. Clementi-Smith.
      "   "   7. Lt & Qmr. S.C.Richards.
      "   "   8. War Diary.
      "   "   9. War Diary.
      "   " 10. File.

CLINICAL CHART.

Army Form B. 181

(To be attached to Case Sheet.)

Corps ______ Military Hospital ______

No. ______ Rank and Name ______ Age ______ Service ______

Disease ______ Date of admission ______ Date of discharge ______ Result ______

Dates of Observation																															
Days of Disease																															
Temperature Fahrenheit	Time A.M. P.M.	Time A.M. P.M.	Time A.M. P.M.	Time A.M. P.M.	Time A.M. P.M.	Time A.M. P.M.	Time A.M. P.M.	Time A.M. P.M.	Time A.M. P.M.	Time A.M. P.M.	Time A.M. P.M.	Time A.M. P.M.	Time A.M. P.M.	Time A.M. P.M.	Time A.M. P.M.	Time A.M. P.M.	Time A.M. P.M.	Time A.M. P.M.	Time A.M. P.M.	Time A.M. P.M.	Time A.M. P.M.	Time A.M. P.M.	Time A.M. P.M.	Time A.M. P.M.	Time A.M. P.M.	Time A.M. P.M.	Time A.M. P.M.	Time A.M. P.M.	Time A.M. P.M.	Time A.M. P.M.	Time A.M. P.M.
·8 ·6 107° ·4 ·2																															
·8 ·6 106° ·4 ·2																															
·8 ·6 105° ·4 ·2																															
·8 ·6 104° ·4 ·2																															
·8 ·6 103° ·4 ·2																															
·8 ·6 102° ·4 ·2																															
·8 ·6 101° ·4 ·2																															
·8 ·6 100° ·4 ·2																															
·8 ·6 99° ·4 ·2																															
·8 ·6 98° ·4 ·2																															
·8 ·6 97° ·4 ·2																															
·8 ·6																															
Pulse per Minute																															
Respirations per Minute																															
Motions per 24 hours																															

(6201) Wt. W. 11421/M1165 2,000,000 12/16 McA & W Ltd. A.F.B. 181 (E. 735)

Signature ______ In charge of case.

To:- A.D.M.S. 59th. Division.

Appendix XVIII

App. III

I have the honour to make the following report and request:-

1.... During the intensive and incessant moves, my chief difficulty has been as regards Horse Transport.

2.... Several months ago I pointed out to the Headquarters of the Division that the present Transport was totally inadequate to convey increased Mob. Stores, of which I gave the cubic contents and weight.
The reply was "Do the best you can".

3.... In addition to excess Mob. Stores, there are always some things, (approx. 3 tons) essential to the working of the Ambulance which have to be carried.

4.... Frequently, as at present, I have been short of Horses through illness, and wagons through accidents so that the crisis becomes still more acute.

5.... Under these circumstances there are only 3 alternatives, all of which have sometimes been employed simultaneously:-
    (a). The creation of a dump ahead of a move, and behind, and its realization to the Unit after the move.   This in the case of Railway journeys is impossible.
    (b). The overworking of horses and men of the Transport in repeated journeys.
    (c). The use of Horsed ambulances and Motor Ambulances for the transporting of stores.

6.... During the past 14 months this Unit has relieved and been relieved by a great number of Ambulances of other divisions, and it has been observed that such incoming and departing Ambulances have very frequently received from their Divisional Supply Column, One, and in some cases 2 lorries for carrying surplus stores. As regards ourselves, however, this proceedure has been the exception and difficult of acquisition, although I am credibly informed, that on moves, a number of Divisional lorries invariably move empty.

7.... In the case of two Field Ambulances, one of which was a Guards Field Ambulance, with the Commanding Officers of which I discussed this problem, I learned as follows:- That in one case they had dumped the complete equipment of one section early in the war, so have been enabled to facilitate their transport since.   In the other case the complete equipment of one Section was accepted by the Divisional Ordnance, on receipt - on the understanding that such equipment would not be indented for during the remainder of the war.

8.... In this connection I would pray that authority for similar action might be given, in order to avoid the great worry and difficulty in Transport, both in action and on the move, and to prevent the inevitable loss and mis-laying of Stores.

Castleston

19/4/18.
Lieut-Col. R.A.M.C., T.F.
O.C. 2/3rd. North Midland Field Ambulance.

Copies (for information) to:-
1. O.C. 2/1st. N.M. Field Ambulance.
2. O.C. 2/2nd. N.M. Field Ambulance.
3. War Diary
4. War Diary.
5. File.

140/2983

2/3rd. Nth. Mid. F.O.

WAR DIARY or INTELLIGENCE SUMMARY

Army Form C. 2118.

2/3 N.M. Fd. Amb.

Place	Date	Hour	Summary of Events and Information	Remarks and references to Appendices
HOUTKERQUE Sheet 27. E.20.B.3.7.	MAY.1.1918		Cleaning of transport wagons. General training of unit. Shorts.	TRAINING
			AP. 30 M. LE COMTE PIERRE D'HESPEL reported for duty as Liaison Officer. Arrangements completed in re Hen's'id App	LIAISON OFFICER
	MAY 2.1918		3 B.M.S moved to WATOU + S.E & encamped in 3 fields "to day"	
	MAY 3-4		Medical stores fetched from Sheet 27 N.12, B.9.9. General training of unit. Bathing. C.& S.	GENERAL
HOSENHILL	MAY 5. 1918		hors of unit by route-march to HOSENHILL near RUBROUCK vide Appendix 1B.	MOVE APP. 1B
ST OMER	MAY 6. 1918		hors of unit by route march to 88 LA BRASS BARRACKS ST OMER when the 178 Inf. Bgr. had billetted ourselves there in Lines hut the Sy Bt. was S.R. Obstructed. App	MOVE APP. 1B
	MAY 7 .18		ST OMER. Bathing of unit & general cleaning. Reloading of wagons. Apart inspection of the infantry of the 178 Bgr. two left (only a skeleton unit + transport remains). Our own disposal is uncertain. Rumours are rife of moving for Italian Division or training Americans App M. LE COMTE D'HESPEL returned to Belgian Mission App	GENERAL
	May. 8.18			

Army Form C. 2118.

WAR DIARY
or
INTELLIGENCE SUMMARY.
(Erase heading not required.)

(2)

Place	Date	Hour	Summary of Events and Information	Remarks and references to Appendices
ECQUES	9/5/18		Route march from ST OMER to ECQUES (6 miles) then debusséd into village the 2/2 N.M.F.R. Billets also taken to day. HQ, Lizard (1st) bn asked for three for one lorry to move to BOURS, 21 miles C.N.O.	MOVE
	10/5/18	6.30 A.M.	Took the road for 21 mile march at THEROUANNE found 8 trees en route two. The unit occupied S. Hamlet to BOURS via PERNES sent to remaining 3rd Bn 2/2 N.M. MOVE to reach SACHIN S.W. of PERNES.	PL. 19
		7.A ECQUES the witnessed than to reach SACHIN S.W. of PERNES 18 MILES C.N.O. via Nhem Pic 19			
BOURS	13/5/18	11th 12th	Unit continued training at BOURS C.N.O.	TRAINING
BOURS 36 B. M. 35 a. 5. 7			Noted 11th Royal Scots Fusiliers & 36 NORTHUMBERLAND FUSILIERS at Sheet 36 B. 1.4.C. Central & 1.6.a. Central (ST. LEONARD) & arranged for evacuation of their sick. Both battalions are composed of B1 & B2 men, are for the most part infit for any distance & are about to dig trenches newly to "B.B." Line.	

C.N.O.

Vol 16

CONFIDENTIAL

WAR DIARY
of
Officer Commanding,
2/3rd North Midland Field Ambulance

from 1-5-18 – to – 31-5-18.

(Volume 5.)

WAR DIARY or INTELLIGENCE SUMMARY

Army Form C. 2118.

Place	Date	Hour	Summary of Events and Information	Remarks and references to Appendices
BOURS	14/5/18		Hospital for 25, 3-4 days sick, 1 a septic Lapstal for 25 establish	DUTY
	15/5/18		Inspection of Lines by 10th Batt. Director of Hvur Lines. Satisfactory CHO	INSPECTION
	17/5/18		Inspection of Motor Ambulances by mess offices 57th D.T. CHO	
			Inspection of Transport Billets Hospitals by DDMS 10th Corps.	
			Conference ADMS 57th Div at P.N. COS re Administration	
			"B.B." time from CAMBLAIN L'ABBÉ to 176th Inf.	CONFERENCE
			Bde. Killed man attacked Talbot central part of the unit	
			from DIVION to ROMBLY CRO	
			Lorries to last 4-5 days the "Volver" the unit Concert Party	CONCERT
			Ses gave concerts to troops in the village CRO	
			M.O.s of 2/5 S.F. 2/6 S.F. 1217 have left Proport to ADMS 31st M.O.s	
	18/5/18		Secretary of CAUCHY-AU-TOUR & LIERES for postions for H.Q. &	
			Show section CRS.	
			CAPT T.E. FLITCROFT left for 31st Div Authority 59 Div	STRENGTH
			The "B.B." Band now shelled this morning 3 Trumpets German	
			In hand of Enemy. I killed 1 wounded CRO	

Army Form C. 2118.

WAR DIARY
or
INTELLIGENCE SUMMARY. (4)
(Erase heading not required.)

Instructions regarding War Diaries and Intelligence Summaries are contained in F.S. Regs., Part II. and the Staff Manual respectively. Title pages will be prepared in manuscript.

Place	Date	Hour	Summary of Events and Information	Remarks and references to Appendices
	18/3/18			STRENGTH
			CAPT T.J. WHITELAW reports for duty from 2/6 N. Staff Regt. Message received 10 P.M. that CAUCHY-AU-TOUR will not be available for billets CMO. Inspection of all villages as an island our line & report thereon to N3/65 in re difficulty of obtaining billets	
	19/5/18		visit to 2 G.G. Royal Mont Regiment at HEUDICOURT & arrangement with O/C No. 8 Canadian F.A. to revert his sick will no 10 Canadian at PUCHEL for No 46) 7 Cy R.E. Cas.	SICK
			CAPTAIN TRISTIAN STOROE ELLIOT awarded the Military Cross	Honours + REWARDS
	20/5/18		1 NCO + 3 men report for duty 59 Div. School SAINS LES PERNES during 19th 26th 2 Horses + 1 Motor Ambulance leave Con	DUTY
			followed 176 Bys Penny W. with the limit + evacuated in emergency of B.1 men shown a wounded cal	DUTY
	2/5/18		arrangement to evacuate Church of 46 labour coy to rest 3 other men evacuated by M.O. daily	DUTY

WAR DIARY
or
INTELLIGENCE SUMMARY
(Erase heading not required.)

Army Form C. 2118.

Place	Date	Hour	Summary of Events and Information	Remarks and references to Appendices
BOURS	21/May/1918		Inspection by O.C. unit of Horse Standings & retaining of horses	INSPECTION
	25/May/1918		Removal of 175 Inf. Bde H.Q. to RAIMBERT.	CMD
	26/May/1918		All the units in the Central sector are being inspected and reported on by the Ambulances (MAZINGHEM & DIVION). In the camp sanitation has progressed satisfactorily. The digging of the B.B. line forges ahead. The 2 G.G. Royal Irish Rgt. have gone advantages in digging water from the 11 R.S.F. & 36 M.F. who have the use of drying rooms. The women GENERAL forward. General health of these B1 Battalions is remarkably good & a spell of summer weather has favoured their first week. CMD	GENERAL
			Repeated but unsuccessful efforts to obtain hills with CAOUTCHOUC-BULB BULLETS. TOUR has been made during the week so that portion is the most suitable to administer to the sick. CMD	CAOUTCHOUC-BULB BULLETS
			During the last few days training of the unit has continued. CMD	

WAR DIARY or INTELLIGENCE SUMMARY

Army Form C. 2118.

Place	Date	Hour	Summary of Events and Information	Remarks and references to Appendices
BOURS.	27/May/18		Final arrangements for collection of wounded rank in Central rest of "B.B." Line were embodied in an order, vide appendix 20. C.Wo	MED. ARRANGEMENTS APPENDIX 20
	29/5/18	pm	Altered arrangements for collection of wounded rick to Decauville accommodation in position vide H.Q. 69 Div. tst Spl. Wilson (Copies ADMS 69 DIV) M.a 9/5/17 vide Appendix 21/5 May 1918	LEAVE APPENDIX 21
"	30/MAY/18		A scheme for evacuation of "B.B." Line, as a defence line has to day been submitted. A.DMS 69 Div. Wp Inspection of Motor Transport by Captain × from G.H.Q. a/o	APPENDIX 22 INSPECTION
RELAY. 36.A. T.2.a.52.00.	30/May/18		After a w/of effects, orders concerning etc the unit received instructions from P.D.M.S. to move H.Q. A RELY × on tent subscription to BOIS- DES-RIETZ (36.B.I.15.b.). The move was satisfactorily completed to day according to orders issued in Appendices 2. G.H.O	MOVE

WAR DIARY
or
INTELLIGENCE SUMMARY.
(Erase heading not required.)

Army Form C. 2118.

Place	Date	Hour	Summary of Events and Information	Remarks and references to Appendices
RELY MAY 31/1918 36.A.7.2.A.50.00			During the night a farm house in RELY occupied by this unit a few minutes 60 yards of train were on fire, the fire burned for 2 hours & gutted the buildings. The fire was caused by an accident to some refugees feeding near an oven, & was not due to the military CHQ	FIRE
			For O.R. proceeded on leave to United Kingdom to-day. O.R.S. The unit has greatly benefited during the last month from rest & good weather & from being out of the actual line. Re-equipment in Equipment & Personnel & M.E. has been effected & the medical service note certain notes have proceeded smoothly	LEAVE

C. Waddoti (T.F.)
R.A.M.C. T. Brookes
Russian N. Mid. T Division
O/c 2/3 N Mid. 59 Division B.E.F.

May. 31. 19 18

Appendix No. 18

Operation Order No. 19.
by
Lt.Col.C.A.Stidston, D.S.O., Commanding.

Ref.Maps. Sheet. 27.
Hazebruck 5A.

1. The 178th Infantry Brigade will move today May 5th by Bus and march route to St.Momelin Area.
2. The 2/3rd North Midland Field Ambulance will move in rear of the Brigade Transport and will be ready to move off from the Camp at 10.30 a.m. One blanket per man will be carried.
3. The Unit will stage for the night of the 5th/6th May at RUBROUCK (Sheet 27 H.14.a.) Distance of the first day's march 12½ miles.
4. All tents belonging to Artillery Reinforcement Camp will be struck and handed in by 8 a.m. All Section tents will be struck and loaded immediately.
5. The Mid-day meal will be issued at 9.30 a.m. and will be carried on the man.
6. Capt.Kingston will remain in charge of the sick and will evacuate them by Daimler car, rejoining the Unit at Rubrouck later in the day.
7. Major T.S.Elliott will proceed in Ford car with the Liaison Officer to Rubrouck at 10 a.m. and complete billeting arrangements.
8. A Rear Guard consisting of L/Cpl.Bryan and two other ranks to be detailed by the S/M. will remain behind with three days' rations to guard the Camp and hand same over to incoming Ambulances of the Division by which they will be rationed and with the last of which they will rejoin Unit in the new area.
9. The 2/3rd North Midland Field Ambulance Headquarters will close at HOUTKERQUE at 11 a.m. and open at RUBROUCK at samehour
10. Brigade Headquarters close at 9 a.m. and open in the new area on arrival.

C.A.Stidston
Lt.Col. R.A.M.C. T.
O.C.2/3rd N.M.Fld.Amblce.

6.0 a.m.
5.5.1918.

Distribution.
No.1 to A.D.M.S.
Nos.2, 3 & 4 to Section Officers.
Nos. 5 & 6 to the S/Ms.
Nos. 7 & 8 War Diary.
No. 9 File.
No.10 O.C.178 Infrantry Brigade Transport.

Appendix No 19

Operation Order No. 20. by
O.C. 2/3rd. North Midland Field Ambulance.

SECRET.   May 9th. 1918.
Map. Lens 11 and Hazebrook 5a.

1. The Unit will move on May 10th to BOURS. Distance 21 mls.
    Reveille.....4.30.a.m. Fall in.......6.15.a.m.
    Breakfast....5.30.a.m. Move off.....6.30.a.m.
2. Route:- THEROUANNE. Starting point of Brigade, Cross Roads ½ mile west of L in LIETTRES 9.26.a.m..... ESTREE-BLANCHE, RELY, AUCHY-AUBOIS, NEDONCHELLE, PERNES, BOURS.
3. Capt. T.E.Flitcroft and S/Sergt. Kendall., will take a Ford Car at 8.0.a.m. and report to Staff-Captain, 178th Infantry Brigade at BLESSY at 8.30.a.m. and will meet incoming Unit.
4. Kits will be handed into the Quartermasters Stores by 5.30.a.m. and blankets in rolls of ten.
5. Midday ration will be issued at 6.0.a.m. from Quartermasters Stores and Carried on the man. Hot meal will be issued on arrival at new destination.
6. One Daimler Car will be at disposal of Major A Mearns for the disposal of sick of Brigade.
7. Horse Transport will follow Unit and all wagons will be loaded as far as possible overnight.
8. In the event of a request for Motor Busses for the personnel eventuating further orders will be issued accordingly.

7.0.p.m.   ....Lt-Col. R.A.M.C., TF.
                 O.C.2/3rd. Nth.Mid. Field Ambulance.

Distribution.
Copy No. 1. A.D.M.S. 59th. Division.
  "   " 2. Headquarters 178th. Inf. Brigade.
  "   " 3. to 7. All Officers of Unit.
  "   " 8 & 9. Two Sergt-Majors.
  "   " 10 & 11. War Diary.
  "   " 12. File.

Appendix. 20 for May 1918

S E C R E T. 2/3rd. NORTH MIDLAND FIELD AMBULANCE.

COLLECTION OF SICK AND WOUNDED IN THE "RD" DIVISION LINE (CENTRAL SECTOR). From ROMELY to DIVION.

MAPS:- Sheet 36b. Sheet 36a. Lens 11. Hazebrook 1a.
ORDERS. (1). Medical Arrangements A.D.M.S. 59th. Division.
(2). Administrative Table, 59th. Division and attached Units.

1... The following is a list of the Units, with Map References, which come under Medical Service of this Field Ambulance.

UNIT.	LOCATION.	Map Reference.
1... 2/5th. Sherwood Foresters.	BOURS.	
2... 2/6th. Sherwood Foresters.	BOURS.	
3... 2/7th. Sherwood Foresters.	BOURS.	
4... R.E. Mechanical Transport.	AUCHEL.	36b/H.24.d.6.4.
5... Machine Gun School.	PALAIS-les-PERNES.	36b/H.15.c.3.5.
6... S.A.A. Section of D.A.C.	BOURS.	36b/A.20.c.3.8.
7... No.4 Co. A.S.C.	BACHEL.	36b/H.1.a.2.5.
8... 30th. Northumberland Fusiliers.	GALLANT STURDAMS.	35b/I.15.b.3.8.
9... 11th. Royal Scots Fusiliers.		35b/I.4.A.7.4.
10... 467th. Field Co. R.E.	AUCHEL.	36b/G.27.b.5.7.
11... 33rd. M.G.Bn. Cheshire Regt.	AUCHEL.	36b/G.27.
12... 178th. Brigade Headquarters.	DIEVAL.	36b/G.14.b.7.3.
13... Chinese series of Groups H.Q.	BURBURE.	36a/F.27.d.4.4.
14... 2nd. G.G.Bn. R. Irish Rifles.	BURIONVILLE.	36a/H.23.d.C.5.
15... 4th. Siege Co. R.E.	LIETTRES RELAIS.	36a/H.21.d.N.C.
16... 560th. Army Troop Co. R.E.	ROMELY.	36a/H.21.a.7.7.
17... No.3. Foreways. CO. R.E.	CAUCHY-a-la-TOUR.	

2... Sick parades of Nos.1, 2 & 3 are held at the Hospital of this Unit at BOURS.

3... Captain Hardy Kingston will take a Daimler Ambulance Car, and leaving BOURS at 9.0.a.m. each day will visit Nos.4,5,6 & 7 in that order.

4... A Horsed Ambulance with four horses will leave BOURS daily at 8.0.a.m. to collect of Nos.8 & 9.

5... One Daimler Ambulance Car will leave BOURS in time to arrive at BURBURE not later than 8.30.a.m., proceed with the Medical Officer of the Chinese Group to collect patients for evacuation and take them to LIETTRES (36a/H.19c.) 2/1st. North Midland Field Ambulance and there deliver them. On the return route this Ambulance Car will call at No.14 in case it might be required.

6... Captain F.J. WHITELAW will take a Daimler Ambulance Car, leaving BOURS at 9.0.a.m. daily and will visit Nos.13,14,15,16 & 17 in that order.

7... One Daimler Ambulance Car will report to the Medical Officer of No.11 by 10.0.a.m. each day for the collection of sick. No.16 is at present administered by the 2/1st. NORTH MIDLAND FIELD AMBULANCE.

8... Captain Hardy Kingston and Captain F.J. Whitelaw will act, when visiting Units detailed to them, as Medical Officers to those Units and will arrange with the respective Commanding Officers for inoculation against Typhoid and for the supply of Drugs and Dressings etc, and will render to the Units concerned all assistance possible.

9... Officer Commanding the Hospital at BOURS will arrange evacuation of sick by Horses Ambulances, completing details of Service with the Transport Sergt-Major.

.................Lt-Col. R.A.M.C.
O.C. 2/3rd. North Midland Field Ambulance.

27/7/18.
DISTRIBUTION.
Copy No. 1. To A.D.M.S. 59th. Division.
"   "   2. " Headquarters, 178th. Infantry Brigade.
Copies Nos.3 to 7 (inclusive). All Officers of 2/3rd. N.M. Field Ambulance.
"   "   8 to 23. Commanding Officers of Units concerned.
"   "   24 to 26. N.C.O.'s, c/o.R.S.M. 2/3rd. N.M. Field Ambulance.
"   "   27 & 28. Sergt-Major of Horse Transport. "
"   "   29 & 30. Hospital. 2/3rd. N.M. Field Ambulance.
"   "   30 & 31. War Diary.
"   "   32 & 33. File.

To:- _____

The undermentioned General Routine orders are published for your information, and guidance when necessary.

(signed) C.A.Stidston.. Lt Col. R.A.M.C.(TF)
July 18th. 1917. O/C 2/3rd North Midland Field Ambulance.

EFFECTS OF WOUNDED, MISSING, AND DECEASED SOLDIERS. (G.R.O. 1358 and 1752.

1. MONEY, PAY BOOKS, IDENTITY DISCS AND ARTICLES OF AN INTRINSIC OR SENTIMENTAL VALUE.
    (a) <u>Sick or Wounded Soldiers</u> -- When a man is sent down Sick or Wounded, any kit, which for any reason, has not been sent down with him, will be examined at the earliest possible moment by a responsible Officer of the Unit to which he belongs, and the man's money, pay book, identity disc and objects of an intrinsic or sentimental value found in the kit will be placed in a package, together with a certificate on Army Form W.3190 (on which the dispatching Officer certifies that he has carried out the instructions laid down in this General Routine Order and the back of which contains spaces for an Inventory) and forwarded as a Registered package through the nearest Field Post Office to the D.A.D.R.T., HAVRE, who will trace the location of the addressee and re-forward the package. If, in the meantime the man has been evacuated to England, his effects will be sent to the Home Record Office of his Unit.
        The Army Form W.3190 certificate is made up in Block pads of original and duplicates, and the duplicate will be retained by the Unit, in case of any question arising afterwards.
    (b) <u>Missing and deceased Soldiers</u> -- Except as stated below, the procedure will be identical to that laid down in 1 (a), but the Officer i/c Burying Parties may sometimes replace the officer of the mans' Unit and he will be responsible, under those conditions for collecting the articles found on the man's body. He will hand them over on the ground, to the Staff Captain of the Brigade concerned, or to an Officer of the Adjutant General's Branch of the Staff.
    EXCEPTIONS.
        (i) A.B.64 of the deceased and missing men will be sent to the D.A.G., Effects Branch.G.H.Q. 3rd Echelon, by registered post under seperate cover (and not together with articles of sentimental and intrinsic value) plainly marking on the outside wrapper thereof " A.B's 64 of deceased and missing men ".
        (ii) Effects of deceased and missing men will be sent to the D.A.G. 3rd Echelon, by registered post through the nearest Field Post Office and NOT to the D.A.D.R.T.., HAVRE.
    (c) <u>Labelling and securing of packages.</u> -- (i) Each package will be sealed and securely fastened. The special label Army Form W.3042, for wounded men's effects, must be used. and Army Form W.3043, for deceased men's kits must be used. Each label will contain information as to the mans name, number, rank, and regiment, and must bear the Censors Stamp, before dispatch.
        (ii) In the event of the dispatch by a Unit of more than one package of effects at the same time, these will be tied up and labelled separately as directed in Clause c (i) and will then be placed in a sack and securely sealed, and dispatched as one Registered package. At the same time a list of the various parcels will also be enclosed in the Sack.

    Note. Personal clothing of Sick, wounded, deceased or missing soldiers must never be sent to the Base.

2. - PUBLIC CLOTHING AND EQUIPMENT.
    (a) <u>Wounded and Sick Soldiers.</u> -- Arms and accoutrements of sick and wounded will, when possible, be taken to Field Ambulances and thence to Casualty Clearing Stations with the men.
    On transfer of the Sick and wounded to Ambulance Trains, the arms, accoutrements, and such articles of equipment as are not

(OVER)

SECRET.

Orders by Lieut-Colonel. C.A.Stidston. D.S.O.
Commdg. 2/3rd. North Midland Field Ambulance.

Appendix 21 for May 18

1. Maps:- Hazebrouck 5a. Lens 11. Sheet 36a. Sheet 36b.
2. .....Reveille.........6.30.a.m.   Parade.......7.0.a.m.
   Breakfast........7.30.a.m.   Parade.......9.0.a.m.
   Dinner..........12.0.noon.   Fall in ......1.30.p.m.
   Move Off.......1.45.p.m.
   Dress....Full Marching Order. Blankets rolled on top of pack.
   The Unit with Transport, less the Tent-sub-division of "B" Section,
   will move by Route March to RELY.
   Route:- PERNES, AUMERAAL, LA CAUCHIETTE, AUCHY-au-BOIS, RELY.
   Distance...11miles.

3. .....ADVANCE PARTY.   An Advance Party consisting of Major T.S. Elliot, Sergt. Tinkler, Ptes Petrie and Court J. will leave, with kit, by the "Chinese" Motor Ambulance at 8.0.a.m. and Proceed to RELY, and arrange billets for the Incoming Unit, with the Billet Warden. This car will then report back to BURBURE and proceed as usual.

4. .....Major A. Mearns will detail an Advance party of 1. N.C.O. and 3 Other Ranks of his Tent Sub-division, who will proceed in the Horsed Ambulance which goes to the 36th. Northumberland Fusiliers at BOIS-des-RIETZ (36b/I.18.b.). The Medical Officer of the 36th. Northumberland Fusiliers will shew this party to the site selected by the A.D.M.S. 59th. Division., and they will pitch thereon 4 Bell Tents, One Operating Tent plus One Operating Tent borrowed from "C" Section.

5. ....Major. Mearns, Capt. Whitelaw and the Tent sub-division of "B" Section will proceed under orders of Major Mearns to BOIS-des-RIETZ, and there establish a Scabies and a General Hospital in the two Operating tents. Major Mearns will arrange all details with the Transport N.C.O for the necessary Transport.

6. .....Evacuation of patients from the present Hospital to C.C.S. will be under the arrangements of Major Mearns, using Horsed Ambulances and should be completed early in the morning.

7. .....Capt. Whitelaw and Capt. Kingston will make their usual rounds and return, Capt. Whitelaw to BOIS-des-RIETZ and Capt. Kingston to the H.Q. of the Ambulance at RELY.

8. .....On Friday 31st. inst., and subsequent days the Sector will be re-arranged into NORTH and SOUTH and administered, vide Medical Arrangements issued recently, as follows:- Northern Sector will be administered from Headquarters, RELY. Major Elliot will take a Ford Car daily and visit Nos 32- 38 and 107 Chinese Companies at FONTS. Capt. Kingston will take a Daimler Car and will visit Units at LES PRESSES, HURIONVILLE, BURBURE and RAMBERT.   SOUTHERN SECTOR. by Major Mearns who will have two Daimler Cars at his disposal and will be responsible for the evacuation of sick from 23rd. Cheshire Regt., AUCHEL., 467th Field Coy. R.E. AUCHEL., 3rd. Foreways Co. R.E. CAUCHY-a-la-TOUR., 11th. Royal Scots Fusiliers on CALONNE- AUCHEL Road, 36th. Northumberland Fusiliers, BOIS-des- RIETZ., and will detail Capt. Whitelaw to visit Headquarters of the Sherwood Foresters at BOURS, Divisional Supply Column at TANGRY, Divisional School at SAINS-les-PERNES, S.A.A.of D.A.C., FIEFS and No. 4. Co. A.S.C. SACHIN.

9. .....The General arrangements re inoculation of Units concerned and Medical Service to them still hold good.

10. ...Major Elliot will arrange a Scabies and General Hospital in Barns at RELY and will administer them with Tent Sub-division of " C" Section.

11. ... All wagons will be loaded ready to move off by 12.0. noon. Officers kits will be loaded on G.S. Wagons

12. ...A Rear Party, to be detailed by the Quartermaster consisting of One N.C.O and 2 Other Ranks will remain with two days rations at BOURS and guard any surplus stores.

13. ...The Horsed Ambulance which proceeds to BOIS-des-RIETZ in the morning will return there at night. The other two Horsed Ambulances will proceed, after evacuating patients to PERNES, to Headquarters at RELY.

14. ....An evening meal will be prepared on the Cooker en route and will be issued on arrival at RELY.

15. ...Headquarters of the Unit will close at BOURS at 2.0.p.m. and re-open at RELY at same time. H.Q. of the Motor Transport of the Unit will be at RELY.

....th. 1918..

...........C Stidston........Lt Col.R.A.M.C..T.F.
O.C.2/3rd. North Midland Field Ambulance.

Army Form B 231.

FIELD STATE.

Unit _____
Place _____
Date _____

To be rendered in accordance with Field Service Regulations, Part II.

FIGHTING STRENGTH

This should not include details attached to unit, or personnel detailed to march with the Train, or any men unfit to go into action with unit

UNIT	Personnel		Horses and Mules		Other Animals	Guns and Ammunition Wagons (stating nature)	Machine Guns	Ambulances	Tool Carts, Technical Carts (stating nature)	Remarks
	Officers	Other Ranks	Riding	Draught and Pack						
(1)	(2)	(3)	(4)	(5)	(6) (7)	(8)	(9)	(10)	(11)	(12)
TOTALS										

RATION STRENGTH

To include Fighting Strength, Personnel detailed to march with the Train, and all Personnel and animals attached for Rations and Forage

Personnel	Horses and Mules		Other Animals	Mechanically Propelled Vehicles					Remarks
Total, all Ranks entitled to Rations.	Heavy Horses	Other Horses and Mules		Motor Cars	Motor Bicycles	Lorries		Tractors	
						3 Ton	30 Cwt.		
(13)	(14)	(15)	(16) (17)	(18)	(19)	(20)	(21)	(22)	(23)

Ammunition with Unit:—
  ·303 inch; approximate number of rounds per Man _____
  ·303 inch; " " " per Machine-Gun _____
  Gun or Howitzer; approximate number of rounds per Gun or Howitzer _____

Supplies with Unit _____
  Approximate number of days' rations for men of ration strength _____
  " " " " forage for Animals " _____
  " " " " fuel and lubricants for Mechanically Propelled Vehicles _____

Signature of Commander _____

SECRET.

Appendix 2a

745/1939.

From. O.C. 2/3rd. North Midland Field Ambulance.

To. A.D.M.S. 50th. Division.

In reply to your 5/355 dated 20/5/15 I have the honour to suggest as follows, subject to your approval please.
1... Map. Sheet 36b and Sheet 36b.
2... Central Sector (the passes from ROMBLY (36a/N.32.c.) to DIVION (36b/I.24.b. Main Dressing Station and Headquarters of Field Ambulance at PERNES. (36b/H.10.d.9.7.
3... Working of an Evacuation Scheme for One Ambulance.
In the event of the present Canadian C.C.S. and 2nd. Sanitary Section having to evacuate the Main Dressing Station would move back to SAINS-les-PERNES (36b/C.16).
Advanced Dressing Stations:- AMETTES (36b/B.4.a) for the Northern half, and FLORINGHEM for the Southern half.
Car Loading posts and banners attached Regimental Aid Posts at RELY (36a/T.2.a), Fosse No.1. (36a/E.26.b), Fosse No.5. (36b/C.1.cent),AUCHEL (26b/C.27.b), CAMBLAIN CHATELAINE (36b/T.1.b.cent).
In the event of a debacle the Main Dressing Station would retire to BOYAVAL (36b/C.15.c) and the Advanced Dressing Stations to NEDONCHELLE. (36b/B.7.e), MAREST (36b/H.254.a.c.).

May 30th. 1915.

....
O.C. 2/3rd. North Midland Field Ambulance.

Lt. Col. R.A.M.C., T.F.

140/3076.

2/3rd Wel. Med. F.A.

June 1918.

CONFIDENTIAL...

WAR DIARY OF

THE

2/3RD NORTH MIDLAND FIELD AMBLCE.

FOR THE MONTH OF

JUNE... 1918.

(Vol. 6.)

To:- A.D.M.S.

    59th Division.

Army Form C. 2118.

WAR DIARY
or
INTELLIGENCE SUMMARY.
(Erase heading not required.)

1. JUNE, 1916.

Vol 17

Place	Date	Hour	Summary of Events and Information	Remarks and references to Appendices
RELY	JUNE 1/16		A carpenter + a two unit lorry proceeded to report to OC	SANITATION
	36.A.T.2	a.50.00	No 22 Sanitary Section PERNES. There to make latrines wood, ablution trestles, meat safes, + grease traps for the relay of RELY, the sanitation of which is as yet unsatisfactory. OAP	
	JUNE 3/1916.		Arrangements are being made to withdraw the sanitary personnel of the Battalion for a course of instruction in sanitation with its unit to replace them temporarily by RAMC personnel. CRO	
	June 5/1916.		Training of the unit continues. Battalion auxiliaries assisting on this section. It is found that in the aircraft + transport work are about 200 men too old. It is regretted that they are left in England. CAP	General
	June 6.1916		Orders have received today for LT-COL. C.P. STIBSTON, O.C. Unit to "report to W.O. for duty on temporary transport to home establishment". This officer has commanded the unit since Aug. 11. 19.16. CMP	DUTY. C.O
	June 7.1916		Major T.S. ELLIOT. M.C. assumes temporary command of the unit. CMP	C.O.

Army Form C. 2118.

WAR DIARY
or
INTELLIGENCE SUMMARY.
(Erase heading not required.)

2. June 1916.

Instructions regarding War Diaries and Intelligence Summaries are contained in F.S. Regs., Part II. and the Staff Manual respectively. Title pages will be prepared in manuscript.

Place	Date	Hour	Summary of Events and Information	Remarks and references to Appendices
RELY	7.6.16	8 a.m.	Temporary Command of the Unit assumed by me at this hour. Full kit inspection this afternoon. Nearly all deficiencies of kit have now been made good.	C.O. Kit inspection
	8.6.16		Shoe & Shirt Major Carrez.	
			Kit & feet inspection. the equipment of all recruits is now complete. Nothing worthy of notice happened this day. M.	Equipments
	9.6.16		This evening about 8.30 p.m. the village of the unit was over a bit enemy photographs (when descending on to RELY — FONTES Rd. On reaching the spot the part a Civilian (French.) cyclist picking off bits most of the literature but he managed to preserve a portion. I am Unnoticed before this. I have this day sent to Div. Hqrs. a summary of the articles & contents it contains not to found in the appendix — 25.	Enemy (Propaganda)
	10.6.16		The papers is printed in very excellent French, & his evidently been compiled by either a Frenchman or a linguist of extra in ordinary statue & intelligence. M.	
	11.6.16		Training of listening Parades Chief work — Sanitation of villages & posting of Orderlies & looking out rubbish also being erected on roadside pits in the village, to prevent	Work
	12.6.16		Croplings of litters scattered about & perish billets. Men will be under the immediate observation of the Billet Warden when the village is un-occupied by troops, & will also be called upon to assist & assist the Warden in the removal of latrines buckets. M.	Billets Latrines.

WAR DIARY
INTELLIGENCE SUMMARY. 3
(Erase heading not required.)

Army Form C. 2118.

June 1918.

Hour, Date, Place	Summary of Events and Information	Remarks and references to Appendices
Rely- June 13. 1918.	8th Cross of 1st Army R.A.M.C. pateol of instructor convened.	R.A.M.C. Cross.
" 14. "	Cpl. Dejeur W.E. adm His work, Lt. Sinclair administration on this course. M.O.	Shelly Troops.
" 15. "	The number sick in 178th C.C.S. Coyto has decreased for to last few days. M.O. History of importance Kehrude. M.O.	
Boyaval " 16. " G.15.c.6.7 / 44.3.	Unit moved at 6 a.m. this morning by route march to BOYAVAL G.15.c.6.7 (44 B) about 9 miles E. BOIS-DE-RIETZ. Tent subdivision moved from independently. Operation orders rec'd October 26. M.C.	Move.
" 17. "	Unit is conventions brood from an accumulated in convention brood. Sunday arrangements are expert to patro. M.C.	Rriete.
" 18. "	Work of unit proceeds. Painting begun improving sanitation. The Rev. J. Grant C.F. (R.C.) reported for duty. M.C.	Work.
" 19. "	The weather has not been a few hours of sun a very dry spell of summery weather. M.C.	

Army Form C. 2118.

WAR DIARY
or
INTELLIGENCE SUMMARY.
(Erase heading not required.)

4.

Hour, Date, Place	Summary of Events and Information	Remarks and references to Appendices
BOYAVAL June 20. 1918	Capt. S.H. Kingston temporarily attached from last night to 13th W. Riding Regt. Fontaine-Les-Boulans. Has taken medical charge of all other details of 178th Bgde in the village & of 36th C.C.B. Northumberland Fusiliers at FREDEFIN. Units under my Medical charge are as follows:— 13th W. Riding Regt. Fontaine-Les-Boulans. Headquarters 178th Brigade " 2/6 Seaforth Feredefin 36th C.C.B. Northumberland Fusiliers FREDEFIN. 11th C.C.B. Royal Scots. LISBOURG. No. 4 Coy. A.S.C. " S.A.A., D.A.C. FIEFS. 59th Div. M.T. Co. TANGRY. 59th Divisional Solart CREPY. An Epidemic of a type of 3-day fever is in progress amongst units of 178th Bgde. The main symptoms are fever up to 104° Fahricle, pains in the back, often gastric symptoms	MEDICAL ARRANGEMENTS FOR UNITS OF 178th INF. BRIGADE. Epidemic

WAR DIARY
INTELLIGENCE SUMMARY

Army Form C. 2118.

Hour, Date, Place	Summary of Events and Information	Remarks and references to Appendices
BOYAVAL June 20. 1918.	and another great produte. The symptoms usually start on the 3rd day + convalescence is rapid. Drugs most useful are - Acid Acetal. Quinine, Stin. Sulphate + Bromide. Units chiefly affected are :- 13th West Riding Regt. 120 sick, 115 Royal Scots 108, Northumberland Fusiliers 284 - Total 95 were admitted to 5th Stationary - Total 95 were admitted to No 191 Aust. + 96 returned to regimental details hospitals - No 191 Field Ambulance Hospitals were established during the day for extra 230 [unreadable] cases. Prophylactic measures were instituted by the ADMS. Transport to Bryalis, conveying 2 horses vis 2 Ingles + level drinks [rest illegible]	Epidemic
" 21. 1918	Capt. to Bishop Thompson struck off to starry of the unit from this date. Capt. Walker [unreadable] to Fortune more Capt. Knights (West Y/S.) [unreadable] of importance to relate M/S.	Story.
" 22. "	Nothing of importance to relate M/S.	

Army Form C. 2118.

WAR DIARY
or
INTELLIGENCE SUMMARY.

(Erase heading not required.)

No. 6

Hour, Date, Place	Summary of Events and Information	Remarks and references to Appendices
BOYAVAL. JUNE 23. 1918.	Colonel O.W.D. STEEL. R.A.M.C. T. assumed command of the Unit.	
June 24th	An outbreak of Measles reported at Torkeare. 6 13 orderlies. The usual precautions were taken. It was subsequently found that the diagnosis had been made by a Friend Interpreter.	
June 28th	Field Ambulance Commanders conference at the A.D.M.S. office at BOMY. The A.D.M.S. explained the probable employment of the Division and gave orders as to policy.	
29th	A number of the time G.P. & O. returned to scene and also the M.O. i/c the Horse Transport personnel.	

(73989) W4141—463. 400,000. 9/14. H.&J,Ltd. Forms/C. 2118/10.

Appendix 26.

OPERATION ORDERS NO.
BY MAJOR T.S.ELLIOT. COMMANDING. 2/3RD.N.M.F.AMB
---:::::::::::::::::::---

1. The Unot will move at 5-55a.m. this morning the 16th inst. to BOYAVAL. G.14 d (44b)
2. Route..WESTREHEM –NEDONCHELLE – FIEFS –BOYAVAL. Distance... 9 miles.
3.   Breakfast..... 5-15 a.m.
           Fall in....... 5-45 a.m.
           Dinner........ 11-0 a.m.
           Tea........... 4-30 p.m.
4. The head of the column will pass the Starting Point. T.7.a.95.65 (36a) at 6-0 a.m.
5. The Quartermaster. Sergt Keeling. Ptes Docherty Bridges and Hurley will move in a Daimler Car at 6-0 a.m. and will on arrival arrange for the Billeting of the Unit.
6. Captain S.H.Kingston will be responsible for the evacuation of all sick men unable to return to duty.
7. A rear party consisting of Captain S.H.Kingston Sergt Tinkler. Corpl Baugh and 6 men will be left to complete removal of baggage complete. Sergt Tinkler will complete the Billeting, certificates and will rejoin the Unit as soon as possible.
8. Captain S.H.Kingston will be responsible that the billets are left clean and all open latrines are filled in. He will obtai obtain a certificate from the Billet Warden to that effect.
9. Officers Kits will be loaded on C.Section Amblce Wagon at 5-30 a.m.

                                Major.R.A.M.C..TF.
           O.C. 2/3rd North Midland Field Amblce.

June 16th 1918.

CONFIDENTIAL

WAR DIARY

of

O.C. 2/3rd NORTH MIDLAND FIELD AMBULANCE.

From:- July 1st 1918 To:- July 31st 1918.

(Volume 7)

WAR DIARY
or
INTELLIGENCE SUMMARY.

(Erase heading not required.)

Army Form C. 2118.

Place	Date	Hour	Summary of Events and Information	Remarks and references to Appendices
BOYAVAL	July 1st		This day the horse transport & vehicles were inspected by the O.C. 59th Divisional Train and by the D.A.D.V.S. who appeared themselves satisfied with the improvement in the condition of the animals. In the evening the Cinema party of the 42nd York Highland Field Ambulance gave an open air performance to the patients and personnel, the limits to the great pleasure of all ranks.	O.S. O.S.
	2nd 3rd		The pandemic of "Spanish Influenza" begins to abate. All patients were removed from Farm to link the locals being very hot. Captain S. Grant L.T. this day proceeded on 14 days leave to U.K.	O.S. O.S.
	4th			
	6th		Late orders received, the repair lorry, at Etaples, was practised this day. She vehicle being available here on the usual search to move in 35 minutes. The horses had to be brought about 300 yards. O.S.	
	7th		This day joined the Unit Captain G.R. Grant M.C. R.M.C. [SR] + 1/7/21. C.R. HEADY. M.O. R.C. U.S.A.	O.S.

Place	Date	Hour	Summary of Events and Information	Remarks and references to Appendices
BOYAVAL	July 9th		Conference of Water masters at the Headquarters of 178th Infantry Brigade at Fontaine-les-Boulons presided over by the A.D.M.S, 59th Division. Colonel C.H. LINDSAY, C.M.S. D.S.O on improving the comfort of the men.	O.S.
	10th		T/S/Sgt Major WOOD. T. of this Unit appointed Hony Lt. + Q.M of the 135th Field Ambulance.	O.S.
	12th		Captain S.H. KINGSTON R.A.M.C. proceeded on 14 days leave to U.K.	O.S.
	13th		The bulk of the personnel engaged in hospital work of	
	14th		the remainder received Div'n Instruction from	
	15th		C.S.M. Major. START 2/9 York & Lancs Regt.	O.S.
	16th		on leave.	
	19th		The horsed transport this day inspected by the D.A.D.V.S. 59th Division who was pleased with the appearance of the animals.	O.S.
	20th		A very exceptional turn-out of the horses, transport, personnel by Major BRIGHT Captain SOOBY A.V.C. & Captain GODDARD A.S.C. during the inspection, there came the D.M.S. 4th Army and A.D.M.S. 59th Division	O.S.

Army Form C. 2118.

WAR DIARY
or
INTELLIGENCE SUMMARY.
(Erase heading not required.)

Instructions regarding War Diaries and Intelligence Summaries are contained in F.S. Regs., Part II. and the Staff Manual respectively. Title pages will be prepared in manuscript.

Place	Date	Hour	Summary of Events and Information	Remarks and references to Appendices
BOYAVAL	July 21st		D.D.M.S. XVII Corps this day inspected the Unit. Park: Horse Lines, most satisfactory & some stock on hand of dental forceps. GS	
BARLY	23rd		This day the Unit marched to Fontaine-les-Boulans & their embussing proceeded via St Pol & Avesnes to BARLY. Much rain.	
	25th		This day the Unit moved by line of march from BARLY to WAILLY [54.S.E] and relieved the 9th Canadian Field Ambulance in the line. Locations. Head quarters R.15.6.5.3. WAILLY Post [4 nursing] R.22.2.9.7. A.D.S. [Major Elliott MC & 23 OR of C sect.ns] M.31.c.2.8 (51 Z) /App I R.A.P.s. Front. Right. S.4.c.8.2. [6RAMC] Support Right S.2.6.5.0 Front. Left M.35.a.1.9 [4 RAMC] Support Left M.29.a.9.2. The A.D.S was situated in a deep dugout but is full view of the enemy, the Officers Bunny is a trench but above ground. Can only be got up to the R.A.P.s in daylight if necessary, but in urgent cases was it considered advisable Their was not much shelling at first & the main point was how B1 personnel lived en route the hardships of living in the trenches. O.C. to A.D.S. & lines. Evacuation working smoothly at present. O Steel Lt Col. Comg 2/3 (W.M) Fld Amb	
	26th, 27th 28, 29th			

SECRET.   Copy No. 15
                      R.A.M.C. ORDERS No. 50.
                               by
                      A.D.M.S., 59th. Division.   App. I

Ref. Sheets:-   July 23rd. 1918.
   1/40,000. 51b. & 51c.

1.   The 59th. Division will relieve the 7th Infantry Brigade,
3rd. Canadian Division in the Line between MERCATEL and NEUVILLE-
VITASSE, on the night of July 25th/26th.
2.   The 2/1st. NORTH MIDLAND FIELD AMBULANCE will relieve No.8.
Canadian Field Ambulance at the Divisional Sick Collecting Station,
LE FERMONT (R.21.c.8.2./51c.) at 10.0.a.m. on July 24th. 1918.
     The O.C. 2/1st., North Midland Field Ambulance will send 2 Officers
and 1 Tent Sub-division to report for duty to O.C. VI Corps M. D.
Station, BAC-du-SUD (Q.31.d.8.7./51c.) at 12.0.noon on the 24th instant.
3.   The 2/2nd North Midland Field Ambulance will relive No.10 Canadian
Field Ambulance at VI Corps Rest Station, Gouy-en-Artois (Q.16.a.7.7./51c)
at 6 p.m. on July 25th.
     The Quartermaster and five Other Ranks should proceed on the
evening of July 24th to report to the O.C. VI Corps Rest Station for
the purpose of learning details and checking stores taken over.
4.   The 2/3rd North Midland Field Ambulance will relive No.9 Canadian
Field Ambulance in the Line with Headquarters and Transport Lines at
R.15.b.5.3./51c.on July 25th.
     The personnel and Ambulance cars of the Canadian Field Ambulance
at the following Stations and Posts will be relieved by similar
personnel etc of the 2/3rd North Midland Field Ambulance by 6 p.m. on
July 25th:-
     (a) Advanced Dressing Station.   M.31.b.2.8. /51b.
     (b) Walking wounded collecting post
         (incourse of construction).   R.29.d.2.7. /51c.
     (c) Car loading Posts.   M.4.d.7.1.   /51b.
     (d)   M.29.c.2.2. /51b.
         Bearer Relay Posts   S.2.b.5.0.   /51b.
     (e) Regimental Aid Posts.
         Support.   (i) Right.   S.2.b.5.0.   /51b.
                         (ii) Left.   M.31.b.2.8. /51b.
         FRONT LINE.   (iii) Right   S.11.c.6.6. /51b.
                         (iv) Left   M.35.a.2.9. /51b.
              Under construction   S.4.a.5.1.   /51b.
5.   METHOD OF EVACUATION.
     The O.C. 2/3rd North Midland Field Ambulance will be responsible
for the evacuation of Sick and Wounded from the Divisional Front back to
the Corps Main Dressing Station. Corps Rest Station or Divisional Sick
Collecting Station.
     Evacuation is by hand carriage or wheeled stretcher carriers
through Bearer Relay Posts to Car Loading Posts and thence by Horsed or
Motor Ambulances to the Advanced Dressing Station, or direct to Corps
Main Dressing Station or Corps Rest Station via WAILLY and BAC-DU-NORD.
     Personnel and Transport.
     In addition to the Personnel and Transport of his own Unit the O.C.
2/3rd North Midland Field Ambulance will have the Bearer Division of the
2/1st North Midland Field Ambulance to assist. This personnel will be
available when required.

= 2 =

The Os.C. 2/1st and 2/2nd North Midland Field Ambulance will each place 1 Horsed Ambulance Wagon and 2 Motor Ambulance Cars at the disposal of the O.C.2/3rd North Midland Field Ambulance to assist with the evacuations from the Front Line.

<u>Local Sick and Wounded.</u>

These will be collected by O.C.2/1st North Midland Field Ambulance at the Sick Collecting Station, WAILLY (R.22.d.3.7. /51c.) where cases requiring only from 3 - 4 days treatment and rest will be retained, the remainder being sent to Corps Main Dressing Station or Corps Rest Station.

6. <u>MEDICAL ARRANGEMENTS.</u>

Wounded, Sick & Accidental (Stretcher Cases) - C.C.S. DOULLENS.
" " " (Sitting Cases) - C.C.S. FREVENT.
Eye Cases - Ear, Nose & Throat - 43 CCS. FREVENT.
    (Special instructions later).
Dental and Denture cases - (To be issued later).
Self inflicted wounds - 46 C.C.S. FILLIEVRES.
N.Y.D.N. cases - 45 C.C.S. AUCHI-les-HESDIN.
Gas Treatment Centre.
(see G.R.Os.3137,3138) - C.M.D.S. Bac-du-Sud.
Scabies Cases - C.R.S. GOUY-en-ARTOIS.
Infectious cases - 21 C.C.S. WAVRANS.
Indians & Chinese - C.C.S. (as for British).
Venereal Cases - C.C.S. receiving sick after being seen by A.P.M.
Dysentery & Diarrhoea - 21 C.C.S. WAVRANS.

<u>Sanitary Sections.</u>
  No.36 H.Q., BAILLEULMONT - Left & Centre Divisional Areas.
  No.70 H.Q., PAS. - Right Divisional Area.
  No.83 H.Q., SUS-St.LEGER - Reserve Area.
<u>Medical Stores</u> - No.15 Advanced Depot - FREVENT.
<u>Oxygen Supply Centre.</u> - No.16 Ad.Dep.Med.Stores. AUXI-le-CHATEAU.
<u>Motor Ambulance Convoy.</u> No.3o. - SUS-St-Leger.
<u>Mobile Laboratory.</u>
  No.33(Hygiene) - attd. No.6 Stat.Hosp. - FREVENT.
  No.10(Bact). - attd. No. 19 C.C.S. - FREVENT.
<u>Mobile X-ray Unit.</u> No.5. attd No.43 C.C.S. FREVENT.

7. The A.D.M.S. Office will close at MONCHY-CAYEAUX at 10 a.m. on 26th July and re-open at BASSEUX at the same hour.

8. ACKNOWLEDGE.
                              (Signed) C.H.LINDSAY.
                                    Colonel A.M.S.
                      <u>A.D.M.S. 59th Division.</u>

Army Form C. 2118.

WAR DIARY
or
INTELLIGENCE SUMMARY.
(Erase heading not required.)

CONFIDENTIAL.

WAR DIARY
OF THE
2/3RD. NORTH MIDLAND
FIELD AMBULANCE

MONTH ENDED AUGUST 31ST 1918.

(Volume. 8.)

Army Form C. 2118.

WAR DIARY
or
INTELLIGENCE SUMMARY.
(Erase heading not required.)

Place	Date	Hour	Summary of Events and Information	Remarks and references to Appendices
WAILLY [R.15.6.5.3] [Sheet 51c S.E.]	August 1st 1918		This day the D.M.S. Third Army and D.D.M.S. VI Corps inspected the Unit. They did not inspect the camp but proceeded direct to A.D.S. FICHEUX, [M.31.b.2.8.Sheet 51.F.S.W.] The D.M.S. expressed satisfaction with the arrangements made at the A.D.S. for reception of sick & wounded.	APP I
	Aug 2nd		A.D.M.S. held conference of Field Ambulance Commanders Major A. MEARNS, R.A.M.C. (T.C.) returned from leave in France.	
	3rd		One O.R. sent to Third Army School of Sanitators.	
	4th		9. O.R. Reinforcement received.	
	5th		Captain S.H. WHITELAW. R.A.M.C. (T.C.) proceeded on temporary duty to 11th Battalion the ROYAL SCOTS FUSILIERS	
	6th		Captain J.R. GRANT, M.C. R.A.M.C.(SR) proceeded on temporary duty to 84th Bde R.F.A.	
	7th		Clinical meeting of Medical Officers at FREVENT attended by Major A. MEARNS & Captain S.H. KINGSTON.	

WAR DIARY
or
INTELLIGENCE SUMMARY.
(Erase heading not required.)

Army Form C. 2118.

Place	Date	Hour	Summary of Events and Information	Remarks and references to Appendices
WAILLY	Aug 8th		Nothing of importance occurred	
	9th		Conference of Field Ambulance commanders with A.D.M.S.	
	10th		Sentence of 28 days F.P. no 2 promulgated in the case of M/102270, Pte HALDANE. H.W. for insolence to an N.C.O. One heavy Enemy Horse drawn Enemy transport artillery activity, but to no avail.	
	11th		Nothing of special importance occurred.	
	12th		59th Divisional Horse show at BASSEUX. The prize of mules and G.S. limbers entered by the Unit secured fourth place in a class of 31 entries. Marks were lost on the painting and polishing of the vehicle, of which no specification had been received.	
	13th		Captain S.H. KINGSTON, RAMC proceeded to No. 3. C.C.S for a course of instruction in Shock and Blood transfusion.	

WAR DIARY
or
INTELLIGENCE SUMMARY.
(Erase heading not required.)

Army Form C. 2118.

Place	Date	Hour	Summary of Events and Information	Remarks and references to Appendices
WAILLY	Aug 14th		S/S. M. MARSH, H.T.A.S.C. reported for duty.	
	15th		Nothing of special importance occurred.	
	16th		Conference of Field Ambulance Commanders at A.D.M.S's office at BASSEUX	
	17th		Nothing of special importance occurred.	
	18th		The personnel at the A.D.S. FICHEUX were relieved. Lieutn. the birs: Major MEARNS & Captain Whitelaw of B Section, replacing Major ELLIOT & Lt. C.K. HEADY of C section	
	19th		A party of one officer and 12 other ranks of the United States Army Medical Corps which had been attached to the A.D.S. for instruction, returned to their units. They expressed themselves as gratified with what they had seen and that they had benefited by their tour of duty.	
	20th		Captain S. H. KINGSTON returned from course of instruction.	

WAR DIARY
or
INTELLIGENCE SUMMARY.
(Erase heading not required.)

Army Form C. 2118.

Place	Date	Hour	Summary of Events and Information	Remarks and references to Appendices
WAILLY	Aug 21st		Heavy hostile night bombing. All cases with S deaths proved through Mein Aid-post in WAILLY.	
	22nd		Information received verbally that we were to attack the following day; the 59th Division to pass through the 57th Division. Preparations were made accordingly. All posts being doubled and reserve of stretcher bearers & medical stores sent to A.D.S. Two cars were provided by the 10th Lowland Field Ambulance.	
	23rd		Attack took place. The utmost secrecy was preserved as written orders were received. A walking wounded collecting post had been established at R.29.a.3.7 [Sheet 51C] where tea & cigarettes were issued and dressings adjusted. Thence cases were sent to the VI Corps Main Dressing Station at Bac-du-Sud [Q.31.a.8.9] by Horse Ambulances & Motor Lorries. The work of evacuation proceeded smoothly. 72 Bearers of the 1/2 Lowland Fd Ambce	

WAR DIARY
or
INTELLIGENCE SUMMARY

Army Form C. 2118.

Place	Date	Hour	Summary of Events and Information	Remarks and references to Appendices
WAILLY	Aug 23rd		performed a great part of the carriage of wounded from the Regimental Aid Posts to the A.D.S. The casualties that passed through our hands during the day were :—	

	Wounded	Gassed
A.D.S.	169	194
W.W.C.P	65	70
Totals	234	264

On the night of the 23rd the Bn. was relieved by the 19th Battn. of 5th Amern. Divn. All ranks returned to WAILLY in the night. App III

| WAILLY | 24th | | At 11 a.m. the Bn. proceeded by line of march to SAULTY and there entrained, arriving at AIRE soon after midnight of the 24th-25th. From AIRE the Bn. marched to MELANOY FARM, [O.31.a central] sheet 36 A. 05 | |
| MELANOY FARM | 25th | | The men were very tired and nothing was done all day. | |

Army Form C. 2118.

WAR DIARY
or
INTELLIGENCE SUMMARY.
(Erase heading not required.)

Place	Date	Hour	Summary of Events and Information	Remarks and references to Appendices
MELANOY FARM TO LIGNE	Aug 26		This day the unit marched to LIGNE [G.11.a.2.8] shown 36th and relieved the 229th Field Ambce. of the 74th division at the XI Corps Rest Station. 1t. C.C.K. HEAD & M.O.R.C. U.S.A & M.D.R.C. U.S.A & a tent subdivision of A section were sent to the M.D.S. at BERGUETTE	App IV
	Aug 27th		This day was spent in getting the various various employment. The Rest Station comprises four groups of tents called A, B & C sections, plus detached buildings as dining room, shops etc. The Camp was intended solely for convalescent cases. No serious cases being admitted. The camp is badly sited on opposite sides of a shallow dingle with the road the lying alongside in the bottom. There was no path. The working arrangements were bad and the ark. have not arrived in. All water had to be brought by water cart as	

WAR DIARY or INTELLIGENCE SUMMARY

Army Form C. 2118.

Place	Date	Hour	Summary of Events and Information	Remarks and references to Appendices
LIGNY contd	Aug 26th		Patients were returned for 14 days, spending 5 days in A section, 5 in B section & 4 in C section. The last 24 hours were spent in special marquees.	
	27th		Nothing of special importance occurred. An employee drowning.	
	28th		D.D.M.S. XI Corps visited the Rest Station	
	29th		D.A.D.M.S. 59th Division visited the camp. Captain S.H. KINGSTON R.A.M.C. returned from No. 3 Canadian C.C.S.	
	30th		A/Cpls Yeatman and Horsley to 2/6th Durham L.I. Infantry for a month course of instruction previous to applying for commissions. D.D.M.S. XI Corps visited the Camp and killed.	
	31st		Captain S. GRANT. C.F. left the Unit.	

Jas J White

O.C. Unit & Capt

[signature] Cav 2/3

C O P Y.   Appendix No. I.

Subject:- Inspection by D.M.S., Third Army.

O.C.,
    2/3rd. N.N.Fd,Ambce.

       The D.M.S., Third Army expressed himself highly satisfied with everything he saw on his inspection of the Field Ambulances yesterday.
       Please make this known to all ranks.

2/8/18.   (sgd) C. H. LINDSAY, Colonel.A.M.S.
664/20/193.   A.D.M.S. 59th. Division

..COPY.. APPENDIX.NO.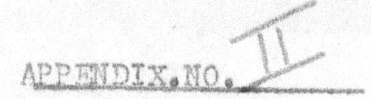

S P E C I A L   O R D E R   O F   T H E   D A Y
BY
FIELD-MARSHAL SIR DOUGLAS HAIG. K.T., G.C.B., G.C.V.O., K.C.I.E.
Commander in Chief. British Armies in France..

The conclusion of the fourth year of the War marks the passing of a period of crisis. We can now with added confidence look forward to the future.

The Revolution in Russia set free large hostile forces on the Eastern Front which were transferred to the West. It was the enemy's intention to use his great numbers thus crea to gain a decisive victory, before the arrival of American Troops should give superiority to the Allies.

The enemy has made his effort to obtain a decision on the Western Front and has failed. The steady stream of American Troops arriving in France has already restored the Balance.

The enemy's first and most powerful blows fell on the British; his superiority of force was nearly three to one. Although he succeeded in pressing back parts of the fronts attacked, the British line remained unbroken. After many days of heroic fighting the glory of which will live for all time in the history of our race, the enemy was held.

At the end of four years of war, the magnificent fighting qualities and spirit of our troops remain of the highest order. I thank them for the devoted bravery and unshaken resolution with which they responded to my appeal at the height of the struggle, and I know that they will show a like steadfastness and courage in whatever they may yet be called upon to perform.

(sgd). D. HAIG. F.M.
Commander-in-Chief.
General Headquarters. British Armies in France.
August 4th. 1918.

(COPY).

App III

59th Division Special Order No. 152.

23.8.18.

The Division has today been relieved on completion of four weeks duty in the front line.

As regards the Infantry Battalions this was their first experience, as such, of life in the trenches, and I wish to express to them my warm appreciation of the soldierly qualities shewn by all ranks during that period. I have been particularly impressed by the spirit of cheerfulness which I have found everywhere, even under difficulties, and with the keenness shewn and progress made in patrolling by night and day.

The excellence of the instruction given in this most important duty was proved by the successful establishment of the line of posts 500 yards in advance of our original front line on the morning of 21st August. This gain of ground was very valuable in view of the operations of 23rd August.

The Division as a whole was put to a high test of unselfish devotion to the common cause on the 22nd and night 22nd/23rd August when it was called on to assist in the preparation of the offensive by the 52nd and 56th Divisions through its own line.

This offensive was completely successful, a result which could not have been achieved without the whole hearted co-operation of the troops of the 176th, 177th and 178th Inf. Brigades., the 59th Div. Engrs. and Pioneer Bn., the 25th Bn. M.G. Corps, the 40th Div. Arty. (attached 59th Division) and the Brigade and Divisional Staffs 59th Division, including the Signal Service, Medical Service and Traffic Controls arranged by the A.P.M.

(Sd). R. WHIGHAM.
Maj. Gen.
Commanding 59th Division.

SECRET.
Copy No. 13

App IV

R.A.M.C. ORDERS No. 53
by
A.D.M.S., 59th DIVISION.

Ref. Maps 36A, 1/40,000.   Aug. 25th, 1918.

1. The 59th Division will take over the line from the 74th DIVISION on August 26th and 27th, 1918. All reliefs to be completed by 6 p.m. on 27/8/18.

2. The 2/1st NORTH MIDLAND FIELD AMBULANCE will relieve the 231st Field Ambulance, 74th Division, at the Divisional Sick Collecting Station and Gas Treatment Centre at HOLINGHEM, O.14.a.3.7. Relief to be completed by 6 p.m. on 27/8/18.

Details of relief to be arranged between Officers Commanding concerned.

Officer Commanding, 2/1st NORTH MIDLAND FIELD AMBULANCE will send one Officer and five other ranks to report to O.C., 231st Field Ambulance by 10 a.m. on 26/8/18. as advance party.

3. The 2/2nd NORTH MIDLAND FIELD AMBULANCE will be in charge of evacuations from the forward area and will relieve the 230th Field Ambulance, 74th Division, with Headquarters at the MAIN DRESSING STATION, BERGETTE, O.15.d.central.

The personnel and ambulance cars of the 230th Field Ambulance at the following stations and posts will be relieved by similar personnel, etc. of the 2/2nd North Midland Field Ambulance by 6 p.m. on 27/8/18. Details of relief to be arranged between Officers Commanding concerned.

ADVANCED DRESSING STATIONS :   P.24.b.5.4.
                                      P.5.a.3.0.
CAR LOADING POSTS :   Q.20.b.4.6.
                                      Q.3.d.7.3.
                                      Q.4.c.2.5.
                                      K.31.c.central.
R.A.P's (Front Line) Right   Q.22.a.5.3.
                      Left   Q.4.c.4.5.
         (Support)   Q.3.a.9.1.

Officer Commanding, 2/2nd NORTH MIDLAND FIELD AMBULANCE will send as an Advance Party 2 Officers and 18 other ranks to report to Officer Commanding 230th Field Ambulance at 10 a.m. on 26/8/18 for the purpose of learning the details of evacuation.

4. The 2/3rd NORTH MIDLAND FIELD AMBULANCE will relieve the 229th Field Ambulance, 74th Division, at the CORPS REST STATION and Officers' Rest Station at LIGNE, G.11.b.3.0. Relief to be completed by 6 p.m. on 26/8/18.

The Quartermaster and 5 other ranks will proceed by car at 8 a.m. on 26/8/18 to report to O.C., XIth Corps Rest Station for the purpose of learning details and checking stores taken over.

5. The O.C. 2/3rd NORTH MIDLAND FIELD AMBULANCE will send one Officer and one Tent Sub-division to report for duty with O.C., 2/2nd North Midland Field Ambulance at the M.D.S. on the evening of the 27th August.

6. Method of Evacuation. The O.C., 2/2nd North Midland Field Ambulance will be responsible for evacuation of sick and wounded from the Divisional front back to the M.D.S., C.R.S. or Divisional Sick Collecting Station.

Evacuation will be by hand carry or wheeled stretcher carriers, where possible, to the Car Loading Posts; thence by motor ambulances to the A.D.S's, and from there to the M.D.S. or Divisional Sick Collecting Station.

7. _Personnel and Transport._ In addition to the personnel and transport of his own Unit, the Officer Commanding, 2/2nd North Midland Field Ambulance will have a Bearer Sub-Division of the 2/1st and 2/3rd North Midland Field Ambulances to assist. This personnel will be available when required.

8. Officers Commanding, 2/1st and 2/3rd North Midland Field Ambulances will each place one Horsed Ambulance Wagon and one Motor Ambulance Car at the disposal of the O.C., 2/2nd North Midland Field Ambulance to assist in the evacuation from the front line.

9. The A.D.M.S. Office will close at NORRENT-FONTES at 6 p.m. on 27/8/18 and reopen at BUSNES at the same hour.

10. ACKNOWLEDGE.

Major for Colonel,
A.D.M.S., 59th Division.

DISTRIBUTION : Copy No.
1. D.M.S. First Army.
2. D.D.M.S. XI Corps.
3. "G" 59th Division.
4. "A" 59th Division.
5. A.D.M.S. 4th Division.
6. A.D.M.S. 61st Division.
7. A.D.M.S. 74th Division.
8. 176th Infantry Brigade.
9. 177th Infantry Brigade.
10. 178th Infantry Brigade.
11. 2/1st N.M.Field Amb.
12. 2/2nd N.M.Field Amb.
13. 2/3rd N.M.Field Amb.
14. 229th Field Amb.
15. 230th Field Amb.
16. 231st Field Amb.
17. Div. Train.
18. Signals.
19. 25th K.R.R.C. (P)
20. 25th M.G. Battn.
21. War Diary.
22. War Diary.
23. File.
24. Spare.

17

Vol 20

160/3259

WAR DIARY
or
INTELLIGENCE SUMMARY.

Army Form C. 2118.

CONFIDENTIAL.

War Diary of
2/3rd North Midland Field Ambce

For Month of

September 1918.

(Volume 9.)

2/3RD (N.M.)
FIELD AMBULANCE
59TH DIVISION

COMMITTEE FOR THE
MEDICAL HISTORY OF THE WAR

WAR DIARY
or
INTELLIGENCE SUMMARY

Place	Date	Hour	Summary of Events and Information	Remarks and references to Appendices
LIGNE	Sept. 1st		This day, Dr HOLLAND ROSE, Litt. D. of Cambridge University, accompanied by the D.D.M.S and D.A.D.M.S., XI Corps, visited the XI Corps Rest Station and lectured in the dining Hut to the patients; the subject being "A sound Peace or an unsound Peace?" The lecturer pointed out that the present was not a time to make peace because small nations like Belgium, Serbia and Luxembourg, were not sufficiently strong to protect their own interests when, therefore, the time shall come for the conditions of peace to be framed, the independance of such small nations must adequately be guaranteed to prevent any further outbreak of war.	
	2nd		The XI Corps Horse. Made inspection of the horses. Dr Skinner to be on order, that when Veterinary Officers and Horse-master visit a Unit, a Commissioned	O.S.

WAR DIARY
or
INTELLIGENCE SUMMARY.

Army Form C. 2118.

Place	Date	Hour	Summary of Events and Information	Remarks and references to Appendices
LIGNE	Sept. 2nd		Officer i/c unit showed the present. It is most unsatisfactory to receive the report of the inspecting officer via the Staff-Sergeant regr. of the Army Service Corps, attached to the O.C. No. 4 Company, 59th Divisional Train inspected animals & vehicles. There was a that this too imperfect.	O.S. O.S.
	3rd		Nothing of special importance occurred.	O.S.
	4.		Major A. MEARNS, R.A.M.C. arranges a very sound concert for the patients, scheme of when took here is the performance.	O.S.
	5.		Nothing of special importance occurred.	O.S.
	6th 7th			
	8th		Major. T. S. ELLIOT, M.C. R.A.M.C. assumed command on the departure of the commanding officer on leave to England.	O.S.

Army Form C. 2118.

WAR DIARY
or
INTELLIGENCE SUMMARY.
(Erase heading not required.)

September 1918.

Instructions regarding War Diaries and Intelligence Summaries are contained in F.S. Regs., Part II. and the Staff Manual respectively. Title pages will be prepared in manuscript.

Place	Date	Hour	Summary of Events and Information	Remarks and references to Appendices
LIGNE G.11.a.2.8.	8.9.18	5pm	Temporary Command of the Unit handed over to me at this time by Lt-Col. O.b.S. Steel M.C. on his proceeding to BOULOGNE en route for U.K. on special leave.	Command
	9.9.18		Nil 9.9.18 to 9.10.18. On J.K.'s days class.	
	10.9.18		Nothing of importance happened. Weather wet + boisterous.	
			Cpl. T. J. WHITELAW detailed by H.Q.M.S. for temporary duty with 1st = 25th = 10th K.R.R.C. relieving Menzies. W. Whitedown to patients M.	Stay K.
	11.9.18		Issue O.R. (Reinforcements) Eleven Strong. M.	Reinforcements
	12.9.18		Drainage of Camp being carried out. Weather still wet + boisterous. M.	Work commenced.
	13.9.18		Escort by patients. Wet. M.	
	14.9.18		Nothing to report. Wet. M.	
	15.9.18		Concert in evening by Sgt. Dir. Concert party — "Crumps" M.	
	16.9.18		Capt. G. R. GRANT M.C. taken Southdown left here at 6-30 a.m. Report to O.C. ½ Rest Ind. Field Amb. at M. Dennis Stn. LESTREM for duty. Relieved W. Cpl. EDWARDS J. proceeded to 11 Corps Gas Schl. M.	Troops duty.
			Sgt. T. J. EVANS Awarded 14 days Special leave U.K. W. Whist drive in P.M.	Leave
	17.9.18		2 Medical Officers available for general duties — Capt. S.H. KINGSTON on sick reporting 59th Dir. Schl. (D.M.S. 5 Army instructions) W. Write let fr 59th Div. Reception Camp daily — Casualty 2/Lt. A.R. PARITY "Movies"	Duties

T2134. Wt. W708—776. 500000. 4/15. Sir J. C. & S.

WAR DIARY
or
INTELLIGENCE SUMMARY
(Erase heading not required.)

Army Form C. 2118.

September 1918.

Place	Date	Hour	Summary of Events and Information	Remarks and references to Appendices
LIGNE G.II.a.2.8.	18.9.18. 19.9.18		Nothing of importance to chronicle — Being Carpenter by patients relieved	Announcemt. Mr.
	20.9.18.		Nothing of pakt — Event of patients	Mr.
	21.9.18.		Cricket match in afternoon — Being Carpet in evening. Lt-Col. A.N.H GRAY, Consulting Physician to Brigt Army Zone paid us our 3rd I.C.T. visit. He left recommendations re (1) Rat. 3 R.I.C.) Duty 21 Inf (3) Outbreak of	Mr. Casualty Disinfectn
	22.9.18		LADDERS huts not 37 Hof. Ox Shes. Sgt T. J. EVANS returned from St Vincent. Col. MILLER, Consulting Physician 5th Army visited Rest Station — Dividcock he admitted latter was unnecessary That no cases of ——— XI Corps. Gas Scarb.	Mr. M. Casualty Physician Mr. Cause Annouced
	23.9.18.		Cpl. GOODMAN Awarded. "Our to gave event attempts to inoculate trops (1) Regimental Sy'/Dir. Our to infected Camps — Indigence to inspected personally all cases — Red. XI Corps infected Camps. DDMS XI Corps etc. (2) Remain by Med. per (3) Exhibits trablits of QM etc. Schemes weekly meeting (3) Exhibits of the up to shang. Control of patients Containing pure drinking water	Mr. Mr. Mr.
	24.9.18		A week with Camp and Dome are Inoc. men had been	Mr. Occurd Ltr

WAR DIARY
or
INTELLIGENCE SUMMARY

Army Form C. 2118.

September 1918

(Erase heading not required.)

Place	Date	Hour	Summary of Events and Information	Remarks and references to Appendices
LIGNE G.11.a.2.8.	25.9.18		The reported to the Rest Station in the Morn — A. line — about 1/3 Bn. marched off to Cambray for R.W.O. Duncan, Cadieu, dental &c. about 1/3 Bn. sick. — Gas cases & use in evacuant. B. " " " — I.C.T.'s + strains — C. " " "	System
	26.9.18		Nothing of importance happened. M.	
	27.9.18		Nothing happened — Cricket match for patients. M.	
	28.9.18		Instructions received this afternoon from D.D.M.S. XI Corps that no more admissions to Corps Rest Station or Officers Rest Station are to take place Patients are to return to duty as they leave. St. Intervals to be packed ready to be removed. Equipment are not to be opened. M.	
	29.9.18		B.Rke. Strin patients. Nothing of importance happened. J.M.	
	30.9.18		S.M. Gray proceeded on leave to U.K. M. Escort by personnel + Convoy party for No. 4. Stationary Hosp. Arras. M.	

Jno. T. Emit
Major RAMC

CONFIDENTIAL.

WAR DIARY

OF

2/3RD NORTH MIDLAND FIELD AMBLCE.

FROM OCTOBER 1ST 1918 TO OCTOBER 31ST. 1918.

VOL. 10.

Army Form C. 2118.

WAR DIARY
INTELLIGENCE SUMMARY
(Erase heading not required.)

October 1918.

Place	Date	Hour	Summary of Events and Information	Remarks and references to Appendices
LIGNE G.11, a.2.8. /36A. XI Corps Rest Station.	1.10.18.		The work of clearing the Rest Station proceeds. About 300 patients in Stye. All Rest patients packed & removed by Corps Ambulance. All officers discharged for Rest Station & Station closed. Major Mirmo & 160 R.B. proceeded to the officers rest station reporting to 2/1 L.b.a.d. M.R. Convoy St Venant, reporting to 54 C.C.S. A.I.R.E.	Clearing Rest Station. Staff Ammunition.
	2.10.18.		One convoy party, to WOLVES gone to shot at 54 C.C.S. A.I.R.E. 240 patients left. Capt. RICHARDS proceeded to Calais en-route to U.K. on convoy 3/10/18. XI Corps Guests party visited Rest Station & gave a Bang Bang Concert shortly in Sgt's K 59 Divn Rest Station, cheerful in 37th Augustinians except 18, which are S. "W" Forces gone in the evening to his station. Capt Church & Evacuate party for move to G.H.K. on 4th June. M.	M.
	3.10.18.		240 patients evacuated by Rail to LA LACQUE, thence by light railway to LA GORGUE. Remainder Patients & ESTAIRES & their Transport moved by road. Rest Station at G.26.d.3.0. on Rail Station. Horse Transport moved via Saint SAILLY-SUR-LA LYS. Arrived Ut 9 am. St VENANT, Sludome & Tx department into Transport & independently. Unit arrived 1-30 p.m. Distance about 28 miles.	Move. See Attached I.
	4.10.18.		Bear party arrived 4-30 p.m. Transport about 1-30 p.m. Into Bury. Distance about 28 miles. — Invigent about 4-30 p.m. Rear party consisting of 1 Sgt & 1 Cpl & 4 men left Rest after closing Rest XI Corps & O.R.Rs. Majr Mirmo, Capt E.R.Pent & Capt Blatchey arrived Unit. W/C	Attached I.

Army Form C. 2118

WAR DIARY
of
INTELLIGENCE SUMMARY.
(Erase heading not required.)

October 1918.

Place	Date	Hour	Summary of Events and Information	Remarks and references to Appendices
LE NOUVEAU MONDE. (ESTAIRES.) G.26.d.3.0.	5.10.18.		Main Dressing Station. Worked from H.F. 4/10 & Depts. 7/10 = 14. Improvements to dressing station carried out. Reinforcements proceeded on leave to U.K. Commencing 6/10. Capt. C.R. Grant M.C. & 2 S.O.R. hrs. have proceeded to 2/1 R.A. of Ant. Capt. W. BAILEY — THOMSON reported for duty. Reported for duty to 2/1 R.A. of Ant. Capt. W. BAILEY — THOMSON reported for duty. M.S. bays included in returns for more forward.	Casualties
	6.10.18.		Frontline moved forward about 1000 yds yesterday afternoon. M.S. Worked for 24 hr = 18.	Casualty work.
	7.10.18.		Worked for last 24 hrs = 27. Grand II — Total = 38. M. Improvements; clearing of bombs & garnets of garbage dumps being carried out. M. All personnel leave have been received from LIGNE & St VENANT. 2.M.S. Herman G. & Watkin J.S. Purcell K 5th Army School of Cookery on Course. Pl. Capt. & Purcell K 5 Army School of Cookery on Course. Pl. Capt. Windebank reported. 60.C.C.S. F.A.	Course.
	8.10.18.		Capt. C.R. Grant R.C. returned to unit. A portion of others moved to rate of pace in this place. Capt. S. GRANT R.C. returned to unit.	
	9.10.18.		M.D.S. Hrs.C.O.7. in preparation to open on 10.10.18. M. Sent on the first 4 least 2 days. Capt. J.H. KINGSTON & the remainder of A Section moved	Rear A.D.S.
	10.10.18.		K H.22.C.O.7. New dressing station closed at 10.00 & re-opened at new Location at H.22.C.O.7/32. This New dressing station closed at 10.00 & re-opened at new Location at H.22.C.O.7/32. Sgt. Johnson, Sgt Downing & Pte Walker proceeded to 2nd Army Rest Camp AUDRESSELLES M.C. Unit moved to new M.D.S. at FLEURBAIX — New C.O.2/31. Completed by 12.30 hrs. M.C.	Move M.C.
	11.10.18.		Lt Command handed over to Lt. Col. O. STEEL on his return from leave. M.C. Capt. W. Bailey — Thomson rec'd on detached duty with 26th Royal Fusiliers.	Mons. Assumg. COMMAND

A.G.L.W. Bailey

John J. Steel Major

WAR DIARY
or
INTELLIGENCE SUMMARY

Army Form C. 2118.

Place	Date	Hour	Summary of Events and Information	Remarks and references to Appendices
FLEURBAIX H.22.c.0.7. Sheet 36.	Oct 12th		All ranks employed on construction work, repairing buildings and roads. The line was handed in that had formerly been a German dressing station. The place kept in good repair and needed much cleaning up. O.S.	
	13th		Nothing of special importance occurred. O.S.	
	14th		Work of improvement & cleaning on went letrine building. O.S.	
	15th		The dressing room was moved into the cellar which gave more accomodation & being dressing-room was used for funeral for men O.S.	
	16th] 17th		Nothing of special importance occurred. O.S.	
	18th 19th		The unit moved to a line of huts & marched to the Hospital at K.19.7. Central [Sheet 36] & Spencer to reinforce B	

Army Form C. 2118.

WAR DIARY
or
INTELLIGENCE SUMMARY.
(Erase heading not required.)

Instructions regarding War Diaries and Intelligence Summaries are contained in F. S. Regs., Part II. and the Staff Manual respectively. Title pages will be prepared in manuscript.

Place	Date	Hour	Summary of Events and Information	Remarks and references to Appendices
K.19.6 central [sheet 36]	Oct 19th		This hospital was situated on the outskirts of LILLE between LAMBRESART and St ANDRE previously been occupied by a German hospital unit. O/S	
			This day Major T.S. ELLIOT proceeded to join LOB the 1st/5th Royal Scots Fusiliers. O/S	
FLERS. L.32.c.6.4 [sheet 36]			This day the unit moved by lime of march to FLERS and opened a Main Dressing Station in the School. Owing to the systematic destruction of all bridges great difficulty was experienced in getting the transport through the outskirts of MADELEINE	O/S
FLERS. L.32.c.6.4	Oct 20		This day the unit moved at 9 a.m. by lime of march to HEMS. [G.25.b.7.7.Sheet 37], taking over the Main Dressing Station from the 2/1st N. Midland Field Ambce.	O/S
HEMS Oct 21st G.25.b.7.7 Sheet 37			This day the unit proceeded by line of march to TEMPLEUVE [H.32.b.5.1 Sheet 37] and opened a main dressing station, relieving the 2/1st N. Midland Field Ambulance.	O/S

WAR DIARY
or
INTELLIGENCE SUMMARY.

Army Form C. 2118.

Place	Date	Hour	Summary of Events and Information	Remarks and references to Appendices
TEMPLEUVE H.32.B.5.1 Sheet 37.	Oct-21st		There was a good deal of hostile shelling during the night and 53 B cases in all, were dealt with, among them several civilians, one of whom fell from third floor to the ground in his night dress except for a cut on the forehead, was not hurt.	
	Oct 22nd		The dressing room was established in the cellars, on account of shelling. By order of the A.D.M.S. 59th Division the hops over the battle than at TEMPLEUVE.	
TEMPLEUVE H.32.B.5.1 Sheet 37.	Oct. 23rd & 24"		Nothing of special importance occurred but there was a good deal of intermittent harassing fire, as a result of which one horse was killed about 50 sick and wounded were dealt with daily.	
	Oct 25th		On account of hostile shellings the line this day moved by Blue B was to CHATEAU de WASMES ["C" Section] and reported the M.D.S. os under Major T.S. ELLIOT N.C	

WAR DIARY
or
INTELLIGENCE SUMMARY.

(Erase heading not required.)

Army Form C. 2118.

Place	Date	Hour	Summary of Events and Information	Remarks and references to Appendices
CHATEAU WASMES [Sheet 37.	Oct 30th		here in charge of the dressing room, which was in a tenth tent on [?] D.D.M.S. XI Corps and A.D.M.S. 59th [Div] visited the train as Motor [horses?] & men employed on general duties.	
TOUFFLERS [G.22.b.9.5 Sheet 37 Oct 31st	Oct 28th		This day the mule teams moved to a large empty house in the village of TOUFFLERS [G.22.b.9.5 Sheet 37] and reopened as a Main Dressing Station.	
	Oct 29th		All hands employed in cleaning the house & making it fit for the reception of cases. Nothing of special importance occurred. D.D.M.S. XI Corps visited the dressing station.	
	Oct 30th		The Horsed Transport moved to a field in TOUFFLERS at G.23.a.2.6 [Sheet 37] on All horses under cover.	

WAR DIARY
or
INTELLIGENCE SUMMARY

Army Form C. 2118.

Place	Date	Hour	Summary of Events and Information	Remarks and references to Appendices
TOUFFLERS [9.22.6.9.5] Sheet 31.	Oct 31st		Captain G. Baillie Thorgon rejoined the Unit from a period of regimental duty. This ended a most of great interest experience as it did a great advance and a change from the devastated area to a country comparatively undamaged and where there were a period of some stores during the last week of this month there crueller heavy rain.	O Ted McCol. Raine 2/3rd. West Riding Field Ambulance

FRIDAY......4th October, 1918.
Orders by Major. T.S.Elliot, M.C. Commanding.

Orderly Officer.......Capt. Kingston.
Orderly Sergeant......Sergt. Johnson.

(Operation Orders)

1. The Unit will Move by road & rail to the M.D.S. at G.26.d.3.0. on the ESTAIRES - SAILLY SUR LA LYS Road.

2. The Horse Transport will proceed separately under orders already issued. They will March off at 5-0 a.m. and will make their long halt at ST VENANT.

3. TIME TABLE.
   - Reveille.   4-15 hours.
   - Parade.   4-30   (fatigue)
   - Breakfast.   5-45
   - March off.   7-00
   - Dinner.   On reaching Camp.

   (Haversack Ration will be carried and water bottles filled)

4. Officers Kits will be ready at Officers Mess at 6-15 hours. Capt. S.H.KINGSTON will be in Command of the Unit on the March. Lieut. HEADY will visit Divisional School and Reception Camp leaving at 8-30 a.m. by car.

5. Sergt FAULKNER and four men detailed by Sergt-Major will remain at Rest Station until all Stores have been removed.

6. A Daimler Car loaded with rations will start at 8-0 hours. Corpl Elliott and Pte Hollis will accompany this car, which will pick up 5 men at G.22.b. and convey them to the CONVENT. ST VENANT. This car will return to the Rest Station on completion.

7. A Motor Cyclist will leave here at 8-0 hours: deliver dispatches at ST VENANT, and then proceed to M.D.S. (G.26.d.3.0. -- 36) remaining there after completion.

8. The Quartermaster will render a certificate that all Billeting Certificates have been rendered and that all outstanding claims have been met.

9. LIEUT. HEADY will be responsible that the Camp and all Billets are left clean and all Latrines emptied or filled in.

T. S. Elliot
Major.R.A.M.C..TF.
O.C. 2/3rd North Midland Field Ambulance.

Appendix I.

Distribution.
1. O.C.
2. Officers Mess.

Operation orders by Major T.S. Elliot, M.C.
Comdg.
2/3rd North Midland Field Ambulance.

App 2

----

1. The Unit will move by Route Marsh to FLEURBAIX (H.22.c.0.7/36) at 10.30 hours 11th October, 1918. Captain W. Bailey-Thomson will be in Command of Unit on March.

2. The Horse Transport will move with the Unit.

3. Sergt. Blake will detail two cars to report at 09.30 outside Officers' Mess. The following will travel in these cars to the new M.D.S.
   Cooks:-   L/Cpl. F.C. Elliott, Ptes. Hollis and Hurley.
   Q.M. Stores.   Pte. Garbett.
   Officers' Mess. L/Cpl. J.H. Elliott, Ptes. Gadd and Petrie.
   Officers' Mess utensils.   Sergeants' Mess Utensils.

   One car to report same place at 10.45 hours. The following will travel by this car.
   Two Officers.
   Sergt. Faulkner. Sergt. Keeling, L/Cpl. Hadley, Pte. W.G. Brown.

4. The move of M.T. Stores and Personnel will be completed by 13.00 hours.

5. Officers' Kits will be loaded on Ambulance Wagons by 10.00 hours.

6. A rear party consisting of Sanitary N.C.O. and three men detailed by the Sergt. Major will remain behind until 12.00 hours and will be responsible for cleanliness of the Camp. They will follow by first available car.

(Signed) THOS. S. ELLIOT.
Major. RAMC. T.
O.C. 2/3rd Nth. Mid. Fld. Amblce.

C O P Y..

App. 3

59TH DIVISION.

The Corps Commander wishes to express his appreciation to the G.O.C. and all ranks of the 59th Division for the work, so cheerfully done by them, frequently under very trying circumstances during the last two months.

The advance and the close persuit of the enemy from LESTREM to the L'ESCAUT has been a very fine achievement, and the fact that constant touch with the enemy has been maintained reflects the greatest credit on the Infantry Brigades, Battalions and on the XIth Corps Mounted Troops which have been attached to the advanced Guards of the Division. The difficulties of crossing the rivers LAWE, DEULE-MARCQ and L'ESCAUT and in making practicable the roads, so skilfully destroted by the enemy, have been sucessfully overcome by the Royal Engineers and Pioneers.

The Field Artillery Brigades have pushed forward with the greatest energy and in spite of every obstacle they have been well forward and have afforded the closest support to their Infantry.

All ranks of all arms have co-operated to bring about this success.

A Division which has shewn such energy and determination cannot be described as a "B" Division, and the Corps Commander directs that henceforth, in the XIth Corps, the 59th Division, shall never be referred to in that manner.

A representation to this effect has also been forwarded to the Army.

(signed) J.BROAD.

B.G... G.S.

XIth Corps.
23/10/18.

To:- O.C. 2/3rd North Midland Field Ambulance.

The attached letter from the Corps Commander is forwarded for information and communication to all ranks

(sd) B.Whitehead. Major for Colonel.
A.M.S..
A.D.M.S. 59th Division..

23/10/18..

NOT TO BE RE-PUBLISHED. RE-PRODUCED OR COMMUNICATED TO THE PRESS.

OPERATION ORDER

BY.

App 4

LIEUT. COL. O. STEEL., M.C. COMDG. 2/3RD NORTH MID. FIELD AMBLCE.

:=:=:=:=:=:=:=:=:=:=:=:=:=:=:=:=:=:

October 24th 1918.

1. The Unit, less "C" Section will move by line of March to TOUFFLERS to-morrow October 25th. Time of starting 09.30 hrs.

2. "C" Section will continue to run the M.D.S. until relieved by the 2/1st North Midland Field Ambulance when they will also proceed to TOUFFLERS.

3. 50 sets of S.D. Clothing for gassed patients will be handed over to O.C. 2/1st North Midland Field Ambulance, and receipt obtained by the Quartermaster.

4. Dinner will be served on arrival at destination.

5. Officers Kits, Mess Kits and Orderly Room equipment to be packed by 08.30 hours.

6. All Billets will be left clean and billeting certificates rendered. On arrival at TOUFFLERS the Unit will re-open as a MAIN DRESSING STATION.

Lt Col. R.A.M.C., TF.
Comdg. 2/3rd North Midland Field Ambulance.

DISTRIBUTION.

H.Q.
Officers Mess.
R. Sergt Major.
S.S. Major Marsh.
War Diary.
File.

140/3601

2/3rd Not Misc F.A.

COMMITTEE FOR THE WAR
10 JAN 1919

WAR DIARY
or
INTELLIGENCE SUMMARY

Army Form C. 2118.

Place	Date	Hour	Summary of Events and Information	Remarks and references to Appendices
TOUFFLERS G.23.a.5.2	November 1st		'C' Section under Major T.S. Elliot M.C. in charge of the Main Dressing Station and Hospital.	
"	2nd		Captain G. GRANT. M.C. R.A.M.C. this day returned from four of duty. With 2/1st W. Midland Field Ambulance. 5 cases of civilian gassed (mostly with phosgene) this day admitted, of which one died.	
"	3rd		Usual Hospital duties.	
"	4th		Captain WHITELAW R.A.M.C. this day returned from leave to U.K. One medical officer proceeds daily to SAILLY-LEZ-LANNOY [G.28.d.sheet 37] to see sick of 57th Divisional Headquarters suffering from "Influenza".	
"	5th		All units held ready to move at short notice in view of the fact that the enemy was reported to have retired.	

Army Form C. 2118.

WAR DIARY
or
INTELLIGENCE SUMMARY.
(Erase heading not required.)

Instructions regarding War Diaries and Intelligence Summaries are contained in F. S. Regs., Part II. and the Staff Manual respectively. Title pages will be prepared in manuscript.

Place	Date	Hour	Summary of Events and Information	Remarks and references to Appendices
TOUFFLERS. G.23.a.5.2. [sheet 37]	Nov. 6th		Captain W. Baillie-Thompson this day reported for duty with the 36th B Station N. Midland and Fusilier. One renewer shown. Arrangements made to buy clothing as all ours were coming in very bad.	M A 3
"	Nov. 7th		Ordinary duties for all ranks. having received that D.M.S Fifth Army would inspect the Main Dressing station. He, however, did not arrive. A.D.M.S. XI Corps visited unit during afternoon.	
"	Nov. 8th		Nothing of special importance occurred. Dispensing room completed.	
"	Nov. 9th		This day unit were verbal instructions to move by line of march to BAILLEUL [sheet 37] to the farm called La HAUT TRIE U. Time of starting Move.	
Bailleul H.18.b.40.99 [sheet 37]			6 p.m. Arrived 6p.m. The Formation did	

WAR DIARY
or
INTELLIGENCE SUMMARY.

(Erase heading not required.)

Army Form C. 2118.

Place	Date	Hour	Summary of Events and Information	Remarks and references to Appendices
BAILLEUL. H.18.b.40.99 [Sheet 37]	Nov.10th		The Unit spent as a Main Dressing Station. It was known that the enemy had retired some distance & that it was expected that the Unit would move in the forenoon on the morrow. G.S. Very great traffic on the road and great difficulty would have been experienced in crossing the river. At 2 P.M. it would have been possible to cross & it being but Unit ordered to stand by. At 8.15 P.m. orders received to send 2 Daimler Cars to Ponstock Bridge at I.14.b.4.6 [Sheet 37] and a party of Bearers with wheeled stretchers to I.S.d.95.25. The purpose being to bring over sick from [Sheet 37] Antrophose by hand. Orders were obeyed. G.S.	The retreat

WAR DIARY
or
INTELLIGENCE SUMMARY

Army Form C. 2118.

Place	Date	Hour	Summary of Events and Information	Remarks and references to Appendices
BATLLEUL H.18.b.40.99. [sheet 37]	Nov. 11th		This day came the news that an Armistice had been arranged, as from 11.00 hours, and that hostilities had, for the moment, ceased. The feelings of thankfulness & relief can easier be imagined than described. The men were prepared to harness that their opponents were now yet on an end, and that they were still learning the King's laughter. In the evening a concert was held attended by all ranks, which to any onlooker.	
	Nov. 12th		Nothing of special importance occurred.	
	Nov. 13th		Captain F. J. WHITELAW sent for temporary duty to the 200th M.G. Battalion.	
	Nov. 14th		Warning order to move on	

Army Form C. 2118.

WAR DIARY
or
INTELLIGENCE SUMMARY.

(Erase heading not required.)

Instructions regarding War Diaries and Intelligence Summaries are contained in F. S. Regs., Part II. and the Staff Manual respectively. Title pages will be prepared in manuscript.

Place	Date	Hour	Summary of Events and Information	Remarks and references to Appendices
La MARAIS M.16.A.centre [Sheet 37]	Nov. 15th		Orders received from 177th Infantry Brigade to move. Unit therefore proceeded by line of March to La MARAIS [8 miles]. Much traffic and many halts in consequence. Horsed transport moved with Unit. O.S.	Move
	Nov. 16th		The Unit this day moved to the town of SECLIN via BOUVINES, PERONNE, FRETIN & AVELIN. Distance about 13 miles. Two men fell out at the end of the march owing to sore feet. The men were billetted in a large factory in the Rue de HOUPLIN, which had formerly been a Jerna [German?] barracks. O.S	Move
SECLIN	Nov. 17th		All ranks employed cleaning billets, repairing harness &c. Verbal instructions this day received from A.D.M.S to open a Divisional Rest Station.	

Army Form C.-2118.

WAR DIARY
or
INTELLIGENCE SUMMARY.

(Erase heading not required.)

Place	Date	Hour	Summary of Events and Information	Remarks and references to Appendices
SECLIN	Nov. 17th		Site for Divisional Rest Station selected in Convent School, Rue St. LOUIS. O.S. The equipment of A. section having been brought into store, by order D.A.D.M.S. the personnel of A. section were posted to B & C sections.	
	Nov. 18th		A. Headquarters section appointed B section and as hereto. A.D.M.S. 59th Div visited the Unit and inspected mens' quarters and horse-lines. Work on new R.I.S. continued. O.S.	Formed O.S.
	Nov. 19th		Work continued on D.R.S. In the evening the Unit was present and listened to lecture on Demonstration and Reconstruction lent out O.S.	
	Nov. 20th		A.D.M.S. 59th Division inspected the Divisional Rest Station. O.S.	

Army Form C.2118.

WAR DIARY
or
INTELLIGENCE SUMMARY.
(Erase heading not required.)

Instructions regarding War Diaries and Intelligence Summaries are contained in F.S. Regs., Part II. and the Staff Manual respectively. Title pages will be prepared in manuscript.

Place	Date	Hour	Summary of Events and Information	Remarks and references to Appendices
SECLIN V.30. central. [Sheet 36]	Nov 21.		70 patients in Hospital this day. O.S. Nothing of special importance occurring. O.S.	P.R. S.
	Nov 22.		Remainder of move to BETHUNE area proceeded. Section of journey between completion O.S.	
	Nov 23		Orders from A.D.M.S. to embus patients & to motor move of Transport when a few O.S.	
	Nov 24th, Nov 25th		Nothing of special importance occurring.	
	Nov 26th		A.D.M.S. visited O.R.S.	
	Nov 27.		Demonstration by A.D.M.S. to Staff Captain of the Division on the use of the Private Delousing O.S.	
	Nov 28th		Billetting parties sent to YOEUX-les-MINES in preparation for the move of the Division to the BETHUNE area. O.S.	
	Nov 29th		The projected move postponed until December 4th & 5th O.S.	

Army Form C. 2118.

WAR DIARY
or
INTELLIGENCE SUMMARY.
(Erase heading not required.)

Place	Date	Hour	Summary of Events and Information	Remarks and references to Appendices
SEELIN [Y.30 central] Shut 36.	Nov 30.		Nothing of special importance occurred. T.S. Bell Lt Col. Comm. O.g. 2/3rd York M'Cant Field Ambulance	

CONFIDENTIAL

WAR DIARY

OF THE

2/3RD NORTH MIDLAND FIELD AMBULANCE...R.A.M.C..TF.

FOR THE MONTH OF

DECEMBER 1918

=:

J. Steel. Lt. Col. RAMC
T.F.
2/3rd. N. Midland. Field Ambce.

WAR DIARY or INTELLIGENCE SUMMARY

Army Form C. 2118.

Place	Date	Hour	Summary of Events and Information	Remarks and references to Appendices
SECLIN. V.30. Sheet 36.	Dec 1st 1918		Morning of special importance occurred	DRS
	Dec 2nd		A.D.M.S. 59th Div. visited D.R.S. & Lt.-Col. K. HEADY. M.O.R.C. U.S.A. this day proceeded to 32nd Div. and was struck off the strength of the unit ors.	
	Dec 3rd		Nothing of special importance occurred	
NOEUX-les-MINES. [K.13.B.5.2. Sheet 44.]	Dec 5th		The unit this day moved by bus to NOEUX-les-MINES, via CARVIN, LENS, & SAILLY-LA-BOURSE, under orders from A.D.M.S. Lucas Appx:J. Horses transport under Major MEARNS R.A.M.C. proceeded by road via CARVIN, HULLUCH & VERMELLES arriving at 4.15.p.m. ors. The unit was ordered to open as a Divisional Rest Station. Accommodation consisting of one large & one small room, was found at the Mairie, personnel being billeted in school adjoining. This unit was blah unsuited for a Divisional Rest Station ors	Appx I MOVE

Army Form C. 2118.

WAR DIARY
or
INTELLIGENCE SUMMARY.
(Erase heading not required)

Place	Date	Hour	Summary of Events and Information	Remarks and references to Appendices
Noeux-les-MINES. K.18.B.5.2. Sheet 44.B	Dec 5th		Lieut. Hosken reported to A.D.M.S. who also informed that the accommodation in Quite inadequate. Suggested that letter should be recommending to D.R.S., D.D.M.S. XI Corps and Patients admitted to A.T.M.S. 59th train visited huts.	App R S.1
"	Dec 6th		A.T.M.S. 59th train visited huts.	
"	Dec 7th		Nothing of special importance occurred.	
"	Dec 8th		Baths repaired & lime washed.	
"	Dec 9th		Baths taken over by 177th Inf. Bde.	
"	Dec 10th		Nothing of special importance occurred.	
"	Dec 11th		Medical arrangements 46[?] Division by A.D.M.S. 59th Div. Divisional area divided for Sanitary purposes between 2/1st & 2/3rd North Midland Field Ambulances.	App 2
"	Dec 12th		A.D.M.S. visited the huts.	
"	Dec 13th		Nothing of special importance occurred.	
"	Dec 14th		Nothing of special importance occurred.	
"	Dec 15th		The Unit this day played the 200th M.G. Batt. at football & very Keen effort a very fine game by 2 goals to one.	

Army Form C. 2118.

WAR DIARY
or
INTELLIGENCE SUMMARY.

(Erase heading not required.)

Instructions regarding War Diaries and Intelligence Summaries are contained in F.S. Regs., Part II. and the Staff Manual respectively. Title pages will be prepared in manuscript.

Place	Date	Hour	Summary of Events and Information	Remarks and references to Appendices
NOEUX-LES-MINES. K.18.3.5.2. (Sheet 44b)	Dec 16		Nothing of special importance occurred. O/S	
			19th orders received to send one Section on detached duty to 1st R. & one Lorry-man working in Workshop are between MAZINGARBE & DOUAI. Verbal instruction from 1st 59th Division to postpone move till to remainder until 18th. O/S	
	Dec 18		Proceeded to MAZINGARBE & found Flash 1/97th huts though many had been lately damaged by civilian at L.22.27.5.0. [Sheet 44b] O/S Huts at MAZINGARBE not available, as reported by the Town. O/S	
	Dec 19		Suitable accommodation found at AIX-NOULETTE at Field Ambulance site at R.22.a.2.5.[44b] Absence of Empty dispatches. O/S	
	Dec 21		Orders from O.M.S. First ARMY cancelling the move to AIX-NOULETTE. O/S	

WAR DIARY
or
INTELLIGENCE SUMMARY.
(Erase heading not required.)

Army Form C. 2118.

Place	Date	Hour	Summary of Events and Information	Remarks and references to Appendices
NOEUX-LES-MINES. K.18.b.5.2. [Sheet 44 z]	Dec 22nd Dec 23rd		Nothing of special importance occurred. O.S.	
	Dec 24th		Preparation for Christmas dinner. Patients transferred to Barker-room for time being. O.S.	
	Dec 25th		The Unit played 201st M.S.B. a match during the morning at association football & beat them by 5 goals to one. The menu dinner pork pies at 4.30 p.m. Pork, baked vegetables + plum pudding was provided. After the meal an impromptu concert was held. Nothing of special importance occurred. O.S.	
	Dec 26th		Coming of R.3 R.A.T. M.S. this day proceeded on leave to U.K. O.S.	
	Dec 27th		Nothing of special importance occurred. O.S.	
	Dec 28th		The Corporals had their Christmas dinner this day at 17.00 hours. O.S. An autopsy on the body of a man of the 1st Essex Regt. was made. O.S.	
	Dec 29th Dec 30th		Warning order to move to Drouvin was received. O.S.	
	Dec 31st		Nothing of special importance occurred. O.S. O.Stil L/Cpl Parrott 2/3rd W. Rid. Fld. Amb.	

E.　　　　　　　SECRET.　　App II　Copy No.

R.A.M.C. ORDERS No. 58.
by
A.D.M.S., 59th Division.

Ref:- Sheets 36 & Hazebrouck 5a.　　　　　December 3rd 1918.

1. The 59th Division will move to the NOEUX-les-MINES - BRUAY Area on 4th, 5th and 6th December.

2. Transport will proceed by road and dismounted troops by bus under Brigade arrangements.

3. (a) Motor Ambulance Cars of 2/2nd and 2/3rd N.M.Fd.Ambces. will proceed as a single convoy in charge of Capt. & Qmr. S.C.Richards, 2/3rd N.M.Fd.Ambce. on the 5th instant, and O.C., 2/2nd N.M.Fd. Ambce. will arrange for his cars to report at H.Q., 2/3rd N.M.Fd. Ambce., SECLIN, at 1800 hours on the 4th instant.
Route :- CARVIN - LENS - SAILLY LABOURSE - NOEUX-les-MINES.
Motor Ambulance Cars of 2/2nd N.M.Fd.Ambce., on arrival at NOEUX-les-MINES, will report to the H.Q. of their Unit in new Area.
(b) O.C., 2/1st N.M.Fd.Ambce. will detail an Officer to accompany the Motor Ambulance Cars of his Unit which will proceed to the new area on the 6th instant.
Route :- SECLIN - CARVIN - LENS - BEUVRY - VAUDRICOURT - NOEUX - BARLIN.
(c) Two days rations will be carried by Drivers and Car Orderlies. 100 yards distance will be maintained between each 5 Motor Ambulance Cars or Cyclists during the journey.

4. The 2/1st NORTH MIDLAND FIELD AMBULANCE will come under the orders of the G.O.C., 176th Infantry Brigade at 1200 hours on the 4th instant.

5. The 2/2nd NORTH MIDLAND FIELD AMBULANCE will come under the orders of the G.O.C., 178th Infantry Brigade at 2200 hours on the 3rd instant.

6. The 2/3rd NORTH MIDLAND FIELD AMBULANCE will close the Divisional Rest Station at SECLIN on the 4th instant and will come under the orders of the G.O.C., 177th Infantry Brigade at 1200 hours on the same date. "C"., 59th Division have been asked to detail a lorry to convey the Spray Bath, Delouser and surplus Medical Stores at the D.R.S., to the new area. (This lorry will report on the morning of the 6th inst).

7. On arrival, the 2/3rd NORTH MIDLAND FIELD AMBULANCE will proceed to open a Divisional Rest Station at NOEUX-les-MINES.

8. On arrival in the new area, each Field Ambulance will arrange for the collection of Sick of their respective Brigade Groups.

9. Map Reference of Headquarters of Unit and Transport Lines will be forwarded to this Office by O.Cs., Field Ambulances as soon after arrival as possible.

10. A.D.M.S., Office will close at WATTIGNIES at 1100 on 6th December, and open at VAUDRICOURT at the same hour.

11. Field Ambulances to acknowledge.

E.A.Lindsay.
Colonel.A.M.S.
A.D.M.S., 59th Division.

Distribution :- NORMAL plus A.D.M.S., 47th Division.
and A.D.M.S., 57th Division.

E.
SECRET.   A.D.M.S., 59th Division No. S.391h.

59th DIVISION.

MEDICAL ARRANGEMENTS No. 7.

App. 2

Ref. Sheet 44b. 1/40,000.   December 11th 1918.

1. O.C., 2/1st NORTH MIDLAND FIELD AMBULANCE will be in charge of the Divisional Rest Station, BRUAY (J.16.d.cent.) where all Sick - except very serious cases - will be treated. Also Convalescent cases discharged from C.C.Ss. will be readmitted and retained until fit to return to their Units. O.C., 2/1st N.M.Fd.Ambce. will keep in touch with O.J., C.C.Ss. etc. and will notify them daily the number of such cases that can be readmitted.

2. O.C., 2/3rd NORTH MIDLAND FIELD AMBULANCE will be in charge of the Divisional Diarrhoea and Scabies Station, NOEUX-les-MINES (K.18.b.5.2.) where all such cases will be sent.

3. Collection of Sick and visiting Units without Medical Officers.

(i) O.C., 2/1st NORTH MIDLAND FIELD AMBULANCE will be responsible for the collection of sick and visiting units without Medical Officer, as follows :-

Unit.	Location.
176th Bde. H.Q.	K.27.c.25.05.
25th Liverpool R.	Q.14.d.90.80.
26th R. Welch Fus.	K.26.b.4.2.
17th R. Sussex R.	J.36.a.9.1.
176th L.T.M.B.	K.27.c.20.15.
No. 2 Coy. A.S.C.	K.33.b.3.9.
No. 4 Coy. A.S.C.	RUITZ.
467 Fd. Coy. R.E.	K.33.b.3.9.
59th D.A.C.	W.5.a.5.8.
S.A.A.Sect., D.A.C.	Q.34.b.7.5.
277th A.F.A. Bde.	ESTREE CAUCHIE.
2/1st N.M.Mob.Vet.Sec.	K.33.a.1.5.
59th M.T.Coy.	Location later.
No. 2 Amer. Lt.R. Co.	VAUDRICOURT. (No Med.Off.)
No. 9 Can. Lt.R. Co.	-do- (No Med.Off.)

(ii) O.C., 2/3rd NORTH MIDLAND FIELD AMBULANCE will be responsible for the collection of Sick and visiting units without Medical Officers as follows :-

Unit.	Location.
59th Div. H.Q.	VAUDRICOURT CHATEAU.
59th Div. Signal Co.	K.4.a.2.9.
177th Bde. H.Q.	L.25.b.5.7.
11th Somerset L.I.	K.24.b.9.8.
15th Essex Regt.	L.19.a.3.5.
2/6th Durham L.I.	L.26.c.05.45.
177th L.T.M.B.	L.25.b.60.05.
59th Div.R.E., H.Q.	K.5.a.6.7.
469 Fd. Co. R.E.	L.25.b.60.05.
470 Fd. Co. R.E.	K.4.b.5.6.
No. 1 Coy. A.S.C.	HOUCHIN.
No. 3 Coy. A.S.C.	BRAQUEMONT.
295 Bde. R.F.A.	Q.5.d.2.2.
296 Bde. R.F.A.	K.10.c.4.0.
250 Div. Emplt. Co.	E.29.c.2.3.
59th Div. Recep. Camp.	FOUQUEREUIL.
200 Bn. M.G.Corps.	NOEUX-les-MINES.
25th K.R.R.C.(P).	K.3.d.3.3.
2nd BG Repair Train.	BARLIN. (No Med.Off.)
1st Can. A.T.Coy. (OUP R.E.Park School.)	COUPIGNY. (No Med.Off.)

/4. Disposal of Cases.

4.   Disposal of Sick, etc.

  (a) Ordinary Sick.   No. 7 C.C.S., AGNEZ-les-DUISANS.
                                               No. 12 Stationary Hosp. St.POL.
  (b) Infectious Diseases.
       (i) All cases except those
            enumerated in (ii).   No. 6 C.C.S., MONTIGNY.
       (ii) Early Scarlet Fever,
            Enteric, Diphtheria
            and Infec. Jaundice
            (Wiel's Disease.)   to receiving C.C.S.
  (c) S.I.W.   No. 6 C.C.S., MONTIGNY.
  (d) N.Y.D.N.   No. 6 C.C.S., MONTIGNY.
  (e) Army Ophthalmic, Dental,
       Ear, Nose & Throat Centres.attd. No. 6 C.C.S.
  (f) Chinese Sick.   to receiving C.C.S.
  (g) Indian Sick.   Lucknow C.C.S., WARLUS.

5.   Sanitary Areas.

       The Divisional Area will be divided into two Sanitary
Areas as under, with Os.C., Field Ambulances acting as S.M.Os. :-
       (i) 2/1st NORTH MIDLAND FIELD AMBULANCE. - Boundary -
BRUAY - HAILLECOURT - RUITZ - BARLIN - COUPIGNY - BOYEFFLES -
BOUVIGNY - to Q.35.d.cent. - Pt.SERVINS - Gd.SERVINS - LES QUATRE
VENTS - ESTREE CAUCHIE - thence along road via HOUDAIN to BRUAY
- all inclusive.
       (ii) 2/3rd NORTH MIDLAND FIELD AMBULANCE. - Boundary -
Railway R.7.d.cent. to R.G.a. thence along Railway to FOUQUEREUIL
- HESDIGNEUL - HOUCHIN (all inclusive) to Cross Roads K.19.b.
thence along Railway K.27. via HERSIN (inclusive) to R.7.d.cent.
       S.M.Os., assisted by O.C., No. 57 Sanitary Section, will
be responsible for the Sanitation of their respective Areas and
will render a Sanitary Report to reach this Office each SATURDAY.

6.   Venereal Cases.
       Attention is drawn to 59th Division Medical Circular -
Venereal Prophylaxis - issued to all concerned today.

7.   Dental Cases.
       Captain MOSBERY, Dental Surgeon, No. 12 Stat. Hospital,
St.POL is placed at the disposal of the 59th Division and will
attend at the Divisional Rest Station, BRUAY, J.16.d.cent. each
MONDAY, WEDNESDAY and FRIDAY at 0900 hours.   Transport for the
Dental Surgeon to and from No. 12 Stat.Hosp. will be arranged by
O.C., 2/1st N.M.Fd.Amb.. Not more than 35 cases will be seen
in one day.

8.   Ophthalmic and Ear,Nose & Throat Cases.
  (a) The Army Ophthalmic and Ear, Nose & Throat Centres are
at No. 6 C.C.S., MONTIGNY.
  (b) Days are allotted as follows :-
       Officers.   Other Ranks.
       FRIDAYS and SATURDAYS.   WEDNESDAYS.
  (c) Urgent cases will be received at any time.
  (d) Not more than 10 Ophthalmic and 4 Ear,Nose & Throat cases
will be sent on one day.
  (e) Cases will be collected on previous day at the 2/3rd North
Midland Field Ambulance, NOEUX-les-MINES, and shown as "detained".
O.C., 2/3rd N.M.Fd.Amb. will notify this Office by 0900 hours by
wire on TUESDAYS for Other Ranks and THURSDAYS and FRIDAYS for
Officers the number of cases collected when arrangements will be
made by this Office for their conveyance by M.A.C. cars to reach
the Centre by 0900 hours the following morning.
  (f) Care must be taken that only suitable cases are sent.
  (g) Patients will take their kit and one day's rations.
  (h) Nominal rolls, in duplicate, will accompany the cases
shewing the Division and Corps from which they come.
  (i) Each patient is to be in possession of his A.B.64.

                                               9/ Locations.

9.   Locations.

A.D.M.S.   VAUDRICOURT. - K.4.a.

2/1st N.M.Fd.Ambce. (i/c Divisional
          Rest Station.)   BRUAY.   - J.16.d.cent.

2/3rd N.M.Fd.Ambce. (i/c Divisional
          Diarrhoea and Scabies Centres.) NOEUX-les-MINES. - K.18.b.5.2.

Advanced Depot Medical Stores. - No. 3 3. - SAVY.
Sanitary Section.   - No. 57.   - HOUDAIN.

---

10.   Field Ambulances and Regimental Medical Officers to acknowledge.

                                            [Signed] C.A. Lindsay
                                            Colonel.A.M.S.
                                            A.D.M.S., 59th Division.

DISTRIBUTION - NORMAL plus All Regimental Medical Officers.
                         A.D.M.S., 47th Division.
                         A.D.M.S., 57th Division.
                         O.Cs., attached Units.

Confidential.

Jan 1914

59 DIV
Box 2888

Vol 24
MO/24-90

WAR DIARY.
of the
2/3rd. North Midland Field Ambulance.
R.A.M.C. (T.)

for the Month of January. 1919.

(Vol. I.)

O.S. Col. McCae R.A.M.C. T.
cdg. 2/3rd North Midland
Field Ambulance.

COMMITTEE FOR THE
MEDICAL HISTORY OF THE WAR
17 MAR 1919
Date

WAR DIARY
or
INTELLIGENCE SUMMARY.

(Erase heading not required.)

Army Form C. 2118.

Instructions regarding War Diaries and Intelligence Summaries are contained in F.S. Regs., Part II. and the Staff Manual respectively. Title pages will be prepared in manuscript.

Place	Date	Hour	Summary of Events and Information	Remarks and references to Appendices
Noeux-les-Mines K.18.Z.6.2. [sheet 44 E].	January 1919 1st		The train continued to be in charge of the transfer of sick and wounded in the collection of sick of the 173rd Infantry Brigade group. O.S.	
"	2nd 3rd 4th 5th		Nothing of special importance occurred. O.S.	
"	6th		Owing to the impending departure of the 176th Infantry Brigade Group, no further cases could be evacuated to the M.R.S. at BRUAY, thus infantry very heavy load in the Ambulance Cars, as cases have to be sent to No. 12 Stationary Hospital at ST. POL. O.S. A.D.M.S. asked for four M.A.C. cars to be attached to Unit. O.S.	
"	7th		Warning orders that move to DOULLENS then cancelled to the Brigade group would move to BRUAY-PORT. O.S.	

WAR DIARY
or
INTELLIGENCE SUMMARY.

(Erase heading not required.)

Army Form C. 2118.

Place	Date	Hour	Summary of Events and Information	Remarks and references to Appendices
NO E A x-60 K. 18. B. 6. 2 (Sheet 44 c)	Jan 19.		MINES: Identification of R.A.M.C personnel retained on what become then what 6 companies of R.A.M.C. limits to and have to have returned home to supervision the health of the troops. O/S	
	Jan 20		S'erupt taken day 96 % all ranks O/S Nothing of special importance occurred. O/S	
	Jan 21		LA 2£ 0. 504 taken on men of limit O/S	
	Jan 22		The enemy trench mortar sent under the direction of MEARNS gave a performance to No. 3. Company 124 Inf. Train on BRACQUEMONT. Off state 57 hit	
	Jan 23		from this entire the visits have been very high. [illegible] the channel to be beyond [illegible] order to have intensity [illegible] by all O/S	

Army Form C. 2118.

WAR DIARY
or
INTELLIGENCE SUMMARY.
(Erase heading not required.)

Place	Date	Hour	Summary of Events and Information	Remarks and references to Appendices
NOEUX-les-MINES K.18.b.6.2. [Sheet 44c]	Jan 24th 1919.		A.D.M.S. 59th Division this day visited unit with regard to drawing up a new Mobilization Stores Table for a Field Ambulance conforming to two Sections. O.S.	
	Jan 25th.		The Unit played the 296th Bde. R.F.A. and drew an 2 goals each. Heavy continued continually wet. O.S.	
	Sunday Jan 26th		Unit paid. O.S.	
	Monday Jan 27th		Dental arrangements received. No.15. C.C.S. opened at R.4.1.7.2. O.S. Our received from 44Dn's 57 FAs to submit 5 names for recommendations. O.S. Sent to A.D.M.S. to ask if it were possible to obtain increase of pay for those men to men doing work of higher nature due to vaccine caused by demobilization. O.S. At 14.30 hours on this day, the G.O.C. 59th Division (cont'd)	

T2134. Wt. W708-776. 500000. 4/15. Sir J. C. & S.

Army Form C. 2118.

WAR DIARY
or
INTELLIGENCE SUMMARY.
(Erase heading not required.)

Instructions regarding War Diaries and Intelligence Summaries are contained in F. S. Regs., Part II and the Staff Manual respectively. Title pages will be prepared in manuscript.

Place	Date	Hour	Summary of Events and Information	Remarks and references to Appendices
NOEUX Les MINES K.18.B.6.2. 1/4.2.	Jan 27th 1919		Major-General SMYTH, V.C, C.B., accompanied by the A.D.M.S, Colonel C.H. LINDSEY, C.M.G, D.S.O, visited the Unit, remaining some 30 minutes. The improvements appeared to be attached & commented on the	
	Jan 28th		Nothing of special importance occurred. O.C.S.	
	Jan 29th		Major T.S. ELLIOT M.C. & Captain T. REYNOLDS R.A.M.C. returned from leave on 1st November. the day received from Ambulance No.19 had been other, while drawing Red Cross Stores in Boulogne. O.C.S. The en out party made their A+M PTRLLS gave to Reinforcement to No 1 by O.S.C. 57.B.L. Train on B.R.L.M. O.S.	
	Jan 30		Nothing of special importance. O.S.	
	Jan 31st		Cold weather continued. Leave & reinforcements stopped. O.S. Col. Vere Amos 2/3rd W. Midland Field Amb.	

CONFIDENTIAL.

WAR DIARY

OF THE

2/3rd NORTH MIDLAND FIELD AMBULANCE

FOR THE MONTH OF

FEBRUARY.... 1919.

(Vol. 2.)

WAR DIARY
or
INTELLIGENCE SUMMARY.

(Erase heading not required.)

Army Form C. 2118.

Place	Date	Hour	Summary of Events and Information	Remarks and references to Appendices
NOEUX les MINES 1919	Feb 1st		Nothing special occurred. o˙s	
	Feb 2nd		K.18.B.6.2 Grant received to sent Captain J. R. GRANT to 57 D.A.C. him paid o˙s. brevis per to move to CALAIS, DUNKIRK or AUDRICQUES. Captain GRANT returned to him, orders to leave being cancelled.	
	Feb 3rd		Nothing of special importance occurred. o˙s	
	Feb 4th		The horses were "malleined" the day by Captain DAWES R.A.V.C. o˙s. Leather treatment to harness withdrawn. o˙s.	
	Feb 5th		Lecture by Sgt trainee Education officer on "Demobilization". o˙s	
	Feb 6th		A.D.M.S. 59th Division invited him o˙s. Lewis photographs.	
	Feb 7th		Major A. & MEARNS this day proceeds to leave in France. o˙s	
	Feb 8th		Nothing of special importance occurred. o˙s	

Army Form C. 2118.

WAR DIARY
or
INTELLIGENCE SUMMARY.
(Erase heading not required.)

Instructions regarding War Diaries and Intelligence Summaries are contained in F. S. Regs., Part II. and the Staff Manual respectively. Title pages will be prepared in manuscript.

Place	Date	Hour	Summary of Events and Information	Remarks and references to Appendices
MOEUX les MINES K.13.b.6.2 (44 b)	Feb 9th	Summary	Intense arty. wire raid. O.S.	
	Feb 10th 11th 12th 13th 14th		Nothing of special importance. O.S.	
	Feb 15th		Unit this day moved by tram to a hutted camp at MINX [K.6.a central 44 b], being relieved by the 115th London Field Ambulance. A very good camp + excellent hori-lines O.S.	
MINX K.6.a central [44 b]	Feb 16th Feb 17th		Unit paid. O.S. Nothing of special importance.	
	Feb 18th		Major A. A. Mearns returned from leave in train. O.S.	
	Feb 19th		Nothing of special importance occurred. O.S.	

WAR DIARY or INTELLIGENCE SUMMARY

Army Form C. 2118.

Place	Date	Hour	Summary of Events and Information	Remarks and references to Appendices
MINX K.18.b.6.2 [44]	Feb 20		Unit employed during day on repairs + camps of various description	
	Feb 21st		Nothing of importance occurred.	
	Feb 22nd		Ten horses marched down to "Y" this day on to divising Camp at BARLIN, 2 which 2 Rates & Light trucks & team drafts O.S. Unit paid O.S.	
	Feb 23rd		Nothing of special importance.	
	Feb 24th		Unit bathed at NOEUX LES MINES.	
	Feb 25th		Fatigue Convoy ty trench tramways to thorny Tattery	
	Feb 26th		"B" Lt. Col. O. Stl. on Special leave for 9 days. Lt. T.C.J.K. McMaster Comd. Co	
	" 27		Nothing of special importance occurred. M.C.	
	28		Weather cold, showery + unsettled. M.C.	

Mo. J. Clark Major Cornel
ADC 2/2 L mid R Regt

CONFIDENTIAL.

WAR DIARY.

for

2/3rd. NORTH MIDLAND FIELD AMBULANCE.

From. March 1st, 1919.
To. March 31st, 1919.

O. Steel: Lt-Col.
R.A.M.C. T.F.

c.dg. 2/3rd. North Midland. Field Ambce.

Army Form C. 2118.

WAR DIARY
or
INTELLIGENCE SUMMARY. MARCH — 1919.
(Erase heading not required.)

Instructions regarding War Diaries and Intelligence Summaries are contained in F. S. Regs., Part II. and the Staff Manual respectively. Title pages will be prepared in manuscript.

Place	Date	Hour	Summary of Events and Information	Remarks and references to Appendices
MINX CAMP.	March 1.		Summer time came into use today at 23-30 hours (winter time) 9/S.	SUMMER TIME.
	2.		Nothing of importance happened — 9/S.	
	3.		Parading of wagons + general checking of equipment. 9/S.	WORK.
	4.		Capt. G. R. GRANT M.C. reported for duty to D/S 2nd Army + relinquished to acting to adjt. of the unit from 4/3/19. Authority 9/S.	STRENGTH.
	5.		Capt. A/Major ALEXANDER MEARNS relinquishes his acting rank + reverts to Captain from date 5/3/19 on reorganisation of the field ambulance on a 2-section basis. (Authority — D.G.M.S. no 78/53 d. 15/2/19. 9/S. NOTE. Reorganisation of the ambulance can not be completed until new establishments 9/2, are received; instructions issued as to disposal of defence Stores + the unit made up to Strength. 9/S.	NEW WAR ESTABLISHMENT
	6.		Warning order received for Transport to proceed by road to CALAIS tomorrow 9/S.	
	7.		Horse Transport under Capt. A. MEARNS M.B. moved en route for MARCK Calais Sheet 13 E.I. — Cabine-Barakes Huns — Sect 9/S.	MOVE. — See Appendix I & II.

Army Form C. 2118.

WAR DIARY
or
INTELLIGENCE SUMMARY.
(Erase heading not required.)

MARCH - 1919.

Place	Date	Hour	Summary of Events and Information	Remarks and references to Appendices
MINX CAMP	March 1st	8	Unit, less Horse Transport moved at 8 am to MARCK (Cris sheet 13 E.1.) In accordance with instructions from A.D.M.S. so Dir by me first night. Left to unit to report to 3/2 First to ascertain which entrance. Temporary command of to unit handed over to Capt. HENRY's in absence. Jus. T.Biffen Major	After letter 11-11
EN ROUTE	March 1st		T/Command taken over by Capt. A. HEFFERNAN who entrained by road with transport & arrived at camp BAUGHEM a 2 mile west of BREBIÉRES. (ADDLOGNE - ST OMER road) No casualties. Horses or vehicles. Remainder of personnel reported from MARCK who is billets and to found to be in position to the scene. W/R was commanded on forming to haul table one ... infrastructure being great absence of matériel. Heavy draft horses used for the road transport. "Allen"	
		10		

WAR DIARY or INTELLIGENCE SUMMARY

Army Form C. 2118.

March 1919

Place	Date	Hour	Summary of Events and Information	Remarks and references to Appendices
BALLINCHER	March 11		Work in camp continued and improved conditions	
	12		rendered after several half days for the shower	
	13		Left for other camp on (11th) Capt. C.C. CRUMMITT taken ill	
	14		At H.Q. 5th Div. formally acquainted the adjutant of bade them an official farewell during which speeches he paid several high tributes to the efficiency ability of all ranks during the 15 months he acted in M.H.S.	
	16		Capt. C.C. CRUMMITT RAMC discharged this de 6 proceeded (Lt B.J. to) Authur Blanton M²/97 AM.Pd. dated 27.2.19 General work and entered 1st Can STEEL reserve over Command General Corm	

Army Form C. 2118.

WAR DIARY
or
INTELLIGENCE SUMMARY.
(Erase heading not required.)

Instructions regarding War Diaries and Intelligence Summaries are contained in F.S. Regs., Part II. and the Staff Manual respectively. Title pages will be prepared in manuscript.

Place	Date	Hour	Summary of Events and Information	Remarks and references to Appendices
BALINGHEM	March 18ᵗʰ 1917		Nothing of special importance occurred. OS	
	20ᵈ		Men paid. OS	
	21ˢᵗ		Orders received from HQMS relating to sending 8 men to CALAIS, 10 to BOULOGNE + 9 to ABBEVILLE. OS	
	22ⁿᵈ		Nothing of special importance occurred. OS	
	23ʳᵈ		Voluntary service held in Reception Room by Lance-Corporal CORNISH HM C. house duties carried out.	
	24ᵗʰ			
	25ᵗʰ		A recent successful surprise + followed by khust trench has been in the Execution from at 8.30 hrs. Our troops were given the providing + then much engaged. The cost was part trai in our Counter guns. OS	
	26ᵗʰ		Nothing of special importance OS	

Place	Date	Hour	Summary of Events and Information	Remarks and references to Appendices
BALING HEM.	March 27th		Inspection & checking to all medical equipment checked prior to loading into transport.	
"	28th		O.R. sent to Calais, Boulogne etc. the rank encamped in general duties at the work of unloading, checking and repacking all equipment has continued.	
"	29th		Checking equipment.	
"	30th		Church service in Recreation Room at 07.30 hours. Major TINKLER, R.A.M.C. Father, L/Cpl. CORNISH & Pt. STAUF. Has day sent to Calais for demobilization.	
"	31st		Here other ranks for demobilization.	

CONFIDENTIAL

WAR DIARY.

of

2/3rd. NORTH MIDLAND FIELD AMBULANCE.

From, April 1st, 1919.
To   April 30th, 1919.

O. Sted. Lt-Col.
R.A.M.C. T.

O/g 2/3rd North Midland
Field Ambulance

G. O. C.
B.T. in F.&F.

    Forwarded, please.
    Kindly acknowledge.

Calais.
3/5/19.

Major, R.A.M.C.
For Colonel, A.M.S.
A.D.M.S.

Army Form C. 2118.

WAR DIARY
or
INTELLIGENCE SUMMARY.
(Erase heading not required.)

Instructions regarding War Diaries and Intelligence Summaries are contained in F. S. Regs., Part II. and the Staff Manual respectively. Title pages will be prepared in manuscript.

Place	Date	Hour	Summary of Events and Information	Remarks and references to Appendices

Army Form C. 2118.

WAR DIARY
or
INTELLIGENCE SUMMARY.

(Erase heading not required.)

Instructions regarding War Diaries and Intelligence Summaries are contained in F. S. Regs., Part II. and the Staff Manual respectively. Title pages will be prepared in manuscript.

Place	Date	Hour	Summary of Events and Information	Remarks and references to Appendices
BALINGHEM	April 27		Nothing of special importance.	
	28		Major A.A. MEARNS took M. through to see the lines D.A.D.M.S. CALAIS.	
			Nothing special.	
	29		Three men in Reinforcements.	
	30		Three men to proceed & relieve men that are south of line 47.	
			O.R.S 66 N.C.Os Rank & File	
			Eng. 2/3 Wind NW change	
			Field Ambulance	

CONFIDENTIAL.

WAR DIARY

of

2/3rd. NORTH MIDLAND FIELD AMBULANCE.

From 1st. May 1919

To 31st. May 1919.

Army Form C. 2118.

WAR DIARY
or
INTELLIGENCE SUMMARY.
(Erase heading not required.)

Instructions regarding War Diaries and Intelligence Summaries are contained in F.S. Regs., Part II. and the Staff Manual respectively. Title pages will be prepared in manuscript.

Place	Date	Hour	Summary of Events and Information	Remarks and references to Appendices
BALINGHEM	May 1st 1919		Unit paid. O.S. Captain to O.M.S. & R. clerks returned from leave to H.Q. O.S. Unit bathed. Clean clothing issued. O.S.	
"	2nd			
"	3rd		Nothing of importance to record. O.S.	
"	4th			
"	5th			
"	6th		Parades as usual.	
"	7th		Pay. Cooks extra duty. Important movement of men known to be on track.	
"	8th		The day held a joyous expectation the link.	
"	9th			
"	10th		Nothing of importance to record. O.S.	
"	"		Officers this day received ment to leave cards to [?] O.S. Lt. O.T.R. O.S.	
"	11th		Nothing of importance to record O.S.	

Army Form C. 2118.

WAR DIARY
or
INTELLIGENCE SUMMARY.
(Erase heading not required.)

Instructions regarding War Diaries and Intelligence Summaries are contained in F. S. Regs., Part II. and the Staff Manual respectively. Title pages will be prepared in manuscript.

Place	Date	Hour	Summary of Events and Information	Remarks and references to Appendices
BALINGHEM	May 10th		A dance held for H.M.Y.M. O.R.'s	
	" 13th		Divine service O.R.'s	
	" 14th		Nothing of special importance to record of interest	
	" 15th			APP.
	" 16		Orders Btn. recd. to proceed to Dunkirk on May 19th. See Appendix I. Train transport to proceed to BEAUMARAIS on May 18th O.R's. Lt-Col. J.W.D. Steel R.A.M.C. (T.F.) assumed command B Unit on departure of Lt-Col. O'BICHARA R.A.M.C. (T.F.) at 12 noon this day.	
	16th		Command taken over from Lt Col J.W.D. Steel at 12 midnight.	
	17th		N.C.O's & Men of Unit attended Previous inspection of R.M.M.C. Penthouse. Hockey match Kingue midnight 7cm.s. R.M.L. 2-4	

WAR DIARY
or
INTELLIGENCE SUMMARY

Army Form C. 2118.

Place	Date	Hour	Summary of Events and Information	Remarks and references to Appendices
BALINGHEM	MAY 17 1919		Horses & men arrivs from 6.? El Pinsonal Transport camp to move unit transport to Dunkerque.	
"	18."		Transport moved off at 09.30 hrs to proceed to Dunkerque, staying night 18-19 at Beaumais. Total Strength 2nd Ech.	APPRX 3
"	19."		Lorries arrived at 9.45 hrs to convey RAMS personnel to Dunkerque. Lorry transport moved off at 10.30 hrs. Lorries moved off at 10.30 hrs. Arrived at MARDYCK Camp S. POL-SUR-MER. (DUNKERQUE) at 16. hours. Personnel Billeted. Transport arrived all complete at 18 hours. Wagon Park at Horses and men (RASC) Billets.	APPRX 4 SBR SBR
DUNKERQUE	MAY 20."		C.O. proceeded to A.D.M.S. DUNKERQUE, for interview at 14.30 hours nothing more of importance occurred.	SBR

Army Form C. 2118.

WAR DIARY
or
INTELLIGENCE SUMMARY.
(Erase heading not required.)

Instructions regarding War Diaries and Intelligence Summaries are contained in F. S. Regs., Part II and the Staff Manual respectively. Title pages will be prepared in manuscript.

Place	Date	Hour	Summary of Events and Information	Remarks and references to Appendices
DUNKERQUE	MAY 21st		BASE	
"	22		M.E.O's men and horse adherence to 5.9th hospital transport him SLR	
"	23		nothing received HR	
"	24		one detachable men sent to No 4 general hospital — HR	
"	25		Wagon cleaned HR	
"	26		nothing of importance received HR	
"	27		Received additional information of form 17E–78R.S. 2 pm. writing R.A.M.C. personnel to present to form re– before 31/5/19 HR	
"	27		Received Regiment allotment from AONS Dunkerque to sever GR for tomorrow HR	
"	28		Eleven O.R with stretchers for general RSLR	

WAR DIARY
INTELLIGENCE SUMMARY

Army Form C. 2118.

Place	Date	Hour	Summary of Events and Information	Remarks and references to Appendices
DUNKERQUE	MAY 28th		Orders received from O.C. No. 10 M.F.A. of 2nd Cavalry Division to proceed 1 Rue de Conigsbrugge, Dunkerque to visit strength & returns of units of 2 A.D. & No. 58 Field Amb.	
"	29th		Have inspected returns & strength of 58 Field Ambce & R.A.S.C. M.T. O.S. personnel employed. R.A.S.C. M.T. convoy of Field Amb. Vehicles. To No 11 by 58 Field Amb. No 11 M.T. complement of motor Lorries reported to H.Q. 58 F.A. A.P.R.	
"	30th		Nothing occurred.	
"	31st		Nothing of special importance occurred. A.P.R.	

sd/ Richard Enyd RAMC
o.c. S/S North Midland Field Amb.

Appendix...1.   A.56/470 . 15.5.19.

1. The Cadre of the 2/3rd. North Midland Field Ambulance will move from Balinghem to Dunkirk in accordance with Communications 916 Q.L. dated 12/5/19.   Move to be completed by 16.00 hours 19th inst. Application for accomodation to be made to Base Commandant, Dunkirk.
2. Two Lorries will report to H.Q. 2/3rd. N.M.Fld. Ambce at 10.00 hours 19th instant, to convey personnel not required to accompany Transport. These lorries will be detailed by O.C. 59th. Div. M.T.Co.   Lorries will proceed direct to DUNKIRK and return on completion.
3. O.C. 59th. Divisional Transport Camp will detail 31 Animals (16 H.D. and 15 L.D.) with Drivers and harness (details of which party have been issued to Units concerned) to report to O.C. 2/3rd. N.M.Field Ambulance, Balinghem, by 18.00 hours on 17th instant.   This party will be in charge of an Officer to be detailed by O.C. 59th. Div. Transport Camp.

O.C. 2/3rd. N.M.Field Ambulance will arrange their accomodation for the night 17th/18th instant.   On 18th inst, the transport of 2/3rd. N.M.Field Ambulance will proceed by Route March to No. Camp Beaumarais, (25th. Kings Liverpools) arriving there by 16.00 hours.   O.C. 25th. Kings Liverpools will arrange for accomodation of this party for night 18th/19th.   On 19th inst, transport will move from BEAUMARAIS to Dunkirk.

Completions to be reported to these Headquarters.

16/5/19.   59th. Division.

===============================

Appendix 2.

Operation Order by Capt. S.C.Richards. Commdg.
2/3rd. North Midland Field Ambce.

1. Transport of Unit will move off at 09.30 hours, to proceed to Dunkirk, staging the night at BEAUMARAIS.   O.C Transport Column will be detailed by O.C. 59th. Div. Transport Camp.

Rations for the day will be carried, also Forage for horses, for 18th and 19th inst.   Stables will be cleaned up and left in a Sanitary Condition.

                    (sgd). S.C.Richards.
18.5.19.   ....Capt. R.A.M.C.,TF.
                    O.C.2/3rd. Nth.Mid.Field Ambulance....

Appendix 3.

Operation Order by Capt. S.C.Richards. Cdg.
2/3rd. North Midland Field Ambce.

1.   The R.A.M.C. personnel not proceeding by road with the Horse Transport will be conveyed today by Motor Lorry to Dunkirk., arriving before 16.00 hours.   Rations for 19th and 20th will be taken in Lorry.
2.   All ranks will fall in, full marching order and two Blankets, at 09.30 hours.   Camp will be cleaned up and be in a Sanitary condition by 09.00 hours to be handed over to R.E.Guard.
                    (sgd). S.C.Richards Capt. R.A.M.C.,T.
19.5.19.   O.C. 2/3rd. North Midland Field Ambce.

Appendix. No.4

Extract from 59th. Divisional Instructions 28/5/19.
" The following Horses in possession of 2/3rd. North Midland Field Ambulance will be dispatched immediately to the following destinations.   1 Ride. to Camp Commdt. 59th. Division.
            2.H.D. to No.5.Base Remounts, Calais.
            4.L.D. to H.Q. 178th. Inf. Brigade to complete
                                    Establishment.

Transfers to be completed by 31/5/19 and completion to be notified this office".

2/3RD NORTH MIDLAND FIELD AMBULANCE.

W A R

D I A R Y

From.

June 1st 1919

to

June 30th 1919

Army Form C. 2118.

WAR DIARY
or
INTELLIGENCE SUMMARY
(Erase heading not required.)

2/3rd (N.M.) FIELD AMBULANCE
59TH DIVISION

Place	Date	Hour	Summary of Events and Information	Remarks and references to Appendices
Margaret Camp S.E. Po2. Sur Mer. DUNKERQUE	June 1st 1919		Nothing of importance occurred. HE	
"	2 "		unit fixed HE	
"	3 "		Nothing to remark at all. 1914 acknowledgmt HE	
"	4 "		nothing HE	
"	5 "		All 1914 men received their 1914 acknowledgmt. Officers received summons to… mother to Equipment General to No 4 General Hospital HE	
"	6 "			
"	7 "		Have men employed to Equipment General send to No 4 General Hospital 42139 Pte Garbett. S.R. 4213, 13 Pte Millman 403. and 42149 Pte Chatten of apparatus A/E/4/4th with Key to unit's Establishment HE	
"	8 "		unit train. motor Sergt. nothing… HE	
"	9 "		nothing occurred or unpoor of view. HE	

2/3ae (N.M.)
Army Form C. 2118.

WAR DIARY
or
INTELLIGENCE SUMMARY.
(Erase heading not required.)

Instructions regarding War Diaries and Intelligence Summaries are contained in F. S. Regs., Part II. and the Staff Manual respectively. Title pages will be prepared in manuscript.

Place	Date	Hour	Summary of Events and Information	Remarks and references to Appendices
S.PO2 SUR.Ner DUNKERQUE	June 10 1919		Orders received for Indian personnel to proceed to England for demobilisation. Five men returned from new General Hospital forming Cadre of unit. HWR	
"	11 "		Equipment turned over/in at Cadre Embarkation Camp. HWR	
"	12 "		G.O.C. 178 Inf. Bde. interviewed all ranks re grievances on demobilisation. When Equipment Guard were coming to Embark these grievances were caused by some of the Bde. Trans. who promised to put them before De Zu Gomel for settlement to G.H.Q. for approximate date when the Equipment Guard would Embark. HWR	
"	" "		Cadre of unit 5 o'Ranks (one of whom promoted to A/CPL unpaid Temporary) proceeded for Dipper. HWR	

Army Form C. 2118.

WAR DIARY
or
INTELLIGENCE SUMMARY.

(Erase heading not required.)

Instructions regarding War Diaries and Intelligence Summaries are contained in F.S. Regs., Part II. and the Staff Manual respectively. Title pages will be prepared in manuscript.

Place	Date	Hour	Summary of Events and Information	Remarks and references to Appendices
St Pol Sur Mer DUNKERQUE	June 13-1919		nothing happened	MR
"	14 "		nothing of importance occurred	MR
"	15 "		nothing of importance occurred	MR
"	16 "		nothing happened	MR
"	17 "		until noon	MR
"	18 "		nothing of importance happened	MR
"	19 "		W.E. was intended to be equipment checked in accordance with letter No. OR.561 (BM) of 1/5/19 the broken motor truck arrived today & is	MR
"	20 "		checking and packing equipment	MR
"	21 "		checking and packing equipment	MR

WAR DIARY
or
INTELLIGENCE SUMMARY.
(Erase heading not required.)

Army Form C. 2118.

2/3rd (N.M.)
FIELD AMBULANCE,
58TH DIVISION

Instructions regarding War Diaries and Intelligence Summaries are contained in F. S. Regs., Part II. and the Staff Manual respectively. Title pages will be prepared in manuscript.

Place	Date	Hour	Summary of Events and Information	Remarks and references to Appendices
3rd Fd Amb Mess DUNKERQUE	June 22 1919		nothing of importance RMR	
	" 23	"	nothing happened RMR	
	" 24	"	nothing of importance occured RMR	
	" 25	"	nothing happened RMR	
	" 26	"	nout fair RMR	
	" 27	"	nothing happened RMR	
	" 28	"	nothing of importance RMR	
	" 29	"	nothing RMR	
	" 30	"	nothing of importance occurred RMR	

1st Richard Eng RAMC(TF)
o/c 2/3 North Midland Field Amb
Equipment Mess

140/5585.

2/0/M. N. hid. 7.a.

July 1919

18 AUG 1919

Army Form C. 2118.

WAR DIARY
or
INTELLIGENCE SUMMARY.
(Erase heading not required.)

Instructions regarding War Diaries and Intelligence Summaries are contained in F. S. Regs., Part II. and the Staff Manual respectively. Title pages will be prepared in manuscript.

Place	Date	Hour	Summary of Events and Information	Remarks and references to Appendices
Hartlock Bks.	1/7/19		Nothing of importance occurred.	AWR
"	2/7/19		Capt. A.C. Richards proceeded on 14 days special leave to U.K.	AWR
"	3/7/19		Half train 3 sections of Ock horse by practice of British drill in Horse & Gardens	AWR
"	4/7/19		Nothing occurred	AWR
"	5/7/19		Nothing occurred	AWR
"	6/7/19		No. 93 Pte Sykes W.A. dispatched for demobilization	AWR
"			to Base details ground.	
"	7/7/19		Nothing noted	AWR
"	8/7/19		Nothing occurred	AWR
"	9/7/19		Received by I.R. No. and Destination for Equipment	AWR
"			viz. Z.F.88 — Ainthee. W.	
"	10/7/19		Nothing occurred	AWR
"	11/7/19		3. R.A.S.C. H.T. Rovers reported for duty to complete	AWR
"			equipment Guard Establishment.	
"	12/7/19		Nothing occurred	AWR
"	13/7/19		Nothing occurred.	AWR

WAR DIARY or INTELLIGENCE SUMMARY

Army Form C. 2118.

Place	Date	Hour	Summary of Events and Information	Remarks and references to Appendices
Hardylot Dunkirk	14/7/19		nothing occurred. HMR	
	15/7/19		nothing occurred. HMR	
	16/7/19		Capt. Crichton returned from leave to U.K. HMR	
	17/7/19		nothing occurred HMR	
	18/7/19		nothing occurred HMR	
	19/7/19		Unit paid HMR	
	20/7/19		9.10. Ambulance ordered inspected Medical & Surgical equipment. HMR	
			nothing occurred HMR	
	21/7/19		nothing occurred HMR	
	22/7/19		Deficiencies to complete Reings. Mob. equipment received from No. 3 Base Depot Medical stores Calais	
	23/7/19		nothing occurred HMR	
	24/7/19		nothing occurred HMR	
	25/7/19		Unit paid HMR	
	26/7/19		nothing occurred HMR	

Army Form C. 2118.

WAR DIARY
or
INTELLIGENCE SUMMARY.
(Erase heading not required.)

Instructions regarding War Diaries and Intelligence Summaries are contained in F. S. Regs., Part II. and the Staff Manual respectively. Title pages will be prepared in manuscript.

Place	Date	Hour	Summary of Events and Information	Remarks and references to Appendices
Hardyck Dunkirk	29/7/19		nothing occurred AMB	
	29/7/19	6/4/19	nothing occurred AMB	
		6/4/19	nothing occurred AMB	
		3/4/19	Orders received from H.Q. 178 Inf Brigade to load wagons & equipment on barge for England. Completed later. AMB	

Capt Turner Capt AMC T.
O.C. 2/3 (MM) Field Ambulance.

7/8

2/3 NM 7th April

WO 30928

WAR DIARY
or
INTELLIGENCE SUMMARY.

Army Form C. 2118.

(Erase heading not required).

Place	Date	Hour	Summary of Events and Information	Remarks and references to Appendices
Marque K	7/8/19		Wagons & equipment commence reed to load on Barges at 09:00 hrs. Completed at 16:00 hours this day. Personnel of this Equipment Group proceed tonight to Boulogne for Demobilization.	Ceased

J W Erskine Lieut RAMC T
O.C. 7B (NF) Field Ambulance.

www.ingramcontent.com/pod-product-compliance
Lightning Source LLC
Chambersburg PA
CBHW080902230426
43663CB00013B/2600